THE TECH-MEDIA HYBRID

THE TECH-MEDIA HYBRID

Google's News Ambition

QUN WANG

Columbia University Press
New York

Columbia University Press
Publishers Since 1893
New York   Chichester, West Sussex
cup.columbia.edu
Copyright © 2026 Columbia University Press
All rights reserved

Library of Congress Cataloging-in-Publication Data

Names: Wang, Qun, 1974– author
Title: The tech-media hybrid : Google's news ambition / Qun Wang.
Description: New York : Columbia University Press, [2026] |
Includes bibliographical references and index.
Identifiers: LCCN 2025028032 (print) | LCCN 2025028033 (ebook) |
ISBN 9780231207263 hardback | ISBN 9780231207270 trade paperback |
ISBN 9780231556897 EPUB | ISBN 9780231564786 PDF
Subjects: LCSH: Google News | Online journalism |
News Web sites
Classification: LCC PN4784.O62 W363 2026 (print) |
LCC PN4784.O62 (ebook)
LC record available at https://lccn.loc.gov/2025028032
LC ebook record available at https://lccn.loc.gov/2025028033

Printed in the United States of America

Cover design: Noah Arlow
Cover images: Shutterstock

GPSR Authorized Representative: Easy Access System Europe,
Mustamäe tee 50, 10621 Tallinn, Estonia, gpsr.requests@
easproject.com

*To those who write and live in your
second language*

and

To my family

In the language that cannot be numbered

CONTENTS

Introduction. Google News: Google and/or News   1

1 Why Was Google Interested in News in the First Place? 9/11, a Turning Point   33

2 The Google News Homepage Over Twenty Years: What Is the "Google Way"?   63

3 Disputes Surrounding Google News: A Global Media-Tech Landscape   97

4 Datafication of News and Media Diversity: Google's Technological Specialization and Its Influence   139

5 A Global Network: Google's Systematic News Initiatives   169

Notes   207
Bibliography   245
Index   277

THE TECH-MEDIA HYBRID

Introduction

GOOGLE NEWS

GOOGLE AND/OR NEWS

HELLO, A NEW DECADE!

As 2021 began, the shock of a series of events related to digital platforms was still lingering: Twitter permanently banned Trump, Amazon suspended the alternative social network Parler from Amazon Web Services, Elon Musk advocated the encrypted messaging app Signal over WhatsApp, and the Reddit army crushed Wall Street through the GameStop rally. Then, in February 2021, Facebook issued a "news ban" on Australian news publishers as a protest against a new law proposed to the Australian Parliament that would require tech companies to pay Australian news organizations for their content. With the "news ban," Australian news publishers' pages were blocked on Meta's platforms. Users and news organizations in Australia were no longer able to post or share news content on Facebook or Instagram. Many news media organizations

INTRODUCTION

covered the story by focusing on the divergence between Facebook and Google. Unlike Facebook, Google agreed to pay select news publishers in Australia and elsewhere. On February 17, 2021, Murdoch's News Corp announced a three-year deal with Google, in which Google agreed to use News Corp's journalism content with "significant payments."[1] The *New York Times* noted, "Facebook and Google ultimately value news differently."[2] A few weeks later, Facebook signed a similar licensing deal with News Corp.[3]

The chaos caused by these events reminded the world that many questions about the digital age remain unanswered, including the relationship between digital platforms and news media, two sectors that play important roles in the world's political, economic, and democratic developments. The disputes between tech giants and Australian news publishers left many wondering: Why do these tech companies have anything to do with news, and in what ways are the tech industry and news industry related? It's not much of a surprise that people would have these questions. Take Google for example; although there have been scattered studies about its news-related features, there has been no systematic and substantive examination of Google's development in the news area over its history. In an effort to fill this gap, let me reintroduce Google, the elephant in the (news)room.

For many, Google is a tech giant and a search engine, but it was also one of the earliest tech companies to invest in news-related business. Since its early history, Google has had a close relationship with the news industry, especially since the launch of its news aggregation service, Google News, in 2002. In its

INTRODUCTION

first two decades, Google's news ambition systematically and continuously developed, and this has had a profound impact on journalism and the news industry. Why was Google, a company that does not produce news, interested in news in the first place? How has Google's news business evolved, and how has its evolution influenced the traditional news industry? Has Google changed news, or has news changed Google? As the world's leading tech company and an important actor in the twenty-first-century information ecosystem, Google is a big part of understanding the changing news environment in the digital age.

Among Google's earliest and most long-lasting products is Google News, one of the first outside of Google's core search function. As a digital news aggregator, Google News does not produce news. Instead, it aggregates news from different sources, presenting news to users through an automated process based on Google's computational algorithms. Since its launch, Google News has had a far-reaching impact on the news industry. As of 2019, Google News included more than eighty thousand news publishers around the world.[4] In 2022, Google reported that Google Search and Google News contributed more than 24 billion clicks per month to publishers' websites.[5] And by 2018, Google News had approximately 150 million unique monthly visitors in the United States.[6] Its news aggregation service, Google claims, invented the "Google way" of experiencing news. What exactly is this "Google way" when it comes to news? This book looks into this idea of the "Google way" from historical, visual, technological, legal, and institutional perspectives.

INTRODUCTION

Given its influence, it's perhaps not surprising that Google's news aggregation service is also one of its most controversial products. As its influence grew, tensions between Google and traditional news media escalated. In the United Kingdom, Rupert Murdoch, the founder of News Corp, publicly accused Google and other technology companies of "stealing" news media's content because they "simply just pick up everything and run with it, steal our stories—we say they steal our stories—they just take them."[7] In the United States, at a 2010 Federal Communications Commission event, "The Future of Media and Information Needs of Communities: Serving the Public Interest in the Digital Era," news executives called news aggregators associated with search engines "the enemy." The then Associated Press general counsel Srinandan Kasi argued that news aggregators' practices threatened the value of original reporting by manipulating the monetization of the news content.[8] The development of Google's news aggregation service and the tension between the "older" and "newer" media sectors reveal complex dynamics in the twenty-first-century media and technology ecosystem. These tensions have fueled ongoing debates about the role and influence of digital platforms. The debate in the regulatory domain is especially heated regarding whether and how digital platforms should be governed. Some seemingly straightforward questions become difficult to answer, such as: What are these digital platforms? How do they work? How do they become what and where they are? Are they technology companies or media companies? This last question is especially fraught. Some scholars and observers point out that platforms strategically position themselves as tech companies

INTRODUCTION

for economic, political, and legal reasons. Identifying themselves as a tech company makes them appealing to the investment community and helps them avoid legal and regulatory constraints. However, as many have argued, these platforms play a de facto role as media companies because of their power to determine what information the public receives through algorithmic gatekeeping and their close relationship with the media industry.[9] In the case of Google, the relationship with the news industry began with the company's launch of its news aggregation service more than two decades ago.

NEWS AGGREGATION

At its most basic, news aggregation is the practice of "collecting information from various sources and piecing it together into a (hopefully, more or less) coherent whole."[10] Aggregation as a practice has long been a staple of newsrooms, from reprinted letters and columns in early American newspapers in the eighteenth and early nineteenth centuries to today's round-up newsletters and summaries of trending stories on social media. In addition to traditional news organizations that practice news aggregation, a group of newer, small organizations who base their business primarily on news aggregation have also emerged in the twenty-first century. These organizations produce secondhand stories based on existing news stories through selecting, editing, and remixing. They then distribute these secondhand stories via various platforms and approaches, such as mobile apps, social media, and newsletters.[11]

INTRODUCTION

In a relatively short amount of time, leading online news aggregators were able to command a considerable share in the US news market. In the early 2010s, seven news aggregators made it to the list of the top twenty-five online news providers in the United States.[12] Studies in 2013 and 2015 showed that the news aggregators Google News, Yahoo! News, and *Huffington Post* were among the most popular news websites.[13] On mobile platforms, Apple introduced its own news aggregation app, Apple News, in 2015, which became another popular digital news aggregator. Unlike Google News, Apple News has a greater focus on magazines rather than newspapers.[14] Other news aggregation apps, such as Pulse, Zite, and News.me, also grew in popularity,[15] but controversies followed. For example, Pulse, a news aggregator app released in 2010, became the best-selling iPad RSS app within a year but soon encountered objections from the *New York Times* for using its RSS feed.[16]

In the digital environment, there are different types of news aggregators. Feed aggregators, such as Google News and Yahoo! News, collect content on a variety of topics from feeds across many different news sources; specialty aggregators, such as Taegan Goddard's Political Wire, which aims to aggregate "all the political news in one place," collect news on specific topics; user-curated aggregators, such as digg.com, sometimes called social news websites, allow users to share and vote on news and usually cover a wide variety of sources; and blog aggregators, such as *Huffington Post* and *Gawker*, repurpose third-party content for a blog site.[17] Some of these aggregators have retired or transformed. For instance, *Gawker* was relaunched in 2021 after its operation ceased in 2016 and then

INTRODUCTION

shut down again in 2023, and *Huffington Post* has expanded far beyond being a blog aggregator and now has its own reporting and video and audio teams. Since the late 2000s, more new players entered the US and global news aggregation market. In addition to Apple News, launched in 2015, there are also Bing News, a news aggregator that Microsoft rolled out in 2008 to compete with Google News; DuckDuckGo News, a feature of DuckDuckGo, a private search engine created in 2008 that claims to be an alternative to Google's search function because it does not track users' information and blocks Google's trackers across the internet; and Facebook News, introduced in 2019, which provides handpicked news by Facebook's own curation and editorial team and personalized news stories.

News aggregation startups and news aggregators associated with traditional news media also emerged. In early 2020, Murdoch's News Corp launched its own news aggregation platform, Knewz, to compete with Google and Facebook, but the service lasted only eighteen months before its shutdown in 2021. While the company attributed the shutdown to the service's not being profitable, observers pointed to other factors that contributed to the low traffic, including the service's bias toward News Corp's own publishers and the new Australian law that resulted in the deals in which Google and Facebook agreed to pay News Corp and other publishers when using their news content on the platforms.[18] In 2020, CNN acquired Canopy, a Brooklyn- and Boston-based private personalization architecture company, to accelerate the development of NewsCo, CNN's own news aggregator.[19] Internationally, China's Toutiao, Japan's SmartNews, India's DailyHunt,

NewsPoint, and InShorts, and Upday in Europe all gained traction in the late 2010s.[20]

Different news aggregators use different methods to manage news. Aggregators may rely more or less on a human approach or machine-based approach. For example, Google News depends primarily on automated, computational algorithms to gather, sort, and rank news, but Yahoo! News combines human editors and algorithms to aggregate news.[21] Some observers also divide aggregators into "pure news aggregators" that only aggregate without producing any original content, such as Google News, The Examiner, Topix, and Bing News, as well as hybrid news aggregators that mix automated aggregation and original reporting, such as Yahoo! News, AOL News, and *Huffington Post*.[22] At the same time, some news aggregators are associated with portals or search engines—such as Yahoo! News, Google News, and Bing News, and others, such as *Huffington Post*, are not. Some news aggregators are platform specific—for example, Pulse is designed for Android mobile devices—and some are community specific: there were more than one hundred local news aggregators in twenty local Dutch communities in the 2010s.[23] Social media websites, such as Twitter and Reddit, compile trending news from different sources and also provide a venue for users to share content from different news organizations. These platforms allow news to be socially aggregated by individual users through following, sharing, voting, and recommending.

While practices of news aggregation differ, there are some common characteristics. For example, news aggregation in the digital era involves limited, if any, original content production.

INTRODUCTION

Content is usually gathered through practices such as "taking," "collating," or "collecting" existing news content, which then is rearranged and repurposed by the aggregator. This process usually involves content from multiple sources. Then, aggregators normally deliver a final product such as a newsletter or published website. So the deliverable of news aggregation involves a collection of content with a sense of wholeness, such as the ideas of "a single place," "a single website," or "a coherent whole."

Through these practices, news content is unbundled and then rebundled. Traditionally, news has always been presented to audience in a package or bundle. For example, news stories that cover different topics and sections were bundled into a newscast or a newspaper and then sold to news audiences as a package. News audiences had to take the whole package even if they were not necessarily interested in every news topic or section included in the bundle. From an economic point of view, product bundling is a common sales strategy to maintain cost and return. By bundling faster-selling news products, such as entertainment news, with slow-selling news products, such as political news, the return on the former could cover the cost of the latter. However, a news aggregator needs to unbundle the original content package, from a newspaper, for instance, because it wouldn't be legally feasible or make any economic or editorial sense for a news aggregator to present the prepackaged news as is. Based on the news aggregation service's own choice, whether through editorial or algorithmic decisions, rebundling happens when the news aggregation service shuffles individual news stories from multiple news

INTRODUCTION

sources and pieces them together into a new whole. This mirrors how iTunes and music-sharing services transformed the record industry, which used to depend on album sales for profit; the digital services introduced new ways of consuming music that allowed customers to buy individual songs, rather than the full albums, and make up their own playlists.[24] Similarly, online news aggregation services' unbundling and rebundling of news have destabilized the news industry's traditional profit model.

GOOGLE NEWS: A COMPLICATED BIO

There is almost no way to *quantify* which news aggregator is the "largest," because ranking systems and individual studies have produced different results, but Google News has clearly been one of the most prominent news aggregators according to various ranking criteria over time. Data from 2018 shows that Google News had about 150 million unique monthly visitors in the United States, almost double the numbers for CNN and the *New York Times* combined.[25] Globally, Google News reported in September 2018 that its service covered 127 countries and sixty-five languages, and as of January 2019, Google News indexed more than eighty thousand news publishers around the world.[26] Moreover, among the "pure aggregators," that is, those that exclusively focus on news aggregation without producing any original content, Google News is the largest with the longest history. Google News was launched in 2002, much earlier than other large news aggregators, such as Bing

INTRODUCTION

News, launched in 2008, and Apple News, rolled out in 2015. Third, Google News is, of course, associated with Google, the world's largest search engine, accounting for over 93 percent of the global search engine market share as of May 2023, overwhelmingly leading the second-place Bing, with a share of less than 3 percent.[27]

As I elaborate on in chapter 4, Google's systems are a finely tuned machine running on complex designs and operations. In these systems, Google on the one hand adopts newsroom ideas and norms, which cover organizational and professional factors. These factors are integrated into Google's news-related algorithm design as key metrics. On the other hand, Google relies on its automated algorithms to "datafy" news: News elements are converted into quantifiable data that can be algorithmically processed. In this datafication process, data are collected at different data points and processed through increasingly complicated metrics, models, and calculations. Along with datafication, human decision making is also at play. Human labor, intelligence, and relationships all shape how Google's algorithms are designed so that they are responsive to different stakeholders' interests and interindustry influences.

Since computational algorithms are automated, they are seemingly free from human editorial interventions and sometimes considered free from bias, but many have come to realize that algorithms, designed by humans, have biases. Search engines have been criticized because they reinforce racism, stereotypes, and other inequalities in established social structures through "algorithmic oppression."[28] Search engines in different countries have been found to be influenced by Western perspectives similarly to how newspapers are influenced, with some of them, such as Yahoo! News, even less likely to cover developing countries than traditional newspaper sites.[29] A search engine native to the local market and one that is not were also found to return different search results, with little overlap, even to the same search queries, indicating that search engines are not neutral but subject to different political and cultural influences.[30] Scholars pointed out that PageRank, the core algorithm that Google uses to sort and rank information, prioritizes popular, authoritative sites by design because the algorithm is based on link structures on the web, in which a site's inbound links are treated as "votes" for this site.[31] These links, however, are not of equal worth: Links from popular sites, for example, have higher-ranking scores, while links from less popular sites have lower scores. Some scholars were concerned that the popularity and authoritativeness of sites are often results of a site's economic power and ability to tap into resources for marketing to attract users. Algorithms using these metrics would reinforce the "rich-get-richer" effect and encourage power imbalances online and offline.[32] Defenders of search engines reply that it takes time, effort, and expertise for a site to become popular and that popularity and quality often come hand in hand.[33]

When it comes to news, algorithms allow news aggregators to control what news the public is exposed to. Like journalistic gatekeeping, which controls the process that transforms "countless bits of information into the limited number of messages that reach people each day,"[34] algorithm-driven news aggregators play a similar role in the digital information environment. What

INTRODUCTION

distinguishes journalistic gatekeeping and algorithmic gatekeeping is that the latter adds another layer of gatekeeping. Journalistic gatekeepers select which of the myriad real-world events to cover and publish. Events that editors don't merit as newsworthy are not covered and thereby obscured from the public. Algorithmic news aggregators set up another gate when they sift through news that's already been published. These aggregators do not respond to world events firsthand but to published works that already have gone through the process of journalistic gatekeeping. Algorithms created by algorithm designers, usually with professional training in fields outside journalism, then further weed out or prioritize certain news. Thus, on platforms like Google News, what initially went through the journalistic gate then goes through the algorithmic gate before it reaches users. This narrower gate arguably reduces news media's gatekeeping and agenda-setting power. Or, at least, this power is now shared by platforms. Given Google's dominance and its de facto status as an entry point to the web for many information searchers, how people access news and what kind of news they are receiving in the digital era is fundamentally shaped by Google's news aggregation service and its algorithm.

Scholars have been trying to measure the effect that Google's news aggregation service has on news media. Their efforts have yielded mixed findings that complicate the answer to questions about whether Google News benefits or harms the news industry. For example, some studies find that traffic to news sites declined when Google News stopped hosting certain news services. In early 2010 and again in 2014, Google News removed content from the Associated Press, which experienced a decline in visits to their site. After Google News shut down its service in Spain in December 2014, declines were recorded as well.[35] News aggregators were also found to have a "business-stealing" effect, since many users tend to stay on the news aggregator platform to get their news without necessarily visiting the homepage of the news organizations that originally produced the content.[36] Just like the front page of a newspaper, a news website's homepage is considered the "cover" of the site: It is supposed to attract the heaviest traffic and therefore have the most commercial value.

As far as Google News' effect on news diversity is concerned, scholars have provided different findings. Some have argued that Google News has promoted diversity through transnational perspectives because it aggregates news sources from around the world, while others have pointed out that in spite of the wide coverage, news presented on Google News still concentrates on Western media.[37] In addition, some scholars point to the fact that Google News regularly recycles content from mainstream news wires, reinforcing their dominance and keeping out other sources.[38] Regarding local media markets, some studies found that Google News benefits small news organizations more than big ones via a "long-tail" effect. These small news organizations may otherwise have difficulty attracting a wider audience given limited awareness, but this has not necessarily led to incentives for local and small newsrooms to do more original reporting.[39]

Researchers also found that Google News has influenced various news genres in different ways. For example, Google News's shutdown in Spain led to a sharp decline in visits to

INTRODUCTION

sports news sites.[40] Other affected news genres included breaking news, hard news, and "scarcity news" (news not widely covered).[41] But there was no significant effect on business outlets.[42] Given these mixed findings, media effect studies alone are not sufficient to understand the complexities involved in the interactions between Google and news. To provide a more comprehensive picture, this book uses multiple research methods to explore the development of the "Google way" by bringing in historical, visual, legal, technological, and institutional perspectives. Before I start Google's story, keep in mind that this book is not only about an individual company but also a reflection on the evolving media and technology environment.

NEWS INDUSTRY AND TECH INDUSTRY: THE EVOLVING RELATIONSHIP

The title of this book's introduction, "Google News: Google and/or News," indicates a complex relationship between the two that can't be limited to the logic of "and" or "or." Google's news endeavor started with its news aggregation service, Google News, which was released in its beta version in 2002. As the name implies, Google News is a hybrid of *Google*—a technology giant and an actor of the "new" media sector—and *news*, the product traditionally created by mass media, representing the "old" media sector. In the twenty-first-century news ecosystem, Google News is an entity that connects the old and new. The hybrid nature of Google News implies that it carries genes from both sides, giving the news aggregator characteristics that are

INTRODUCTION

both similar to and different from either sector. This hybridity is not just a simple form of combination but reflects a complex interplay of the media and technology sectors. This interplay has also changed over time.

A 2017 report by the Tow Center for Digital Journalism at the Columbia Journalism School stated that platform companies were using their technological power to "reengineer" journalism in areas such as publishing, distributing, and monetizing. This echoed the center's earlier warning that social media and platform companies were "swallowing journalism" and "eating the world."[43] A year later, another report found that the relationship between publishers and platforms could be defined as both "friends" and "foes" and was shaped by both competition and collaboration.[44] In the following year, many news publishers were found to be ready to announce the end of the "platform era," driven by their "heightened distrust" toward tech platforms.[45] The rapidly shifting power dynamics between the media sector and technology sector is the backdrop against which Google's news enterprise has been evolving. How can we see through the ups and downs and grasp the larger trends when the Google-news relationship keeps transforming? What are the driving forces behind these trends? Drawing on discussions across sociology, technology and innovation, media evolution, and journalism studies, I begin with a focus on normalization and differentiation processes and waves of convergence and divergence in the tech-media landscape to explore the trends that shape the pushes and pulls transcending individual phenomena and events. These changing trends can help us understand the big picture before I start Google's story in chapter 1.

INTRODUCTION

NORMALIZATION AND CONVERGENCE

In the 2000 book *Politics as Usual*, the authors argued that a newer social sector's development is shaped by the existing norms and rules of established social sectors. Take cyberspace, for example, noted the authors: It is no longer a "strange realm," as it was in the eyes of revolutionists, but a space ruled by politics as usual because the internet has been normalized by established rules and practices that are applied in ordinary politics and commercial activities in the real world.[46] For sociologists, normalization is a process in which practices become routinely embedded in everyday life and incorporated into social contexts.[47] Social practices tend to be oriented to social orders maintained by sets of shared norms, values, and meanings, especially when a new social practice first emerges, because it has a comparatively low *legitimacy*. That was the case when Google, a nontraditional actor in the news area, entered the news ecosystem. Organizational scholars have long found that organizational legitimacy contributes to the higher survival rate among young organizations.[48] In seeking to increase its legitimacy, the social entity tends to normalize existing social routines to justify its existence and create congruence between the entity and the larger social environment, through mechanisms such as obtaining recognition from higher authorities or prestigious organizations in an industry, seeking endorsement from other actors in the field, and forging external relationship building.[49]

One of the common ways to gain legitimacy is to adopt, that is, to reproduce existing social practices in new social routines to serve similar or different purposes. There are different forms of adoption, from simulation to appropriation. Journalism studies have recorded plenty of examples of journalists normalizing technologies like hyperlinks, blogging, and Twitter to reinforce a traditional journalistic role, such as gatekeeping, or introduce and legitimize new roles, such as that of news marketer or communication facilitator.[50] From a media and technology evolution perspective, Manovich argued, after its initial stage of simulation, the new medium enters a new stage of media hybridization.[51] The new medium or technology selectively absorbs aspects of existing media through "a particularly novel combination of media types" to grow into "new species."[52] This hybridization stage involves appropriation, or "deep remixability," in that new technology remixes not only content from different media but also "their fundamental techniques, working methods, and ways of representation and expression."[53] In the news-tech relationship, different forms of normalization have pushed the two industries closer and resulted in convergence, "a movement directed towards, or terminating in, the same point, a 'coming together of things that were previously separate.'"[54]

Two Waves of Convergence

As early as the 1980s, the newspaper industry started experimenting with electronic publishing as an alternative to traditional publishing,[55] and by the early 1990s, some newspapers had started their online publishing. But it was not until around 1994 that the news industry as a whole adopted the internet

INTRODUCTION

into its core business, when "the Internet became a household word and subscribing to a service like America Online began to become mainstream."[56] News media's early digital transition can be roughly divided into two phases: the first from the mid-1990s to the mid-2000s and the second from the mid-2000s to the mid-2010s.[57]

The first wave of convergence across the news and tech sectors took various forms during the early stage of the media industry's digital transformation. The most common practice was to create a digital version of the print edition so that traditional news media could have an online presence.[58] Later, new technologies and features, such as hyperlinks and blogging, were adopted into journalists' everyday work.[59] The cultural convergence that merged top-down and bottom-up journalism inspired by the digital participatory culture was also reflected in newsroom routines.[60] By mid-2000s, convergence was so pervasive that a survey conducted in 2008 among news directors and editors of top news organizations in the United States found that webvergence, in which news teams produced multimedia content to feed the news organization's own website, had become a dominant form of media convergence in US newsrooms.[61] More than 97 percent of broadcast respondents and more than 99 percent of newspaper respondents acknowledged the increasing importance of their organizations' news websites.

The second wave of convergence was between journalism and tech platform companies such as Google and Facebook.[62] There was no clear landmark indicating where the second wave of convergence started, but over the second decade of the

INTRODUCTION

twenty-first century, the news industry developed a deep engagement with the newer generation of tech companies, that is, digital platforms, including search engines, social media, and other digital and mobile platforms. In early 2016, news publishers were found to have a detached attitude toward platforms, seeing them as mere distribution channels. This complacency, a common stage in media evolution,[63] was rather short, and just a year later, a survey across 1,025 newsrooms in the United States and Canada revealed that the convergence between journalism and platforms went deeper. The vast majority of the news organizations had taken steps, through major or minor changes in newsroom routines, budgets, workflow, and content production, to adapt to the growth of digital platforms. At that time, these news publishers consistently posted their content on major digital platforms at high volume, averaging 1,800 items per week for each publisher.[64]

Other technological trends were also incorporated in the news industry during the second wave of convergence, from computational and data journalism to mobile journalism and multimedia journalism. Big data and techniques of data processing and data analysis, such as data mining and data visualization, were applied in investigative journalism.[65] Specific examples included the design of computational applications that converted large volume of raw data into an editable map, which illustrated the trend of the unemployment in the United Kingdom, by the *Guardian* and the application of the computer-assisted reporting supported by data processing and data analysis to disclose public issues from school spending and urban services to demographic matters and local business by

INTRODUCTION

the *Chicago Tribune*.⁶⁶ Immersive journalism that involved emerging technologies such as virtual reality (VR), augmented reality (AR), and mixed reality (MR) to provide "first-person experience of the events or situation described in news stories" were adopted in journalism as well,⁶⁷ such as the *New York Times*' virtual reality initiative.⁶⁸ AI (artificial intelligence) technologies, such as natural language processing and machine learning, were also integrated via the use of chatbots, such as the ones that the BBC uses for conversational journalism and that news publishers created for home assistants' automated content.⁶⁹

In media and journalism studies, normalization has been studied from the traditional media sector's perspective, but does normalization also happen the other way around? Does the tech sector normalize ideas and practices from the news sector, especially in areas that intersect the two sectors, like Google's news aggregation service? If so, under what circumstances and with what implications? This book will explore these questions.

DIFFERENTIATION AND DIVERGENCE

Differentiation theory is a framework that originated in sociology. Sociologists held that modern societies evolve into specialized social structures, with social units tending to differentiate from one another during the process of modernization.⁷⁰ Social systems differentiated from one another by their exclusive, specialized functions. This gives social systems a certain degree of autonomy; it also requires their interdependence to make sense of the existence of each social system and to ensure society runs smoothly as a whole.

Differentiation can be a response to situations in which the status quo of established social sectors is challenged. For example, in the media realm, when new media sectors grew, existing media institutions often responded with strong *resistance* to such disruption. Resistance came in different forms, from rhetorical resistance, which aimed to define public discourse; economic resistance, which controlled resources to undermine the new sector's economic viability; legal resistance, which pursued protections from the court; to institutional resistance, which executed counterpressure through allyship.[71] When the efforts of resistance are no longer effective, these media institutions seek to change in order to survive. Such changes are termed *differentiating* shifts in media evolution theories.[72] At the stage of media differentiation, incumbent media institutions specialize their media content, target audience, or advertising strategies for competitive advantage.[73]

In order to differentiate itself from other social sectors, a social unit often has to increase the *specialization* of its functions and resources to ensure its relevance and irreplaceability and to avoid overlap with other social sectors. As specialization grows, it results in a stronger demand for *autonomy* so the social sector can sustain its independence, for "the absence of autonomy would mean the absence of an institution."[74] To have autonomy means that a social institution is able to "largely set their own course" and manage pressure from other social

INTRODUCTION

institutions.[75] In the case of media differentiation, Hallin and Mancini argue that media differentiation is not the media's breaking off from other social institutions but the rise of the media logic that gradually gained priority over the logics of other established social institutions, which once defined and controlled social orders and norms. Between the news and tech industries, differentiation has resulted in two waves of divergence.

TWO WAVES OF DIVERGENCE

The first wave of divergence happened in the first decade of the twenty-first century when new forms of the division of labor emerged; in fact, the adoption of new digital technologies in newsrooms provided the very conditions for such division. In converged newsrooms, there were frontline journalists and editors responsible for traditional journalism duties on the one hand and online journalists, web producers, online art designers, and engineers who worked for the online news on the other hand.[76] Working in the same workspace but with different specializations, these news workers created boundaries within boundaries to maintain autonomy. The identity clash between online journalists and their print counterparts was studied during the news media's digital transformation at that time.[77] Print journalists saw themselves as legitimate news professionals but considered their online colleagues to be people who "do not have sources" and who create "secondhand journalism."[78] At that time, online journalists struggled with scarce employment opportunities and low professional status. As new values associated with digital journalism, such as immediacy, interactivity, and participation, gained greater prominence in mainstream newsrooms, online journalists increased their legitimacy.

The very understanding of journalism changed along with the distinction between traditional journalism and digital journalism. For example, while traditional journalism considered news the final product of journalism work, digital journalism created a "journalism as process" model in which news became a starting point of news making; once news is produced, it could be repurposed and redistributed by audience and news workers.[79] Industrywide, the decline of newspaper circulation and news media's loss of ad revenue correlated with tech companies' economic growth, which created distinct economic scenarios for the two sectors.[80] In the larger communication industry, there was also a wave of breakups among the mergers and acquisitions that had aimed to create cross-sector power in the telecommunication, information, and media sectors. These breakup cases included the separation of Viacom and CBS in 2006, the splitting of AOL from Time Warner in 2009, and News Corporation's sale of MySpace in 2011.

The second wave of divergence began around the mid- to late-2010s, when news media were able to "wrestle back a degree of control" and "retain some autonomy."[81] Compared to the heavy dependence on digital platforms for distribution during the press-platform convergence stage, a report tracking twelve large, well-resourced news outlets over an eighteen-month period in 2017–2018 found "sharp adjustments."[82] Many news publishers no longer produced content exclusively for

INTRODUCTION

digital platforms; instead, they became more cautious and reflective about platform products. For example, in 2018, two years after Facebook launched Instant Article, a product that allowed news publishers to distribute fast, interactive articles within the Facebook mobile app, the majority of Facebook's launch partners abandoned the product because the publishers realized that they wanted to drive audiences back to their own websites rather than leave them to Facebook. Among such publishers were the *New York Times*, *Vox*, and the *Washington Post*, with their publish rate for Facebook Instant Article dropping more than 80 percent over 2017–2018.[83] In addition, a series of scandals associated with tech companies, such as the spread of false information on their platforms, data privacy breaches, the censorship of certain political perspectives, and foreign government interference in the 2016 US elections, were broken by news media. News coverage of these issues has largely shaped the public discourse about digital platforms and contributed to the change in the regulatory climate in the United States. Congress has held a number of hearings on these issues since 2017, including one in June 2019, when Congress investigated large platforms' dominance in digital markets and their influence on the US news media industry.[84]

INSTITUTIONALIZATION

The several waves of convergence and divergence established the backdrop against which Google's news business developed over the past two decades. This book documents key moments in Google's news-related development that speak to these dynamics. Google's evolution in the news area demonstrates that normalization and differentiation are not linear processes but results of the pushes and pulls in the media and technology landscape. It is through the dialectics of normalization and differentiation that Google seeks to establish an institutional identity. Institutionalization happens based on three pillars—the regulative pillar that sets the rules for how things work; the normative pillar that defines what is "right," "appropriate," or "preferred" through a prescriptive, evaluative, and obligatory manner; and the cultural-cognitive pillar that constructs symbolic systems consisting of "common schemas, frames, and other shared symbolic representations that guide behavior."[85] These three pillars point to the areas where institutional power can develop. As this book illustrates, the decades-long interaction between Google and the news industry reflects the contest and negotiations of their respective institutional power.

The news industry, as an established social institution, is strong across the three dimensions. The technology industry, as shown in the various waves of convergence, is powerful in the regulative dimension. We can see many examples of the impact of the tech sector's regulative power, such as the ubiquitous web presence as a norm, newsrooms' adoption of SEO rules, the influence of ranking and recommendation algorithms on news content's visibility, and how the promotion of data analytics shapes the data-driven mindset in the news industry.[86] These technological rules largely defined the information infrastructure and have been adopted as the default logics in the digital world. Such regulative power is coercive, in

INTRODUCTION

that it produces FOMO (fear of missing out). By setting the digital rules, tech companies have a lock-in effect on the parties that interact with them.[87] In other words, rules are defined and reinforced when they are being followed. The technology companies' regulative power is also strengthened by their economic success—as of 2019, Google, Facebook, and Amazon accounted for over 70 percent of the digital advertising market share.[88]

The normative and cultural-cognitive pillars, however, are not as strong for the tech industry. So far, it lacks a clear and self-driven sense of what is "right," with respect to both social responsibility and ethical principles. Tech companies often advocate ideas such as universal access to information and free expression, but these ideas have not been fully established with legitimacy; instead, scandals associated with these companies have resulted in their advocacy for such ideals often being criticized as "PR stunts."[89] Tech companies also use the idea of "platforms" to portray themselves as both neutral intermediaries and progressive egalitarians. There was pushback against this idea as well when it is viewed as strategic framing to serve self-interest in order to seek a "regulatory sweet spot between legislative protections that benefit them and obligations that do not."[90] For example, as platforms, these companies can enjoy the safe harbor provided by Section 230 of the 1996 Communications Decency Act, which immunizes them from legal liability for the content published on their platforms.[91] To this point, these discourses have yet to be translated into normative and cultural-cognitive legitimacy or help the tech sector establish a strong institutional identity. In a 2018 survey, 79 percent

INTRODUCTION

of the US respondents believed that technology companies should be regulated the same way as media companies,[92] indicating the public's perception of a blurry boundary between the media and tech sectors.

At the institutional level, the relationship between the news and tech industries has been transforming over the past two decades. This book aims to use Google, a leading actor in the tech and media landscape, as a vantage point to examine this relationship, which is dynamic, relational, and dialectical in nature, through the lens of normalization and differentiation. I focus on key elements involved in the processes of normalization and differentiation, including *legitimacy, resistance, specialization*, and *autonomy*, to explore the trends and underlying logics that shape Google's development in the news area, with institutionalization as a complementary dimension for the analysis. Legitimacy is a type of social capital related to the "generalized perception or assumption that the actions of an entity are desirable, proper, or appropriate within some socially constructed system of norms, values, beliefs, and definitions."[93] A social actor may put up resistance when facing disruption or perceiving pressure or threat. Specialization involves a process in which a social actor identifies and optimizes unique resources that distinguish it from other social actors in order to help it gain competition advantages over other social actors. Autonomy is a "matter of the institutional actors' ability to pursue their own institutional ends with manageable pressure from other social institutions."[94] It is about a social actor's capability of executing self-control and maintaining independence to prevent its incorporation into other social sectors.

INTRODUCTION

Normalization often involves a low level of legitimacy and low urgency for autonomy. A new social actor usually has low legitimacy. Through the adoption of existing social practices, it pursues local validity in a given area before it can gain general validity. At the normalization stage, the demand for legitimacy is more urgent than that for autonomy because the social actor relies on other social actors for recognition. On the other hand, a high level of resistance, high level of specialization, and high demand for autonomy can lead to differentiation. The growth of specialization works as an internal force that provides the conditions for a social actor to distinguish itself from other social actors. When the internal force is combined with external pressure, such as strong resistance, it will urge the social actor to pursue a high demand for autonomy. How has Google's evolution vis-à-vis the news industry been shaped by normalization and differentiation over the past two decades plus? Would these trends affect Google's institutional power? After going through these social processes, how is the "Google way" of experiencing news defined? How has the media-tech hybridity played out in Google's news ambitions? These questions will guide the book to present a story about how the world's largest search engine has changed and been changed by news.

THE PLAN OF THE BOOK

Where did Google's news endeavor start? Why was Google interested in news in the first place? Chapter 1, "Why Was

INTRODUCTION

Google Interested in News in the First Place? 9/11, a Turning Point," addresses these questions. It examines under what historical circumstances Google's news aggregation service emerged and what it looked like during its early history. After the events of 9/11, Google realized that news was a special type of information with both social and economic value. This realization motivated Google, a company that was new to the news environment, and with low levels of legitimacy at the time, to integrate news business into its search business, which transformed its role from that of a pure search engine.

Chapter 2, "Google News Homepage Over Twenty Years: What Is the "Google Way?," draws on thousands of archived web pages and uses them as a "fossil record" to demonstrate how Google News's homepage has changed since its emergence and what those changes imply. Using visual and archival analysis, this is the first effort to systematically and comprehensively record and analyze Google News's homepage changes via a longitudinal approach. These changes reveal rich information about how Google understands news, how Google deals with its relationship with the news industry, and how Google positions itself in the news environment. This chapter also identifies the first time that Google introduced the idea of the "Google way" and examines how the "Google way" was defined and redefined throughout the evolution of the Google News website.

From a global perspective, chapter 3, "Disputes Surrounding Google News: A Global Media-Tech Landscape," examines institutional resistance by discussing disputes between news organizations and Google in different countries across

INTRODUCTION

the globe. News publishers worldwide were concerned about the growing power of Google and its impact on news media. They adopted different approaches and relied on various legal frameworks to resist Google. These disputes and Google's responses reflected the power contest between Google and the news industry, which outlined a complex global media and technology landscape. The power dynamics at the global level have informed the regulatory developments toward platform governance, which urged Google to pursue autonomy.

Chapters 4 and 5 go beyond Google News as a single platform and take Google as a whole as the focus of analysis. Chapter 4, "Datafication of News and Media Diversity: Google's Technological Specialization and Its Influence," focuses on Google's news-related technologies and algorithms, which largely define Google's specialization and also represent an important source of Google's power. The chapter first adopts an innovative approach—patent analysis—to investigate the key technological innovation areas in which Google invested and the long-term trends over the past twenty years, as well as the determining factors, workflow, and logics of Google's news-related algorithm. Chapter 4 also explores how the "Google way" datafies the news in its algorithm systems and discusses the implications of the datafication process. Drawing on the analysis of Google's video search results during the COVID-19 pandemic, the second half of this chapter discusses how the datafication of news affects the output end through the lens of media diversity. The study also illustrates that news has been deeply integrated into Google platforms other than Google News.

INTRODUCTION

Chapter 5, "A Global Network: Google's Systematic News Initiatives," provides an overview of Google's news-related initiatives and its global partnership network. Despite the tension between Google and news publishers worldwide, Google's news effort has not been stopped. In this chapter, I propose the N-D-N framework to conceptualize the decades-long Google-news relationship and its implications for the AI era. For Google, technological and economic power alone is not enough to deal with established social institutions such as the news industry. Google has been working to systematically enhance its institutional power. In what areas is Google's institutional power growing and in what areas it is still weak relative to the news industry? The final chapter explores these questions.

Chapter One

WHY WAS GOOGLE INTERESTED IN NEWS IN THE FIRST PLACE?

9/11, A TURNING POINT

GOOGLE'S NEWS ambition started with Google News, launched in 2002, almost seven years before the launch of Bing News, thirteen years before Apple News, and seventeen years before Facebook News. As a search engine, why was Google interested in news in the first place? How did Google's news plan get started over two decades ago? This chapter traces the origin and the early history of Google's engagement with news. As I will show in this chapter, the events on September 11, 2001, were a milestone for the transformation of the web in general and Google in particular. What happened on that day, especially the news paralysis on the web, the tremendous demand for news, and an online culture that encouraged a public service role during a national emergency, set the historical context within which Google shifted its role as a pure search engine and started to integrate news business into Google business.

WHY WAS GOOGLE INTERESTED IN NEWS?

PRE-9/11: THE EARLY SEARCH LANDSCAPE

Google was launched in 1998, when the search market was dominated by web portals and the first generation of search engines. Yahoo!, rolled out four years before Google, was the dominant player on the search market, and users turned to Yahoo! as the gateway of the internet. Instead of crawling the web as many later search engines did, Yahoo!'s model was to create a web directory to help users find things on the nascent web. Under the directory model, websites were submitted to Yahoo!, and Yahoo!'s editors manually reviewed them and decided which sites to list in their directory. These editors also decided how to write the description of each website and how much time they wanted to spend processing the listings.[1] Yahoo! editors then cataloged the selected websites into categories by topic, which were organized in a hierarchical structure. To find a piece of information, users needed to browse through the hierarchy to locate the relevant category. For example, if a user needed to find information about the civil rights movement, he/she could go through the hierarchy of "Arts>Humanities>History>US History>20th Century>Civil Rights Movement."

In the second half of the 1990s, a crowded pack of crawler-based search engines developed rapidly. Unlike Yahoo!'s web directory model, the core technology of these search engines was a piece of search software that crawled the web automatically to collect information from the indexed pages, whether it was webpage titles, URLs, or the full text of web sites. Among the popular search engines at that time was Lycos, one of the most visited search tools on the web in the late 1990s, with the

WHY WAS GOOGLE INTERESTED IN NEWS?

largest index, 60 million documents at the end of 1996; InfoSeek, a search engine that served more than 7 million visitors per month by September 1997; and AltaVista, the first searchable full-text database, which had 80 million hits per day by the end of 1997.[2] Compared to web directories, the automated search technology created much larger indexes and became the mainstream strategy in the search industry. Even Yahoo! had to partner with spider-compiled search engines to support its web directory.

As the internet grew rapidly, the two search models—the web directory model and the search engine model—both showed limitations regarding the effectiveness of information search. On the one hand, early search engines increasingly returned irrelevant information because of flaws in algorithm design and keyword matching techniques. Some of the results were commercially biased because they were auctioned to the highest bidder. On the other hand, Yahoo!'s web directory model was expensive and criticized as being subjective. Since it depended on human editors to select and compile web pages, Yahoo! also had trouble keeping pace with the ever-increasing scale of the web, and there were long delays in listing new sites.[3] The directory returned a growing number of links that were unfound, broken, or erroneous, what was known as "link rot," because of the highly dynamic development on the web, with countless of new webpages being added every day and existing ones being moved around or deleted.[4] It was against this backdrop that in 1998 the Open Directory Project (ODP) was rolled out as an improved approach, representing "a resurgence of human-compiled Web directories, in the process,

WHY WAS GOOGLE INTERESTED IN NEWS?

toppling spider-compiled search engines from their dominant positions as principal gateways to the Internet."[5]

ODP was an open-source web directory. Unlike Yahoo!, the ODP recruited a vast army of volunteer editors to work with its editorial team to categorize web pages. When the ODP project ended in 2017, it had about 92,000 editors, who had listed more than 3.8 million websites in over one million categories in ninety languages.[6] Inspired by the open-source model, the ODP envisioned a "republic of the Web." "Instead of fighting the explosive growth of the Internet," it stated, "the Open Directory provides the means for the Internet to organize itself. As the Internet grows, so do the number of net-citizens. These citizens can each organize a small portion of the Web and present it back to the rest of the population, culling out the bad and useless and keeping only the best content."[7]

In the following couple of years since its launch, the ODP directory was adopted by many search engines, among them Google.

A YOUNG GOOGLE

By the time Google was founded, many early search engines had been purchased by traditional media companies and telecommunications giants and had become portals supported by corporate advertising.[8] For example, InfoSeek was purchased by Disney in 1998; Excite was sold to the broadband provider @ Home Network in 1999; NewHoo, the precursor of the ODP, was acquired by Netscape in 1998 and then by AOL in 1999. In an unsettled search landscape, Google was able to gain a

WHY WAS GOOGLE INTERESTED IN NEWS?

foothold with its innovative search technology. In 1998, with the goal of "bringing order to the Web," Google developed a new algorithmic system called PageRank for its key web search tool.[9] Instead of seeing the web as a hierarchical structure, PageRank paid attention to the interlinked nature of the web by calculating the number, importance, and relation of the links through an analysis of the linked parties and the linking directions. The PageRank algorithm allowed Google to rank search results based on a webpage's importance and relevance scores and return search results that better matched users' search queries. In the early history of the search engine industry, PageRank helped Google secure its place in the search market. Google's search algorithm was so successful that in 2000 Yahoo! added Google as its fourth search engine partner, after Open Text, AltaVista, and Inktomi.[10] This partnership with Yahoo! increased young Google's legitimacy, so Google immediately announced the news on its own website homepage—"Yahoo! Selects Google as Search Engine Provider." Later, Google obtained more legitimacy in the digital information environment after becoming the provider of search results for the then-popular sites AOL and Netscape.

Despite its popularity, Google's search technology did not replace the directory model entirely. In fact, Google adopted the ODP directory in 2000, and on its homepage, Google provided users with two search models: One was Google's web search, in which users input search terms in the search window to get the search results returned by Google, and the other was Google Web Directory, powered by PageRank-based ranking algorithms on top of the ODP data, allowing users to browse

WHY WAS GOOGLE INTERESTED IN NEWS?

web pages by category. When using Google Web Directory, users could choose whether they wanted to view the results in Google PageRank order or alphabetical order. Alphabetical order was the convention of the web directory model whereas Google's PageRank order ranked "the highest quality pages to appear first as top results for any Google directory category" based on relevance and importance. "The good news is that you don't need to choose between the two," Google told its users, because Google's web search was "likely the fastest way to find information on a specific subject," and the directory model was "particularly useful when you're not sure how to narrow your search from a broad category."[11]

There were a few considerations about Google's adoption of the directory model. First, compared to other search engines, Google was still a newcomer in the search industry. As discussed earlier, when a social innovation first emerges, it seeks to increase its legitimacy through the adoption of existing social routines or by endorsement from established social actors. Google's adoption of the ODP directory to complement its search and ranking systems, just like the publicity of its partnerships with Yahoo! and other popular web portals that Google promoted on its homepage, can be seen as efforts in pursuing legitimacy. Google realized that the directory model was helpful for users to understand how topics within a specific area are related and to grasp the scope of a given category, such as the number of newspapers in California. The strength of the model, Google found, was in the trust of human judgment. Google advised its users, "You might prefer to use the directory when you only want to see sites that have been evaluated by an editor." The trust in human editors in terms of their expertise, judgment, and ethics was shared by users as the world was transitioning from a traditional media era to the digital age. At that time, Google did not seek to completely replace the directory model with its algorithm-driven web search model but aimed to provide users with "both human judgment and a sophisticated ranking algorithm."[12] Google's decision reflected its needs of integrating widely accepted norms into its new routines for legitimacy, the manifestation of normalization that characterized Google's early history in both the tech and news domains.

Second, in the late 1990s and early 2000s, many users had not established the habit of using the web search method to find information online when Yahoo!'s directory model was still widely used. As Google realized, some users had trouble identifying relevant search terms or tended not to seek anything specific on the web but just wanted to learn something in general. This search behavior was typical in the early history of the internet, and such needs could be accommodated by the directory model when information on the web was still manually manageable. But as the web grew exponentially, users' search needs became more sophisticated. Instead of just searching for webpages in general, users demanded something more specific to help them navigate the sea of information on the web. By providing both the directory and web search models, Google used the opportunity to train users to transition to a new search habit, that is, using Google's search tool to pinpoint specific information based on users' queries. The search function was also integrated into the directory model, which allowed users to search within a particular category; for

WHY WAS GOOGLE INTERESTED IN NEWS?

example, users could search for something in the news category only. These technologies prepared Google to develop its own way of managing news soon after.

In the search world before 9/11, the human-compiled search and the automated, algorithm-powered search alternated as the dominant model to organize and search for information on the web. The dynamics also left room for new, alternative ways to emerge. Google, by introducing its specialized search technology, carved out a niche in the search ecosystem, then in flux, which helped prevent the company from being purchased by traditional communication industries through mergers and acquisitions and avoid the fate of many then-popular search engines during a period of time when these search engines became part of the vertical integration and "downgraded" as "a simple requirement for doing business."[13] To ensure its irreplaceability, Google had to distinguish itself from other popular search models. In a short "Why Use Google" page, for example, the company used the expression "unlike other search engines" three times. When compared to other search engines, it claimed that Google's search method was "what a search service should be," something that was not edited, not based on a limited directory, and not about a list of results auctioned to the highest bidder, "but a thoughtful method of organizing the Internet according to its own structure."[14]

SEARCH ENGINE AND NEWS

With its innovative technology, Google established itself as one of the leading search engines in the years before 9/11, but

WHY WAS GOOGLE INTERESTED IN NEWS?

Google showed little interest in news at that time. Search sites back then normally had the news as one of the categories in their indexes, but news was not treated any differently from other types of online information. The news category often focused on indexed news websites, not news content per se, which means that even if news content was available on the web, it was not easy for users to find updated news via Google. It's reported that on the day Princess Diana of the British royal family died in a car crash, a user spent hours searching the news until he finally found updated information through InfoSeek.[15]

Among the search services that were popular before 9/11, Yahoo! was an early adopter of news. Beginning in 1996, Yahoo! introduced a variety of news-related features on its homepage. In addition to the news category in the Yahoo! directory that listed news sites across genres and types, there was also a separate tag "News Headlines" displayed on the top of its homepage, which provided stories from a select number of news sources. Later, an "In the News" section in the body of Yahoo!'s homepage that provided full coverage of certain news topics was added. These news-related practices constituted Yahoo! News, which was essentially the site's news aggregator. In line with its directory model, Yahoo!'s news aggregation service adopted traditional newsrooms' practices that relied on human editors to select and manage news. Yahoo! made it clear that Yahoo! editors had complete editorial control over news resources displayed on the site and that they made the final decisions on which links to list.[16]

Unlike Yahoo!, there were no news-related features on Google's homepage before 9/11. Rather, Google had a simplistic

WHY WAS GOOGLE INTERESTED IN NEWS?

interface that highlighted its search window, sometimes with a few simple links to Google's own information pages, such as the about page, hiring page, feedback page, etc. It was only after Google adopted the ODP directory in 2000 that the "News" category became available in Google's Web Directory, although news was still not given any priority or displayed on the site's homepage. To get news on Google's platform, users had to click on a link that read "or browse web pages by category" to find the news category, at least one level deeper from the homepage.

In the "News" category, there were as many as twenty-three subcategories, covering different news genres, such as breaking news, sports, and satire, and different media forms, such as newspapers, magazines, televisions, and radio. A feature on Google's web directory was searching within a specific category. Using Google's advanced search, users could "Search only in News." This feature later led to an expanded, standalone service, which eventually evolved into Google News. When a news category search was combined with Google's ranking algorithms, Google users were able to browse search results within the directory that were ranked by importance and relevance scores made available by Google's PageRank algorithm. According to Google, this meant that "the most relevant and highly-regarded sites on any topic are listed first" and that users didn't have to be "buried deep within a list of other pages."[17] The category search function, benefiting from the web directory model that structured online resources into categories, allowed users to search within the news category, which laid the technological ground for Google's news aggregation service to emerge. While news was not initially given high priority, Google's position on news changed dramatically after 9/11, when the company decided to integrate news business into Google business.

9/11

9/11 changed Google's relationship with news permanently. For young Google and the web in general, 9/11 was a defining moment in their evolution. In several interviews, Krishna Bharat, the founder of Google News, acknowledged that Google News was born in the wake of the 9/11 tragedy. What happened on September 11 that motivated Google to adopt news into its search business? What did Google learn about news on and after 9/11? What were the driving forces behind Google's decision to enter the news market?

NEWS PARALYSIS

On the morning of September 11, 2001, two hijacked airplanes were crashed into the twin towers of the World Trade Center in lower Manhattan in New York City, followed by a series of terror attacks in Arlington County, Virginia, and Washington, DC. The attacks that killed 2,993 people and injured over 8,900 others was the largest terrorist attack on US soil.[18]

After the attacks, many Americans swarmed onto news websites to find out what happened. This sudden surge in traffic caused a "news paralysis" on the internet,[19] referring to a

WHY WAS GOOGLE INTERESTED IN NEWS?

situation when major news outlets' websites—such as cnn.com, abcnews.com, and msnbc.com—went down from excessive online traffic. Later that day, some news sites decided to present their sites in plain text as much as they could to reduce pressure on servers. It was reported that between 8 p.m. September 11 and 6 p.m. September 12, nytimes.com was available only 77 percent of the time and that it took an average of one hundred seconds to download something from the site, much slower than usual.[20] While some news sites were available, oftentimes they only provided limited information, which was described as "posttraumatic haiku": "The election was called off. The airports were closed. The United Nations building was evacuated."[21]

The news paralysis did not only occur on news organization websites. After the attacks, millions of users also turned to Google to search for related information. During an emergency like 9/11, Google's web search model made more sense than the directory model because it could direct information seekers to something specific about the attacks, such as queries about the World Trade Center. Using the directory model, the same user would have to go through the hierarchy, "Business>International Business and Trade>Services>Information News> Current Events>Economy and Business>Globalization and Free Trade," to find information about the World Trade Center. Nevertheless, Google was not able to return information relevant to the attacks from the search query "New York Twin Towers" (another name for the World Trade Center). The search results returned had nothing to do with the 9/11 attacks. The first search result was about WTCA On-Line, a business website of

WHY WAS GOOGLE INTERESTED IN NEWS?

the World Trade Centers Association for trade information, followed by a WTCA website about online catalogs and events, and then the information about the World Trade Center Boston (figure 1.1). The return of the irrelevant search results was because Google's index had been crawled a month earlier, long before the 9/11 attacks happened,[22] and so it failed to link users to the proper breaking news about the attacks. This embarrassing situation revealed that Google's search system was not treating news as a unique type of online information and did not recognize the timeliness of news and its significance in people's everyday lives, especially when breaking news occurred.

ONLINE NEWS DEMAND

In the immediate aftermath of the attacks, the demand for online news skyrocketed. Nearly 40 percent of all internet-equipped households accessed news websites online on September 11, increased from 12 percent before 9/11. Between 9 a.m. and 10 a.m. that day, MSNBC.com experienced a 500 percent increase in traffic; CNN.com saw a 450 percent increase in traffic.[23] Before 9/11, MSNBC.com had a record of 6.5 million unique visitors after the presidential election in 2000; that number nearly doubled on September 11, 2001. Nytimes.com also saw a surge in its page views on that day, reaching 11.5 million, compared with its 5.7 million daily average and its previous record of 9.6 million, set on the day after the 2000 presidential election.[24]

News-related searches also soared on Google to about sixty times greater than the previous day.[25] Over 80 percent of the

WHY WAS GOOGLE INTERESTED IN NEWS?

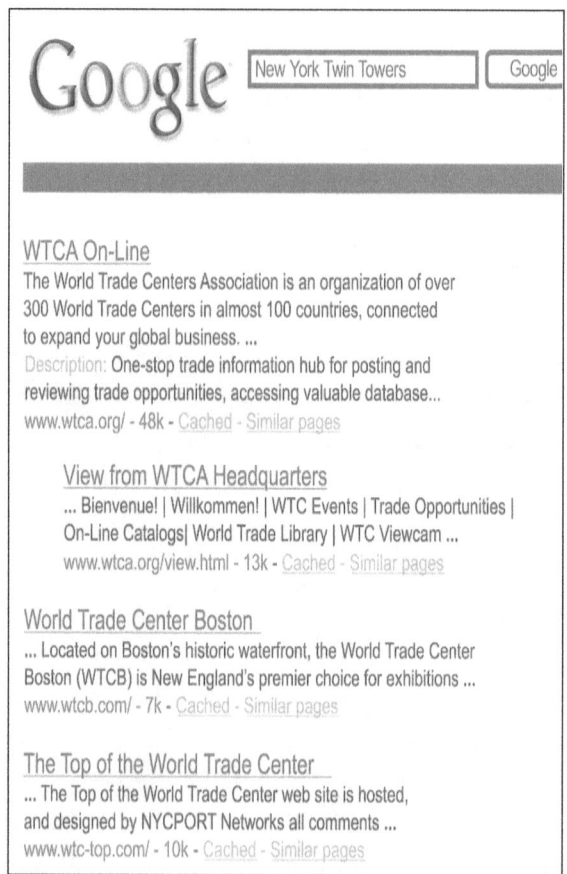

FIGURE 1.1. Google's Search Results for "New York Twin Towers" on September 11, 2001.

Source: Google, "The Evolution of Search," YouTube video, 2011, https://www.youtube.com/watch?v=mTBShTwCnD4.

top five hundred search queries on Google were related to the 9/11 attacks. The top ten queries on that day were "CNN," "World Trade Center," "BBC," "Pentagon," "MSNBC," "Osama Bin Laden," "Nostradamus,"[26] "American Airlines,"

WHY WAS GOOGLE INTERESTED IN NEWS?

"FBI," and "Barbara Olson."[27] In this list, three of the ten top search queries were news media outlets, and all of them held top positions on the list: CNN, no. 1 on the list; the BBC, no. 3; and MSNBC, no. 5. Between 6:26 a.m. and 7:06 a.m. Pacific Daylight Time that morning—between forty and eighty minutes after the attacks—the number of searches for "cnn" reached a peak, averaging six thousand queries per minute, far more than other top search queries, such as "world trade center," "pentagon," "nostradamus," and "osama bin laden" (figure 1.2).[28] It is an established social routine that in a time of crisis people turn to news media as their primary, reliable source for timely, verified, and authoritative information to help them navigate the situation. Amid the sea of information on the web, timeliness, authoritativeness, and reliability were distinctive and irreplaceable characteristics that distinguished news from other types of online information. These characteristics of news spoke to the news's social function that addresses the public's informational, emotional, and practical needs during a national emergency.

GOOGLE'S NEW ROLE

The bottlenecks, delays, and other technical issues did not stop the traffic to news sites from growing, suggesting that "the value individuals placed on accessing these sites was greater than the problems associated with gaining access."[29] Google's ineffectiveness in providing relevant search results on September 11 taught it an important lesson about the flaws in its algorithm design in responding to news and fundamentally changed the place of news in Google's search function.

WHY WAS GOOGLE INTERESTED IN NEWS?

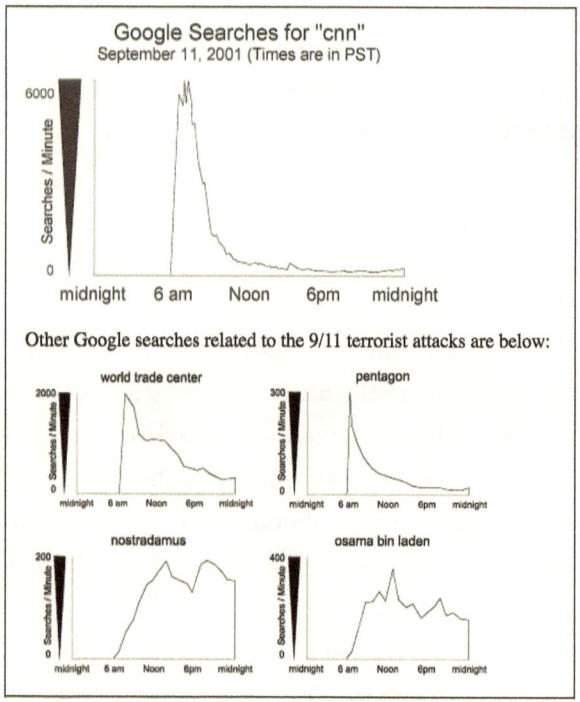

FIGURE 1.2. Google search statistics from 9/11/2001.
Source: "Google Search Statistics from 9/11/01," Google, 2001, https://archive.google.com/press/zeitgeist/9-11-search.html.

After the attacks, Google displayed on its homepage a short message: "If you are looking for news, you will find the most current information on TV or radio." This message read as if Google was pushing users to traditional media, rather than keeping them on its own platform. But shortly after, Google removed the short message. Instead, it told users that many news websites are not available because of high demand, and on its homepage, Google started to offer links to news

WHY WAS GOOGLE INTERESTED IN NEWS?

sources such as the *Washington Post,* Yahoo! News, CNN, ABC News, the *New York Times,* MSNBC, and the BBC. Later, in expanding the list, Google moved to brand itself as an intermediary between information seekers and news sources and successfully kept users on its own platform even if users did not submit any search queries. By doing so, observers pointed out, Google's role transformed from a pure search engine to a portal.[30]

Search engines and portals provide information for users in different ways. Searching is a user-initiated act, in which the search engine returns results only when the user makes a search request. Portals, on the other hand, proactively present information even if the user did not request anything specific. In this regard, portals play a gatekeeping role similar to news media: Both select and present information for the user, and their selection and presentation suggest what is important and what the public should know about. With this role transformation on September 11, Google adopted the journalistic role of informing the public, not by producing news directly but by serving users through the aggregation of news information on its own platform, a role different from its identity as a pure search engine. After witnessing the news paralysis on the web and the public's strong demand for authoritative and reliable news during the national emergency, Google quickly seized the opportunity to take on a new, intermediary role as a news aggregator. By providing links to news sources on its own platform, Google "trained millions of people to expect Google.com to deliver breaking news,"[31] which also unlocked a new market for the company. Indeed, on its homepage, Google

WHY WAS GOOGLE INTERESTED IN NEWS?

didn't miss the opportunity to remind users: "Make Google Your Homepage!"

Google decided to escalate its new role on the following day, when a news folder—"google.com/news"—was set up under google.com. On Google's homepage, a link with the words "News links and support information regarding attacks" led users to google.com/news, where Google compiled "links to news sites and support resources related to the terrorist attacks on the US." Later in September, the link was renamed "News and Resources." Strictly speaking, the link was about "news *sources* and resources," as it listed a collection of news sources with their links rather than specific news stories. The "News and Resources" link was on Google's homepage for about a year, until Google News (beta) was officially introduced in September 2002.

On September 12, 2001, the day after the attacks, news sources listed on google.com/news increased to thirty-four. Over half were news sources outside the United States, including internationally known news brands such as BBC News as well as other news outlets from around the world, including *Pravda* (Russia) and *Asahi Shimbun* (Japan). The US news sources CNET.com, FOX News, MSNBC, NPR, the *New York Post*, *Salon*, Time.com, and *USA Today* were added to the list. By September 12, news sources that were among Google's top-ten search queries on September 11—CNN, BBC, and MSNBC—were all included in Google's /news folder.

In addition to news sources, the page also provided a list of support resources, including emergency assistance, such as the American Red Cross and America's Blood Centers;

WHY WAS GOOGLE INTERESTED IN NEWS?

transportation, such as American Airlines, United Airlines, and Amtrak; government and public databases, such as Pentagon Updates and the World Trade Center Survivor Database; user input sites, such as Report Terrorist Activity and Report You're Safe; donation sites, such as Donate via Yahoo! and Donate via Amazon; and other emergency contact info. In the aftermath of a disaster, the news media, in their public service role, usually provide the public with information about these resources; when Google compiled these public resources on its own "News and Resources" page, the search engine also adopted this journalistic role. Observers pointed out that this "entirely new role" of Google hinted that "someone at Google was playing the role of editor, selecting major, authoritative sources, and updating the content to match users' needs as they changed over time."[32] This "entirely new role" signified the start of Google's ambition in the news area.

9/11 AND THE WEB

9/11 had a profound effect on internet users' online behavior and how they used the internet for news. About a year after 9/11, the Pew Research Center issued a report based on findings of a daily tracking survey among 1,527 internet users. The report found that 66 percent of American internet users used the internet to get news.[33] Among the respondents, 32 percent reported that they had gotten news online more frequently after September 11, 2001. The percentage in the category of using the internet to "get news" was much higher than all other

WHY WAS GOOGLE INTERESTED IN NEWS?

categories, including "send or read email" (13 percent), "get health information" (9 percent), "use government agency websites" (17 percent), "get mental health information" (12 percent), and "make donations online" (26 percent). Among the internet users who reported they had increased their use of the internet to get news, 43 percent of them gave 9/11 as a major reason for the change. In the post-9/11 online world, it seemed, if Google's goal was to organize the web, it had to do something with news, which had become one of the most important components of the web's information ecosystem.

A new media technology needs a watershed moment to claim its role and legitimacy, especially in its early history. 9/11 was one such defining moment for the web to come into its own.[34] On the web, the massive and urgent need for informational, emotional, and practical support during and after 9/11 was translated into the demand for news. 9/11 was the most significant "newsworthy" event since the internet became a household tool. It was through this historical moment that the web claimed its role as a major platform for news. The evolution of the web provided the environment for Google to establish the legitimacy it needed to enter the news market.

NEWS WAS "KING"

The events on September 11 resulted in the rise of "amateur journalism." Many websites that were not news oriented by design—from music lists, humor sites, game communities, and local community websites—became sources of citizen journalism. Their work ranged from eyewitness accounts,

WHY WAS GOOGLE INTERESTED IN NEWS?

firsthand pictures, pleas for information about missing friends and relatives, and commentary and analysis. In the wake of a national emergency, journalism's public service mission was shared by amateur journalists on the web. As one blogger-turned–citizen journalist reflected, "[The experience] makes me feel like I'm doing something useful for those that can't do anything."[35] Indeed, news was one of the most "useful" things during those days.

Slashdot.org, a site featuring discussion forums that primarily focused on technology-and-science-related "news for nerds," was one of the earliest sites on the web that posted news facts about the 9/11 attacks. On 9:12 a.m., only twenty-three minutes after the first attack happened, Rob Malda, also known as "CmdrTaco," the founder of the site, shared a post on Slashdot (figure 1.3). In the post, he reported some raw facts about the attacks and later provided updates, something he said he normally wouldn't consider doing on this platform.[36] On Fark.com, a weblog that allowed users to submit and comment on comedy stories, editor Drew Curtis also made a statement addressing the transformation of the site's role during 9/11: "One thing we've had trouble with in the past few days is making a smooth transition from a comedy news site to a *real* news site." The blog site posted 157 entries regarding the 9/11 attacks during the days following September 11. Curtis claimed, "We really hadn't ever thought we would need to, and probably wouldn't have except for the fact that on 9/11 every major news site went down and someone had to pick up the slack."[37] In these examples, web users were clearly aware of the boundary between "real news" and non-news content, but 9/11

WHY WAS GOOGLE INTERESTED IN NEWS?

was such an event that many actors on the web broke the boundary voluntarily in the hopes of doing something "useful" for the public.

During a national crisis, especially when mainstream news media were unavailable, producing news to inform the public became a duty for many non-news actors online. Slashdot and Fark had a significant surge in users on and after 9/11, tripling their normal peak-hour traffic. Slashdot estimated that its editors received at least five times as many emails as FoxNews.com did between September 11 and September 12.[38] "This week," many software, open-source, and information sites realized, "news has been the undisputed traffic

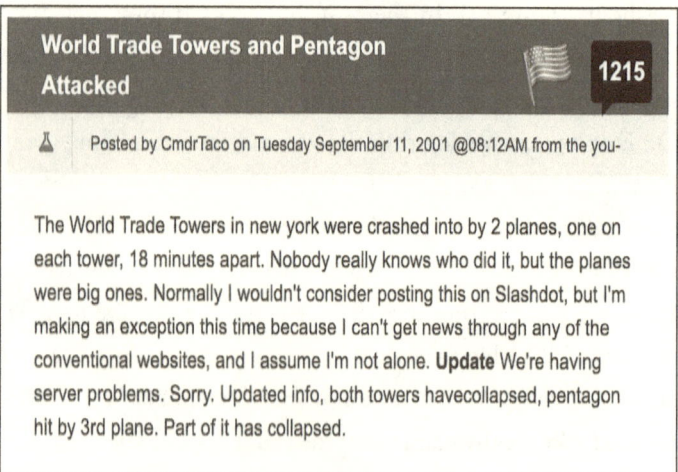

FIGURE 1.3. Slashdot.org on September 11, 2001.
Source: "World Trade Towers and Pentagon Attacked," Slashdot.org, September 11, 2001, https://slashdot.org/story/01/09/11/1314258/world-trade-towers-and-pentagon-attacked.

WHY WAS GOOGLE INTERESTED IN NEWS?

king."³⁹ An online news market that was both socially and commercially important became more and more visible in the aftermath of 9/11.

NEWS AGGREGATION ON THE WEB

Over night, thousands of "September 11" websites emerged online.⁴⁰ A common practice of these website owners was to aggregate online news. They pooled, organized, and presented information from different sources that they saw as important for users. As discussed in the introduction, aggregation was already a practice of traditional news media in the pre-internet era and then was even more widely adopted across newsrooms in the wake of 9/11. For example, BBC America compiled eyewitness accounts and information about 9/11 from thousands of audience emails.⁴¹ Many local media and most metropolitan newspapers aggregated news by "packaging news, background, and commentary in ways that only a major print newspaper can do effectively."⁴² The practice of news aggregation during and after 9/11 also gave many non-news sites the opportunity to better understand what journalism is as a profession, especially in terms of accuracy and accountability. On September 13, Fark.com posted a rumored story about CNN using ten-year-old footage to fake the images of Palestinians dancing in the street after the 9/11 attacks. The story was proven untrue when Reuters and CNN both confirmed that the footage had been taken on September 11, 2001.⁴³ In the website's statement, the editor of Fark.com noted: "That was [the] first time that I realized we'd passed from being a fun silly website to being a

WHY WAS GOOGLE INTERESTED IN NEWS?

real source of news for people. This whole journalistic integrity thing really hadn't applied before."[44] The wide adoption of news aggregation as a common practice online lay the ground for Google to experiment with its own news aggregation service.

GOOGLE NEWS FOUNDER AND MOTIVATION

Google News's founder Krishna Bharat had told interviewers that it was the news experience during 9/11 that motivated him to create the news aggregator. The technical issues that caused the "news paralysis" on September 11 motivated Bharat to consider what Google could do to address these problems technologically. Bharat also noticed how news media failed to provide new developments about 9/11 in a timely and in-depth way after the attacks happened. "After Sept. 11," said Bharat, "when all the newspapers were recording who, what, when, where—there was a big question of why. Why did this happen? What's going to happen in the future?"[45] Indeed, the wire copy was the main source of many news websites on September 11. The overreliance on a few mainstream news wires was already a concern before 9/11.[46] Inspired by the public's desire for more perspectives about the attacks, Bharat called for multiperspectival news that would allow the public to learn about a news topic from different sources and different points of view. "Bringing those views together seemed like a good *social* function."[47] Bharat commented, "Helping people understand multiple points of view, and hence becoming wiser for it—whether they agree with it or not—just understanding there is another

WHY WAS GOOGLE INTERESTED IN NEWS?

point of view is enlightening."[48] Bharat imagined news as an experience. In the digital context, according to Bharat, a journalist's job is to create news as an overall experience rather than a simple product. The news audience's experience is like a customer's experience at a Starbucks, Bharat said. "You think you're there for coffee, but you're really there for the full experience."[49] The "full experience" was not just the coffee but the music, the collegiality, the reading space, the aroma, and the brand. "You pay for coffee, sure; but the whole experience is what counts."[50]

That both the technological competency and the social function of news are critical for journalism was a good lesson for both new media players like Google and the traditional news industry. At a time when the public's trust in journalism was declining, Bharat's vision of news that is technologically advanced and multiperspectival became the early vision of the "Google way" of experiencing news. For Bharat, a PhD in computer science and a member of Google's then ten-person research lab, the means of providing the new news experience in the digital age was largely technological. "Fundamentally," Bharat said in one interview referring to the Google way of handling news, "I wanted to build a tool that would automate this."[51]

EARLY FORM OF GOOGLE NEWS

In December 2001, only three months after the 9/11 attacks, Bharat gave an internal demonstration of his dynamic news project, which became the prototype of Google News. In the pilot project, twenty news sources were crawled once an hour. The most recent stories on selected topics were returned, and the entire process was automated. Building on the success of this initial presentation, Bharat and his team worked to cover more news sources until Google News (Beta) was introduced publicly a few months later.[52]

Bharat's dynamic news project was very different from Google's /news folder (google.com/news) introduced on September 12, 2001. The latter listed only a collection of news sources with links. When a user clicked on the link, the user was directed to the news source's website, rather than any specific news story. In this regard, Google's /news folder was more of a *news source* aggregator than it was a *news* aggregation service. Bharat's model was a true news aggregator that collected news *articles* from different sources. Google's PageRank algorithm and its ability to pinpoint specific information differentiated it from the traditional web directory model. When this technology was applied to news aggregation, news stories were presented by headlines rather than just the news sources' names. This deep linking technology connected users to individual articles by debundling the news packages that the traditional news industry tried to sell to audience. Bharat's dynamic news provided a new way for users to experience news—it was automated, story based, and run by Google's ranking algorithms, independent of human editors. Here, users could get news without having to search anything; they were also able to access individual news stories through Google, bypassing a news media's website homepage. These approaches, while considered innovative,

WHY WAS GOOGLE INTERESTED IN NEWS?

didn't encounter resistance at the time, but they later became a central issue when disputes between Google and the news industry flared up.

In late January 2002, four months after 9/11, Google gave the news aggregation page a public trial and named it "Google Headline News." Google Headline News was a text-based news aggregation page. It was the first public appearance of an early form of Google News, but back then it was not yet a standalone service. A link on google.com/news directed users to Google Headline News. Google Headline News adopted the section-based structure that news media used to organize news on their websites. News stories from 155 news sources were categorized into "Headline News," "World News," "US News," "Business News," "Entertainment News," "Science and Technology News," and "Sports News." Most of these news categories were kept the same on Google News throughout its history.

After the public trial, Google's news aggregation service quickly attracted a large group of dedicated users, about seventy thousand a day.[53] Within the following few months, the news team integrated users' feedback, upgraded hardware, designed a user-friendly interface, and fine-tuned algorithms. As early as March 2002, Google News Search (Beta) was available under the URL news.google.com. In September 2002, when Americans were commemorating the first anniversary of 9/11, Google News was formally introduced to them on Google's homepage as a standalone service, with the slogan: "Get your news the Google way—Try Google News." The launch of Google News was a culmination of a year-long

WHY WAS GOOGLE INTERESTED IN NEWS?

process in which Google made a series of adjustments on how it handled news on its platform. These frequent adjustments, made over a short period of time, revealed Google's changing perception of news as a special type of online information and as a business. After 9/11, observers were wondering where Google would go next. Would 9/11 set a precedent for Google in terms of how news should be handled in its search system? Will Google's news-related service be permanent? Will Google use human editors or make deals with the traditional media industry?[54] These were the questions Google had to answer after 9/11.

CHAPTER FLASHBACK AND DISCUSSION

9/11 was the moment in the early history of Google when Google found its interest in news. Before 9/11, the search community was shuffling its leading actors between the directory model and the automation model. Google's PageRank algorithm introduced a new way to search the web and return search results ranked by relevance and importance scores. The algorithm helped pinpoint specific pieces of information fast without having to going through the hierarchies of the web directory. While Google attempted to distinguish itself from other search models at that time, its technology had not yet become the dominant replacement for the ODP directory. By integrating the directory model into its own routines, Google also adopted associated norms and values, which emphasized the role of human editors and their editorial expertise as a

WHY WAS GOOGLE INTERESTED IN NEWS?

widely accepted and trusted approach to evaluate content on the web. To gain more legitimacy, Google, as a newcomer in the search community, also sought endorsement from existing companies, including the then-dominant web navigation site Yahoo! and other popular portals. With low legitimacy, specialization that was still developing, and a national emergency that helped shield Google from large-scale resistance from the news industry against its news aggregation practices, normalization became a main trend at this stage, where Google, as a young company in both the tech and news fields, gave its top priority to legitimacy growth.

Before 9/11, Google did not pay special attention to news, treating it as one among many of the categories in the web directory. On September 11, the "news paralysis" on the web after mainstream news websites were overwhelmed by heavy traffic, the irrelevant search results returned by Google itself, and the strong demand for online news helped Google realize that news was a particular type of online information with unique social and economic value. Google quickly adopted news into its service and implemented some early news aggregation practices by compiling news-related information on its search platform. These practices transformed Google's role from that of a pure search engine and let Google take on an intermediate role between users and news. This shift in Google's role trained internet users to develop a new habit of getting their breaking news via Google, which also unlocked a new business for Google. More than a decade after 9/11, when Facebook integrated news into its social media business, critics said Facebook's interest in news was driven by business motives, rather than a public service mission.⁵⁵ Compared to the newer-generation digital platforms born after 9/11, Google's early engagement with news started under different historical circumstances. September 11 was the first time that "the Internet was viewed as an alternative channel for obtaining in-depth news and information."⁵⁶ During the national emergency, there was a strong culture on the web that prompted many to take up journalism's public service role. Google was just one of the many actors online that responded to this sentiment. After September 11, Google found itself at a historical crossroad where the company needed to decide whether it wanted to deepen the normalization of news in its post-9/11 development.

Chapter Two

THE GOOGLE NEWS HOMEPAGE OVER TWENTY YEARS

WHAT IS THE "GOOGLE WAY"?

CHAPTER 1 ended by asking where Google would go after 9/11. Would the news-related features Google offered during 9/11 be temporary or permanent? Would Google return to its role as a pure search engine, or would it continue its transformation into something else? In this chapter—based on over six thousand archived web pages and visual and historical analysis—I provide a longitudinal examination of the evolution of the Google News homepage over twenty years. The analysis shows that Google's interest in news is far from temporary; rather, it worked to promote the idea—"Get your news the Google way." Google News has since grown into one of the most visited news aggregation services in the United States, with more than 193 million unique monthly visitors; it indexes over eighty thousand news sources worldwide and covers 125 countries. A clear answer to the question of what the "Google way" is has remained elusive, but how the Google News homepage has changed over time holds clues about Google's altered position regarding its news service. From 2002 to 2022, twenty years after Google first dabbled in the news area, Google News has experienced at least four homepage overhauls, through which Google experimented with different ways of incorporating news business into Google business. The "Google way" of experiencing news has been defined and redefined along the way.

WHEN "GOOGLE NEWS" WAS "GOOGLE NEWS SEARCH"

Google News, located at the URL news.google.com, was officially rolled out in September 2002. Six months before the official launch, an early version called "Google News Search (BETA)" appeared with the same URL; that's only five months after 9/11. Figure 2.1 shows what the website looked like in March 2002: It had a simplistic header and footer, with a single-page, long-scrolling main body section on a white background. The website's logo was "Google News Search," rather than "Google News," appearing in the header section of the webpage, with the search box directly below. Next to the search box, there were links to general tips about using Google as a search engine. The slogan "Search and browse the latest headlines" appeared under the search box. At the bottom of the webpage was a simplistic footer section, with only two links, one directing users to the homepage of Google search and the other to "All About Google."

Except for the Google logo on the very top of the page—rendered in the classic Google color combination of six letters in blue, red, yellow, blue, green, and red—the page featured mostly blue and black text, with hyperlinks that turned red when the cursor hovered over them. Other informational text was displayed with white text on a red background (e.g., the name of news sections on red dividers) or red text on white background, as in the slogan "Search and browse the latest headlines." The main body of the Google News Search webpage was a one-column area that set out a list of news headlines from different news sources. The area was split by red rules, containing white type, into seven topic-based blocks—"Headline News," "World News," "US News," "Business News," "Entertainment News," "Technology News," and "Sports News"—sections that were introduced in the testing version as well. Other than the "Headline News" section, which had eight news topics, each topic-based section covered five news stories. Each of those news stories was presented by a headline, displayed in blue, that served as a hyperlink to an article about that story. At that time, only the headline, the news source's name, and the publication date were made available on news.google.com, with the headline clickable, linking to the original news story on the news provider's website. The display did not include news snippets, photographs, or videos—elements that later sparked legal disputes, as will be discussed in chapter 3.

The March 2002 version reflects that Google was not very clear back then about what its news service should be. The website, named "Google News Search" and not "Google News," combined news searching and browsing, which made the platform half news search engine and half news

THE GOOGLE NEWS HOMEPAGE OVER TWENTY YEARS

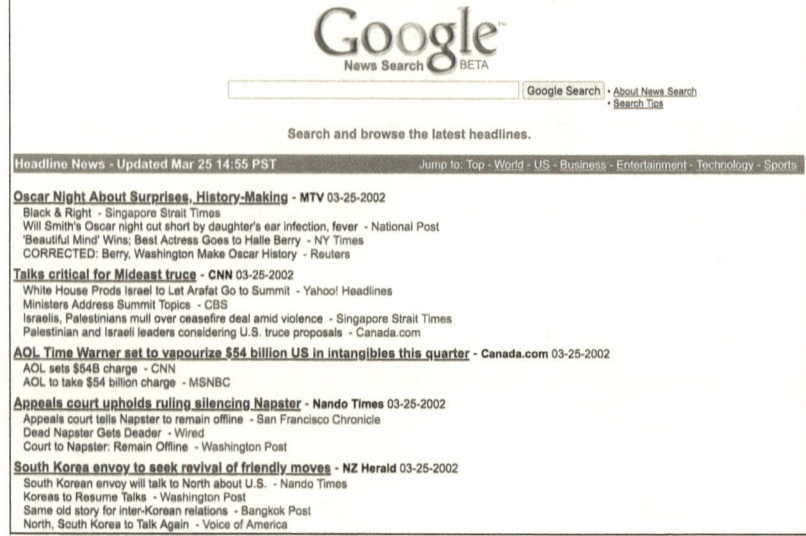

FIGURE 2.1. Google News Search (BETA) homepage in March 2002.

Images are for illustration purposes. They do not show the entire homepage. Webpages were originally in color but converted to black and white for printing purposes.
Source: Internet Archive.

aggregator. Google introduced this service as "a novel approach to news" that presented information culled from news sources worldwide, like what a news aggregator would do, and automatically put related stories together in the same search result, like what a search engine would do.[1] The novelty at that time featured automated, cross-source crawling and ranking, but this time Google improved its crawl technique based on lessons learned during 9/11, when Google had failed to provide

- 66 -

relevant information about the attacks because of its low crawl rate.[2] For the March 2002 version, Google stressed that its technologies were now able to provide continuous updates throughout the day that allowed users to keep up with the most recent developments of news events. The improved crawling technology addressed timeliness as a key characteristic of online news and helped Google engage with news more deeply. By crawling news sources more frequently, it also collected exponentially more news data, which was a prerequisite for news to become a standalone Google service. Google's deeper convergence with news and its shifting views on the place of news in its business can also be seen in the changes to the Google News logo design (figure 2.2). In September 2002, the logo was changed from "Google News Search" to "Google News" and then "Google news" in 2009, with the word "news" in lowercase. The Google News logo changed again several times after that, as well. In the 2011 version, "Google" and "News" were split apart, but the logo then was changed back to "Google News" as one term again in 2017. These changes in the Google News logo design revealed Google's attempts to fit news in its search business and to define the company's position in both the search and news industries. As will be elaborated in chapter 3, a legal case could also be made depending on whether Google News was defined as a search engine or a news aggregator because search engines and news aggregators are subject to different legal requirements and exemptions in different countries.

In early 2002, when Google News was Google News Search, the news items were presented in a list of headlines

FIGURE 2.2. Google News logo changes. From top to bottom: March 2002, September 2002, 2009, 2011, and 2017.
Source: Internet Archive. Compiled by author.

and news sources. At its most basic level, the list, according to the various definitions of news aggregation discussed in the introduction, was what a news aggregator was supposed to do. If, however, as Bharat envisioned, news was not a final product but an "experience," this machine-generated, all-text list did not provide a very interesting news experience. Users would have to scroll down the list, find a news headline that interested them, and click on it, all text. The news industry, on the other hand, was experimenting with different design trends on their websites, involving multimedia elements beyond text. For example, in 2001, ABCNews.com used information modules that "eliminated cumbersome scrolling by departmentalizing information in a smaller space."[3] In addition to text, the modular layout, a standard in modern newspaper design, was filled with visuals and interactive features. On the webpage, users could engage with news audio and videos, webcasts, and community events (figure 2.3, left). Compared to Google's machine-generated textual rundown, this news site gave users a richer experience. In fact, the traditional newspaper industry has a long history in content presentation to better engage readers, which inspired many website design trends.[4] Some of the design ideas that news media used for their websites in the early 2000s were adopted by Google in September 2002 when Google News Beta was launched, but the layout changes of Google News over the years reveal much more than just the changing trends related to website design. Since March 2002, when Google rolled out its news service under the URL news.google.com, the website homepage has undergone four major redesigns. These changes witnessed the long evolution of the

THE GOOGLE NEWS HOMEPAGE OVER TWENTY YEARS

FIGURE 2.3. Left: Homepage of ABCNews.com in 2002. Right: Homepage of Google News Search (Beta) in 2002.
Source: Internet Archive.

website; they also reflect how Google handled news and defined the "Google way" differently at different times.

GOOGLE NEWS' MAJOR REDESIGNS

Since news.google.com went live in the spring of 2002, the Google News homepage had four major redesigns, in the fall of 2002, and then in 2010, 2017, and 2022. What did these changes signify, and how did these changes reflect the definition and redefinition of the "Google way"? In what follows, I

▪ 70 ▪

will address these questions through the examination of the long-term evolution of the Google News website.

The Google News homepage has generally included the header section on the very top (sometimes it's a two-level area with a search and function section below the header), the main body of the homepage (depending on the design, there could be one, two, or three columns in this area), and the footer section. Next, the visual and archival analysis will focus on these areas.

GOOGLE NEWS IN THE FALL OF 2002

In September 2002, when users entered news.google.com, they found that the homepage looked very different than it did six months ago. This version abandoned the previous one-column, list-like style in favor of a multicolumn design structured with modules, a design trend many news websites were adopting at that time. The most notable difference was that the name of the website had changed. "Search" was removed from the website name; it was now "Google News," not "Google News Search." With the name change, this version downplayed the search function. While the search box was still available at the top of the webpage, the search function was not highlighted in the "About" page, as it had been in March. Google News was introduced as a "news service" rather than a search service.

Meanwhile, news was listed on Google's main page with other four Google services: Web, Images, Groups, and Directory. This change indicated the rising status of Google News within the company, as Google only promotes select products on its main page. In the following years, Google News never left the products list that Google promoted on its main page, which reflected the strong status of this service and the deeper normalization of news into Google's core business. On its main page, Google exhorted, "Get your news the Google Way—Try Google News!" This was the first time the "Google way" was announced. What is the "Google way," exactly? Google did not define it explicitly, but Google News's "About" page pointed out something "highly unusual" that helped users understand that what the "Google way" was, foremost, was that it featured "a news service compiled solely by computer algorithms without human intervention."[5] Google stressed: "While this may lead to some occasionally unusual and contradictory groupings, it is exactly this variety that makes Google News a valuable source of information on the important issues of the day."[6] According to Google's description, the novelty of the "Google way" also spoke to the scale ("culled from approximately 4,000 news sources worldwide"), the frequency of updates ("updated continuously throughout the day, so you will see new stories each time you check the page"), the ranking function ("automatically arranged to present the most relevant news first"), and the access to multiple perspectives ("from thousands of sources worldwide—enabling you to see how different news organizations are reporting the same story").[7]

In the September 2002 version, the layout of the Google News homepage was organized based on news sections listed in the navigation bar: "World," "U.S.," "Business," "Sci/Tech," "Sports," "Entertainment," and "Health," the last of which was new to this version. These news sections have remained mostly unchanged throughout the years and became the standard template of Google News. The use of news sections is a common practice of traditional news media, which Google News adopted to organize news and to lay out its webpage structure. Observers found that even the color codes that Google used were similar to those of news media, such as *USA Today*.[8] Unlike the March version, which only listed news headlines, sources, and publication time, the September page also provided a short snippet for each news item. As many other news websites did, photos were added. The combination of these elements would later become controversial and trigger copyright disputes in different countries, as I will discuss in chapter 3.

A new feature for this version is the "In the News" section (figure 2.4, arrow 1), which included ten specific terms, known as "named entities" in the field of natural language processing. These terms often include names of people (e.g., President Bush), places (e.g., Gaza City), and topics (e.g., homeland security). In many cases, they reflect the popular search terms that Google users were querying. When clicking on a named entity, users get a group of related news stories across various news sources. For Google News users, this is a different way of getting news because with its grouping technology, Google unbundled the original news arrangements, in which the news was selected, arranged, and packaged by news editors. Debundled news was then rebundled by Google's own grouping algorithm, using named entities. In journalism, how news was presented as a bundle was an editorial decision: The length, size, placement, and the accompanying visual elements of a news item in relation to other news items in the news package can say much about the editors' interpretation of the nature, importance, and priority of that news item. These editorial decisions establish the news media's agenda-setting power by informing the public of what's newsworthy, what's not, and to what extent. By debundling the news, Google challenged the news media's editorial power, and by rebundling, Google introduced a new way, the "Google way," for users to experience news.

On the Google News homepage, the use of named entities survived the next few major redesigns. In Google's algorithm systems, named entities served as the building blocks to tag and cluster data extracted from news (see details in chapter 4).

FIGURE 2.-4. "In the News" on the Google News (BETA) homepage in September 2002.
Source: Internet Archive, emphasis mine.

Unambiguous named entities are especially important to improve accuracy and relevance of the search results.[9] One way to identify unambiguous named entities is to use what Google calls the "knowledge base" to extract factual information unique to a given term. Google's knowledge base pools information from reputable sources such as news feeds and structured webpages such as Wikipedia.[10] News is particularly relevant here because named entities can be extracted from the 5Ws that journalists are trained to identify clearly in their news stories. Once users learned how to use named entities to find news, data about their news use patterns could be fed back into Google's algorithm systems to analyze users' preferences and interests. The more users use named entities to find news, the better they could follow and refine Google's algorithm across its products, in other words, reinforce both Google's algorithmic design and its product design. This is not completely different from the traditional media industry's vertical integration strategy, in which media companies promote their own media products across business channels that they also own in order to maximize profit. The media industry often does this by owning both the production and the distribution links of the supply chain. For example, the Walt Disney Company, an American media and entertainment conglomerate, can produce films and then market them via the television networks the company owns.[11] In the case of digital vertical integration, platform companies maximize their profit and power through the privatization of data flow and the effect of user lock-in, in which users become overdependent on these companies' products or services, on the one hand, and contribute data to reinforce the dominance of such products and services, on the other.[12]

THE GOOGLE NEWS HOMEPAGE OVER TWENTY YEARS

GOOGLE NEWS REDESIGN IN 2010

Google considered the Google News homepage overhaul in 2010 the biggest since the site's official launch in 2002.[13] In this version, an additional column on the right-hand side was added (figure 2.5, arrow 1) besides the navigation panel on the left side and the news stream in the middle column. This space served as an arena of negotiation to balance the interests of different stakeholders in the digital news environment, including Google, news publishers, regulators, and users. While this column featured "Most popular" stories among users, it also accommodated "Editors' Picks" from news publishers. Google also used this space for features to respond to external pressures from the news industry, the regulatory community, and

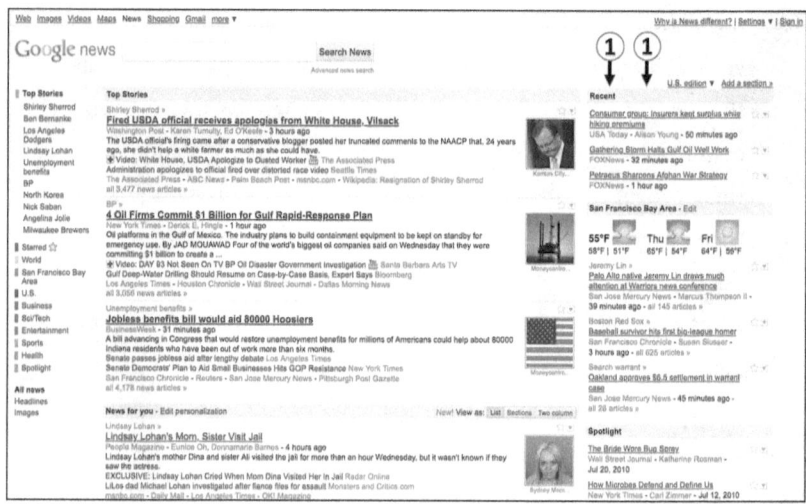

FIGURE 2.5. The Google News homepage in 2010.
Source: Internet Archive, emphasis mine.

the general public. As Google explained, these features catered to interests of different parties, letting "*readers* get the news they're interested in from the sources they trust, and *publishers* receive higher traffic to their websites."[14] By balancing these interests, this space often presented the outcome of editorial, rather than algorithmic, decisions.

When first appeared in the 2010 redesign, this right-hand side column was a busy area with as many as six features, including:

- "Recent": A segment that displayed a small group of breaking news items shortly after they were published by their original news sources.
- Special topic: A place for special news sections as well as Google's self-promotion. Over the years, Google News introduced dozens of special news sections covering elections, the COVID-19 pandemic, the Academy Awards, and the Olympic Games. Probably a legacy of Google's 9/11 experience, crisis response to disastrous events in different parts of the world often appeared in this section, such as the China earthquake in 2008, Gulf of Mexico oil spill in 2010, flooding in Pakistan in 2010, etc. Google's own products, such as Google Maps, were promoted along with the crisis response. In some cases, Google would play an editorial role to boost certain news events; for example, it would recommend Olympic Games–related news to users even if user data showed that they were not particularly interested in sports.[15] This space also functioned as Google's PR bulletin board to publicize its own news; for example, the news about Google News's founder Krishna Bharat engaging

with the journalism community was presented here several times. These practices leave room for human intervention on a platform that Google claimed to be "a news service compiled solely by computer algorithms without human intervention."

- Local coverage: A segment that presented local weather and local news based on the geolocation of the user, an extension of the Local News section introduced in 2008. Before that, Google's local search feature had little to do with news but focused on local information such as directions to a nearby pharmacy or reviews of a neighborhood restaurant. The Local news section has been gaining more priority on the Google News homepage since then and became one of the standard news sections in 2018. Google also developed a deal with the Local Media Consortium, an organization representing more than 1,600 local media outlets in the United States, to build its local network.[16] Google's increasing attention to local news on the one hand reflected local news' informational and economic value, given that 89 percent of Americans get local news online and that local information is people's most important daily information need;[17] on the other hand, it was a response to external pressure, such as that from the News Media Alliance, a nonprofit organization representing over 2,200 member organizations in America's news and magazine industries. The organization has been advocating for new laws to regulate major digital platforms and protect local media,[18] including the Journalism Competition and Preservation Act that aims to provide a forty-eight-month temporary safe harbor for small news publishers to collectively negotiate with dominant online platforms over the terms of using these publishers' content. The development of the Local section on Google News is another example of Google's nonalgorithmic intervention in response to dynamics in the large digital news environment.

- "Spotlight": As opposed to quick updates or breaking news, this feature aggregated long-form, in-depth feature stories of "lasting value," such as "investigative journalism, opinion pieces, special-interest articles, and other stories of enduring appeal."[19] It was claimed that the stories were selected by an undisclosed algorithm, but observers found that Spotlight news was overwhelmingly dominated by mainstream news sources.[20] This feature was considered an effort of Google to offer another element of traditional news media's portfolio, in which Google "steps back from the ever-quickening news cycle" to value "in-depth pieces of lasting value," a news product often considered an important asset of quality journalism.[21]
- Google gadget: A place to introduce Google's own products, ones considered useful to create new ways of consuming news. For example, Google promoted its Fast Flip here, which allowed users to quickly flip through news pages online, simulating the experience at a newsstand.
- "Most popular": A segment with ten stories "most popular" among readers, although Google didn't specify how the "most popular" stories were selected.

The new right-hand-side column was like a mini news website that mirrored various conventional journalistic practices, from breaking news and special news sections to long-form journalism and local news. Specific features in this right-hand column changed from time to time, but this column created a space separate from Google's regular, algorithm-run news stream. Here, features were rolled out to accommodate news publishers' needs. For example, the "Editors' Picks" feature that Google introduced in 2011 allowed Google's news partners to choose their work to be displayed in this area. Google made it clear that this content was not picked by algorithm— "Editors' Picks will always be just that—picks provided by publishers themselves, and not by Google."[22] Observers pointed out that publishers could submit anything that they thought "simply worth reading" and that the point of "Editors' picks" was that "they [news publishers] can choose."[23] Features like this gave back a degree of control to news organizations and changed Google News's stance as a service generated entirely by computer algorithms.

"Fact check" is another feature that was introduced in the right-hand column. This feature had a short history on Google News. Introduced as a news label during the 2016 US presidential election cycle, this feature was seen as a response to criticisms about the role of social media and digital platforms in the spread of mis- and disinformation during the election.[24] To "divine fact from fiction, wisdom from spin," Google News asked news publishers to use ClaimReview[25] techniques and "commonly accepted criteria" to label fact-checking content with standardized data, including the claim being fact checked, the source of the claim, the identification of the fact checker, and the fact-checking conclusion (true or false).[26] In 2017, "Fact check" became an independent, dedicated section in the right-hand side column on the Google News homepage.[27] A small group of fact checkers, such as *PolitiFact*, Snopes.com, the *Washington Post*, and FactCheck.org appeared frequently in this section. During the COVID-19 pandemic, health fact checkers, such as Health Feedback from the World Health Organization, joined this section as well. Google claimed that fact checkers in this section are "algorithmically determined,"[28] but Google also maintains a close relationship with the fact-checking community. For example, Google funded the Fact-Check Insights global database run by Duke Reporters' Lab and the International Fact-Checking Network at Poynter Institute, a nonprofit journalism organization. These examples from the right-hand column on the Google News homepage demonstrated Google's susceptibility to interindustry dynamics as well as influences from the broader sociopolitical environment. These social factors contribute to a fluid idea of the "Google way," which at this stage drifted further from Google's initial vision of a news experience that's entirely algorithm controlled and free from human intervention.

In the redesigned 2010 version, a set of social networking features were introduced on the Google News homepage that allowed users to email and share news via Google Reader (a web feed reader operated by Google), Facebook, Twitter, and Google Buzz (a short-lived sharing tool introduced in 2010 that allowed Google users to network with Gmail contacts). Google's efforts in the social media domain were considered the company's endeavor to compete with Facebook and Twitter when these social media companies rose to become Google's rivals in the digital advertisement market. Over the years, however, Google was unable to develop a clear purpose or effective strategies for its social networking service. On the Google News homepage, the social features were inconsistent, jumping from one tool to another. Steps to integrate social functions into Google News started as early as 2006, when the "Most Popular" section was introduced. The section was then changed into "Most Shared" in 2010 and disappeared in 2016. The criteria for the "most popular" or "most shared" were never clear.[29] Other social features phased out one after another as well. For example, the aforementioned Google Reader was retired in 2013; Google Buzz was shut down in 2011 and the place filled by Google's "+1" button, a function that was designed for users to recommend news content. In 2012, the "+1" feature was gone, replaced by Google+, Google's own social networking system. But Google+ never gained the traction the company expected. Observers pointed out that without both the first mover's advantage on the social media market and substantial differentiation from existing services, Google faced dire odds in competing with established social media platforms. The data breach crisis associated with Google+ and a few wrong moves that damaged users' confidence about the product led to low usage and engagement.[30] Google disclosed that "90 percent of Google+ user sessions are less than five seconds."[31] Google+ was finally shut down in 2018. After several failed attempts, Google's own social features vanished entirely on today's Google News. It could be argued that Google's unsuccessful social media ambition played a role in shaping the "Google way," which tends to be different from the social media way of dealing with news. Google, unlike its social media rivals, who rely on user-driven momentum as their main source of power, seems to channel more effort into maintaining a close relationship with the news industry. This is in contrast to Facebook's deprioritization of news on its platform at a few points of its development and Twitter's exodus of news professionals from the platform after Elon Musk's takeover.

GOOGLE NEWS REDESIGN IN 2017–2018

A new version of Google News, with a "clean and uncluttered" user interface, was introduced in June 2017.[32] In this new version, the homepage was segmented into card-shaped areas, and news stories were displayed in various "news cards." Except news photos at the very front of each news card, most of the elements on the homepage involved white or light-gray backgrounds and black text. Perhaps the most important change that contributed to the "uncluttered" look was that the news snippet for each story was no longer available. Each news card only showed headlines, publisher names, and article labels (figure 2.6).

Although without Google's official explanation about why this change was adopted in the United States, the removal of news snippets on Google News—a change occurring in the aftermath of a wave of copyright disputes surrounding Google's news aggregation service and subsequent regulatory actions, especially in Europe (see chapter 3)—appeared to be a ripple effect of the European cases. One of the concerns of the European news publishers who sued Google for copyright violation was that the combination of the headline, photo, and snippet that Google News made available on its platform provided "more than enough" for users to understand the news and therefore significantly reduced the likelihood of users' visiting publishers' websites. By doing so, they argued, Google's news aggregation practices harmed news publishers' economic interest. It was against this backdrop that Google News removed all news snippets in its 2017 redesign, after fifteen years of using them. Changes like this reflected the tension and negotiation between Google and the traditional news industry.

Another change in the 2017 version of the Google News homepage was the addition of article labels throughout the news stream. Article labels are "predefined, generally understood terms" tagged on news stories to describe the nature of the news content.[33] According to Google, publishers could embed appropriate tags in HTML markup when they opted in to Google News. These labels used to be applied only in the "Top Stories" section but then appeared throughout the whole news stream because "people have told us," noted Google, that "these labels identify important facets of a story and provide more context."[34]

Labels used on the Google News homepage over the years have included "Most Referenced," "Fact Check," "Trending," "Opinion," "Satires," "Press Release," "Featured," "Live Updating," "Highly Cited," "Local Source," "In Depth," "Trending On Google⁺," "Wikipedia," "From Germany [or other locations]," "International," etc. Similar labels have traditionally been used by news media to tell readers about the nature and

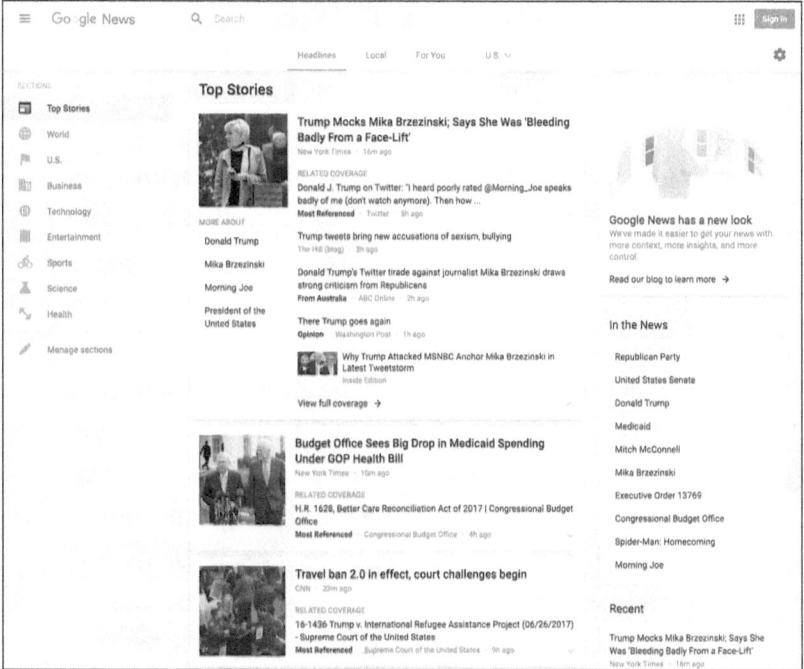

FIGURE 2.6. The Google News homepage in 2017.
Source: Internet Archive.

characteristics of news content.[35] Here, once again, Google adopted newsroom ideas, as the product manager of Google News said, to let users "see additional context on stories immediately even as you are scanning."[36] Labels, like named entities, served to help Google's algorithm decide how news can be clustered, placed, and ranked. Note also that by following Google's rules to create labels via HTML markup, news publishers opted in to Google's datafication process, because these metadata were fed into Google's algorithm to process news (see chapter 4). This type of data is useful in training Google's machine learning systems and enhancing Google's deep linking technology because the more contextual information, the more likely Google is able to pinpoint what the news users were looking for. The deep linking technology that sent users to specific content (such as a news article) rather than a general destination (such as a news website) eventually became a growing concern for news publishers, who argued that deep linking reduced the likelihood of users' browsing a news website as a whole.

After the 2017 redesign, the Google News homepage did not change much in 2018 in terms of the look, but the 2018 Google News was introduced to the public as a "re-imagined," AI-powered news aggregator supported by real-time artificial intelligence and machine learning technologies.[37] Unlike generative AI, which gained significant prominence in 2022 and which can now be used to produce information for the front end (see chapter 5), AI technology back then was primarily utilized in the back end for tasks such as data processing and model training. On the Google News homepage, users wouldn't see the direct manifestations of the AI-powered changes except for some features that involved personalization.

Personalization has a long history on Google News, involving both front-end and back-end models. Depending on the role of the participants in the process of personalization and the degree of user agency involved, some scholars distinguish between these two models of personalization as user-initiated customization versus system-initiated personalization, or active versus passive personalization.[38] In the case of Google News, front-end approaches give users explicit options to customize certain elements on the webpage so they can get preferred news feeds. Back-end personalization, on the other hand, is undertaken usually without users' knowledge. Google's AI algorithms can use contextual user information to make news recommendations based on what the user did in the past and in different social settings, what the user's social networks look like, and what larger communities the user belongs to. Over the years, the personalization choices available for users to customize the Google News webpage stayed largely the same, but the back-end technologies evolved substantially. It can be argued that the unparalleled development of the two personalization models lessened rather than strengthened user agency because it trained users to be lazier, not smarter. Users can play with a few simple options to customize the news page but leave more sophisticated decisions to the back-end algorithm. This is, in fact, explicitly what Google told its users: Google's news recommendation "allows you to be even *lazier* (you don't need to configure your preferences)."[39]

Early personalization on Google News was carried out in the form of user-initiated customization. The earliest attempt dated back to 2002, when users were able to choose their preferred way, that is, a text version versus a graphical version, to view the news page. About three years after the website's official launch, in 2005, Google News users were introduced to a feature called "Customize this page" for the first time, where more customization options were provided. For example, users could create a standard section, choose an international edition, or add a custom section; they could also decide how many news stories (one to nine) to see on the customized news page.

Then from 2006 to 2010, Google News promoted several front-end personalization features. In addition to those just mentioned, users could set news source preferences and geolocation information. In 2010, the new "News for you" section became the "new heart" of the redesigned Google News.[40] Here, users could choose from three view options (list, sections, two-column), search and add news topics to follow, choose how often they would like to read news from each section (never, sometimes, always), and rearrange the order of the news sections. These front-end personalization features gave users limited—and often basic—options to customize the news feeds or the layout of the news page, but personalization since then has become more granular, drilling down from the news-section level to the individual-article level.

Scholars' findings are mixed over whether news personalization contributes to the forming or popping of filter bubbles.[41] Meanwhile, news professionals are concerned about losing editorial control over journalistic work, especially when personalization algorithms do not align with journalistic values.[42] If personalization allows users to prioritize fun, popular content over less popular but important news content, journalists worry that the journalistic mission of serving the public interest and the democratic project may be at stake. While debates about news personalization were going on, Google News, when it was redesigned in 2018, introduced a "Full Coverage" feature as a "unpersonalized" section, where news content is "the same for everyone," so users can have "an unfiltered view of news."[43] It was reported that features like this were offered to present publisher-curated content,[44] another space for editorial, rather than algorithmic, decisions, offering yet another illustration of the continual negotiation between Google and the news industry.

At first, personalization features on Google News did not require any personally identifying information. Starting in late 2005, users were asked to sign in to use these features. In the years that followed, more features on the website, such as "For you," "Favorites," and "Saved searches," required the user to sign in to enable personalized search and setup. The sign-in requirement would give Google direct access to a greater quantity of and more precise user data from the back end. While front-end personalization can be observed on the homepage, back-end operations are often invisible to users. According to Google's privacy policy and terms,[45] Google collected various types of user information, including personal information (e.g., name, email address, account password, payment information), login information (e.g., web request, IP address, browser information, cookies), and user communications (e.g., emails). Google also combined user information associated with the Google account with information from other Google services and third parties for contextual user data; for example, Google News recommended news stories "read by many other users who've also read similar stories as you in the past."[46] Google could also collect and manipulate information obtained by third-party applications and gadgets, location data, and advertising cookies; user communications, such as the content of SMS messages; deleted information; user information shared by Google partners; YouTube information, comments, and posts; user information used for Google Analytics; photos,

THE GOOGLE NEWS HOMEPAGE OVER TWENTY YEARS

videos, docs, spreadsheets, and related information from publicly accessible sources; information stored even without signing into a Google account; and more. After 2018, as Google News became more AI-driven, contextual user information played an increasingly important role in training and optimizing Google's AI technology.

In the 2022 Google News redesign, customization was introduced as one of the highlights. The customization function in the new Google News looked almost the same as the one rolled out seventeen years earlier (figure 2.7). What's different is the back-end technology, which had advanced markedly since then, while remaining largely invisible to users. Also less noticeable to many users is that this time around, sign-in, or giving away user data in exchange for Google's services, was more readily taken for granted than seventeen years ago.

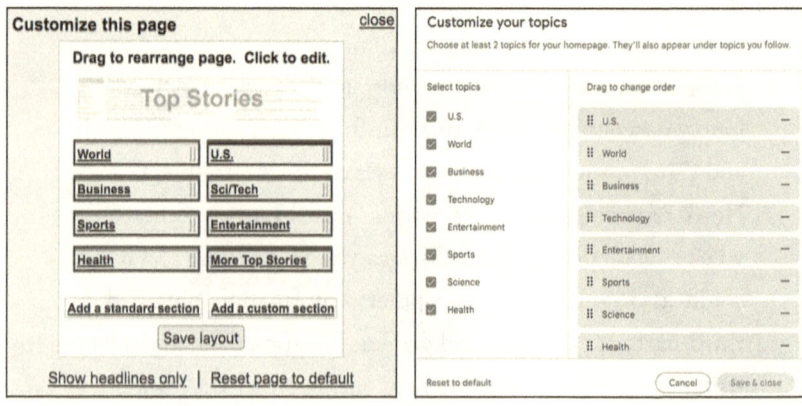

FIGURE 2.7. Left: "Customize this page" in March 2005. Right: "Customize your topics" in 2022.
Source: L: Internet Archive; R: Google News.

THE GOOGLE NEWS HOMEPAGE OVER TWENTY YEARS

GOOGLE NEWS REDESIGN IN 2022–2023

On June 22, 2022, Google announced another redesign. Scrolling down the page, users would find that the previous three-column layout had been replaced by a pane of news cards (see figure 2.8). Some observers found that the new design made Google News look more like a newspaper's front page.[47] Indeed, if readers open a newspaper's homepage, say nytimes.com, next to Google News's window, they might see some similarities. On the new homepage, items that used to be located in the left-hand navigation panel were moved to the header section below the search window, including "Home," "For you," "Following," and nine news sections. In the footer section, Google reminded users to sign in to get news based off of their personal interests. In the main body of the webpage, news cards were organized under separate headings.

In this version, Google continues to emphasize the idea of "you" to center the users. This emphasis can be seen from sections such as "For you," "Your briefing," and "Your topics," where users can receive personalized news service. The biggest change in this round of redesign came from "News Showcase," a new feature rolled out in the United States in the summer of 2023 that signified Google's adjustment to its relationship with news publishers in the wake of the changing regulatory climate inside and outside the United States.

News Showcase is a section on Google News that presents "stories selected by newsroom editors" (figure 2.9). Since Google pays its news partners for their participation in News Showcase, the feature is widely seen as the company's response

THE GOOGLE NEWS HOMEPAGE OVER TWENTY YEARS

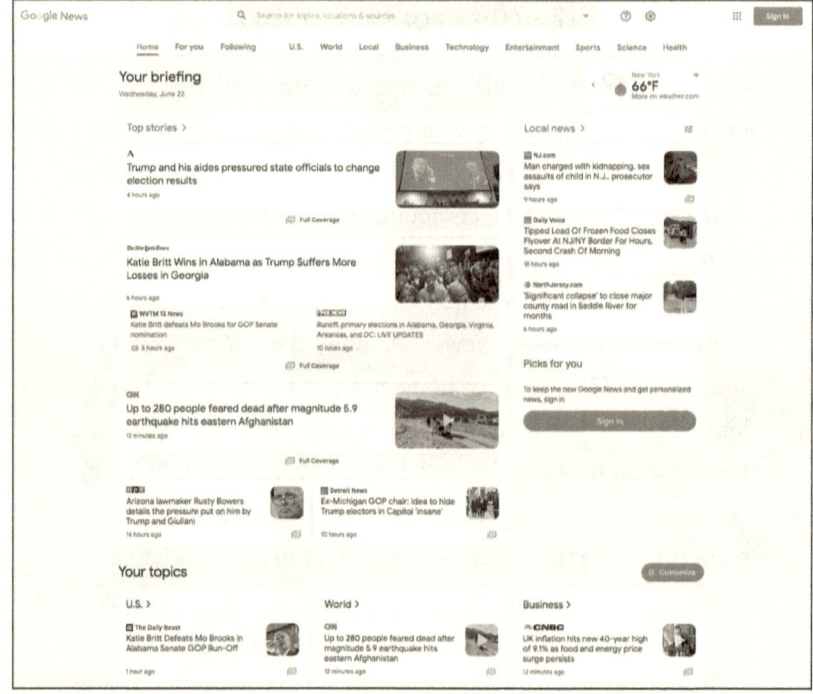

FIGURE 2.8. The Google News homepage in 2022.
Source: Google News.

to the legislative efforts in different parts of the world that require tech platforms to compensate news publishers for using their content.[48] Starting 2020, News Showcase was rolled out in markets outside the United States as Google's licensing program, but its domestic launch was three years later when similar legislation was proposed in the United States. In California, a new bill, the California Journalism Preservation Act, passed the California Senate Judiciary Committee in June

2023; this bill would require tech companies to pay Californian news media for the right to distribute news content on their platforms.[49] A week later, Google announced its plan to launch News Showcase in the United States. To prevent the proposed legislation, Google also struck a deal with California lawmakers to fund newsrooms in the state, which involved a $250 million commitment.[50]

News Showcase allows Google's partner news publishers to choose their own news stories and present them in a content package, or news Panels, using templates in such formats as "news rundown," "timeline," "bullets," "related articles," "extended access," and "follow publisher." It was reported that News Showcase does not involve any ranking algorithm; instead, news publishers have full control over what content to present and how—"publishers never had this kind of opportunity or control over the presentation of their content on Google News in the past," stated observers.[51] By inviting the creation of news packages, this feature was the furthest that Google News had gone since its birth. The change transformed the "Google way" from "a novel approach to news" that debundled and rebundled news packages through algorithm-driven news aggregation to a negotiated outcome among Google, the news industry, and the regulatory authorities, culminating in the invitation to news bundles to return to its platform. With the new redesign, Google offered to help news media increase traffic, engagement, and subscription gains through features like "Following" and "Google Reader Revenue Manager."[52] The "Google way" has become a series of strategic maneuvers that aim to serve Google's two-sided market, which, on the one hand, promises user-customers with algorithm-generated, personalized news experience that's different from the traditional way of consuming news, and, on the other hand, caters to news publisher–customers to satisfy their economic interests and ease Google's external pressure.

FIGURE 2.9. News Showcase on Google News in 2023.
Source: Google News.

As of June 2022, Google News reported that its service is available in over 125 countries and forty languages.[53] This grew from the five international editions that Google News listed on its homepage in 2003: Australia, Canada, India, New Zealand, and the United Kingdom. The list expanded to sixty-three countries by 2009, eighty-one in 2017, and then 125 in 2022. From five countries to 125 countries, the growth of international coverage enhanced Google's reach and legitimacy in the global media landscape, which was supported by an expanding web of global news sources that Google indexes. When Google News was launched in 2002, it searched and browsed four thousand news sources. That number grew to more than eighty thousand news publishers around the world as of January 2019. Meanwhile, studies found that news content presented on Google News was dominated by Western perspectives and concentrated on a small number of large, legacy media outlets that are often based in metro areas such as New York City, Washington, and Los Angeles.[54] Source concentration deviated from Google News's initial imagination of the "Google way," in which users can access multiperspectival news across sources worldwide thanks to bias-free algorithms. This issue about source diversity and other aspects of media diversity will be discussed in more detail in chapter 4, in the context of COVID-19 pandemic.

CHAPTER FLASHBACK AND DISCUSSION

When Google News was launched, Google proudly declared, "Get your news the Google way!" What is the "Google way?"

Google never answered that question explicitly. The decades-long evolution of Google News and the four major redesigns on its homepage reveal a fluid idea of the "Google way." Initially, the "Google way" was branded as a "novel approach to news" that aggregates news across news sources worldwide "solely by computer algorithms without human intervention." This approach allowed Google to debundle and rebundle the news packages arranged by news media, which disrupted news media's gatekeeping and agenda-setting power. Through each redesign over the past more than two decades, however, the "Google way" has drifted from its original vision and become a means to maneuver between various stakeholders in the digital news environment. This process witnessed the evolution of Google's technological specialization, through which news was reimagined; it also documented how Google's news ambition responded to the inter-industry, cross-stakeholder power dynamics. News and technology, as demonstrated by these interactions, are hybridized through the "Google way." Algorithm, like news, is a "network of actions upon actions"[55] and decisions upon decisions. The evolution of the Google News homepage over the past two decades provides a window to observe these developments, and the next few chapters will continue to explore the deeper reasons for and implications of them. The "Google way," whether as a proactive or reactive approach to news, has shaped the digital news environment profoundly in terms of the economy of news, media diversity, and the institutional developments of the tech and news sectors.

Chapter Three

DISPUTES SURROUNDING GOOGLE NEWS

A GLOBAL MEDIA-TECH LANDSCAPE

THIS CHAPTER focuses on the resistance that Google has encountered from the news industry. Google's expanding efforts after 9/11 alerted the news industry that the company's interests in news were not just a temporary response to 9/11 but an investment that would only grow larger. As the "Google way" increased its influence, news publishers worldwide began to resist. This chapter will analyze the disputes between Google and news publishers in different parts of the world. These disputes revealed traditional news industry's concerns facing Google's rise and how Google coped with challenges coming from the news industry, all unfolding within a complex global media and technology landscape.

On February 24, 2021, Australia passed the News Media and Digital Platforms Mandatory Bargaining Code. Under the new law, Google is required to sign licensing agreements with Australian publishers for news content that appears on

Google's platforms. In the days leading up to the passage of the new law, Google threatened to shut down its search engine in Australia, but one week before the law was passed, Google signed commercial agreements with major Australian publishers such as Nine Entertainment, an Australian media company that owns a TV network, radio stations, and several newspapers and digital properties, and Seven West, one of Australia's leading integrated media companies, with businesses in broadcast television, publishing, and online media. The deals were reported to be worth over AU$60 million ($46 million) annually.[1] Google also signed a three-year agreement with News Corp, a global media corporation that operates primarily in the United States, Australia, and the United Kingdom, with News Corp Australia being one of Australia's largest media organizations. With this deal, News Corp will receive "significant payments" from Google when the tech company uses news content from News Corp publications such as the *Wall Street Journal*, the *Times* (London), and the *Australian*.[2]

As observers predicted, the Australian law inspired similar legislation around the world. On April 5, 2022, Canada introduced "Australia-style" legislation called the Online News Act, or House of Commons Bill C-18, that required platforms such as Google to make fair deals with Canadian news businesses, which will be assessed by the Canadian Radio–Television and Telecommunications Commission. If the deals were not approved, mandatory bargaining and final-offer arbitration will be processed by the regulator.[3] These recent regulatory developments focusing on news, in which Google is one of the main addressees, were in fact the follow-up to many earlier disputes between Google and news publishers in different parts of the world. In this chapter, I will examine these disputes, starting with the EU countries France, Belgium, Italy, Germany, and Spain, followed by cases from the United States and the United Kingdom, and then Brazil and beyond. In each case, I will identify the resisters involved in the disputes, the approaches that the resisters pursued, the main arguments and counterarguments of the involved parties, and the consequences of these disputes (table 3.1). Each case has its unique aspects, but together these cases outline the resistance against the "Google way," which evolved over time and concerned various areas related to Google's power and influence, from copyright and antitrust issues to technology and business model issues. These disputes reflected the complex interplay of the industrial, national, and regional interests in the global media-tech landscape.

FRANCE

European publishers were the first to pursue legal actions against Google. In March 2005, Agence France Presse (AFP), the world's third-largest news agency, reporting in French, English, Arabic, Portuguese, Spanish, and German and headquartered in Paris, France, filed a copyright lawsuit against Google in the United States and France. The AFP lawsuit, which was closely watched in the media industry, charged Google News with copyright violation by using AFP's news content without permission. The litigation process lasted for

TABLE 3.1 Disputes surrounding Google and its news service

Country	Year	Resister	Means of resistance	Main issues	Consequences
France	2005	AFP	Litigation	Copyright	Settlement; Google agreed to pay after new EUCD
Belgium	2006	Copiepresse	Litigation	Copyright	Settlement
Italy	2009	FIEG	Official complaint	Antitrust	Settlement
Germany	2012	VG Media	Litigation	Copyright	New legislation
Spain	2014	AEDE	Lobbying	Copyright	New legislation; Google News shutdown in 2014; return in 2022
United States	2009	AP	Commercial negotiation	Compensation	Contractual agreements
United Kingdom	2010	News Corp.	Market approaches	Compensation	Payment agreement
Brazil	2009	ANJ	Collective boycott; lobbying	Disinformation	New bill; Google agreed to pay
Other countries	2021–2024	News publishers and regulators in Australia, Canada, South Africa, and Indonesia	Lobbying; advocating; public discourse	Compensation	New laws; investigations

two years. In April 2007, the case was settled by the US District Court for the District of Columbia after the two parties jointly dismissed their respective claims and counterclaims. The AFP and Google signed a licensing agreement that allowed Google News to use AFP's news content in "innovative, new ways."[4] In the aftermath of *Agence France Presse v. Google Inc.*, Google agreed to create a €60 million fund to help French publishers with their internet presence and online revenue. With the agreement, Google was able to host French publishers' news content and was temporarily free from the threat of legislation regarding a "Google tax."[5]

One of the foci of the AFP lawsuit was the copyrightability of news. While AFP claimed copyright over its news headlines, leads, and images, Google argued that news was not protected by copyright law. The dispute hinged on the nature of journalistic content and practice. In the history of copyright, as I will elaborate later in this chapter, there have been inconsistent understandings of the nature of news. Article 2(8) of the Berne Convention, for example, said that the copyright protection should not apply to "news of the day or miscellaneous facts having the character of mere items of press information."[6] The debate about the copyrightability of news also reflected the different journalism culture in the United States and France. Fact-based reporting and objectivity are in the core values and norms of American journalism, but these ideas have never developed in Europe as fully as in the United States.[7] French journalism traditionally has a strong political-literary character, which involves a considerable amount of creative work, with writing that mixes descriptive, normative, and commentary statements.[8]

In the lawsuit, Google held that news stories report "facts" and that facts are not copyrightable, but AFP insisted that journalistic work has both expressive value and factual value.[9] The minimal threshold of copyrightability, argued AFP, is "originality," and news meets the two conditions of originality: independence and creativity. AFP claimed that news is "independently created by the author (as opposed to copied from other works)" and possesses "some minimal level of creativity."[10] According to AFP, the copyright is in the original expression in news rather than the facts themselves. Based on this argument, when Google uses AFP's news content on its news aggregation service, it copied both the facts and the expression of the facts, hence constituting infringement of copyright.

The copyrightability of specific news elements, such as headlines, news leads, and news images, were also debated. Google insisted that these news elements, rather than copyrighted work, are simply components with practical functionalities in its algorithm system. News headlines, for instance, are ordinary statements of the news events, and news images are merely "another link to a story."[11] Google argued that AFP headlines were too short to be protected. Without a substantial length, Google held that the headlines could not hold protectable expressions and that AFP headlines were only titles that functioned as labels for news stories. According to 37 C. F. R. § 202.1(a), Google pointed out, titles are words and short phrases that are not subject to copyright.[12] AFP defended the copyrightability of headlines, claiming that headlines differ from titles because the former involves originality and creativity while the latter would be only an identifier of the news story. In the expert report that AFP submitted to the court, AFP illustrated that while "Planes Crash Into Downtown Office Buildings" (a mock headline) might serve as an identifier of a news story, the actual headlines news professionals created for that news—such as "War at Home" (a headline in the *Dallas Morning News* on September 11, 2001) and "Terror Beyond Belief" (a headline of the Newark, New Jersey, *Star Ledger* on September 11, 2001)—while short in length, provided readers with rich information that was far beyond the mere facts.[13]

Google also viewed the news-making process as a series of discrete activities based on the division of labor in newsrooms: Editors assign tasks, reporters cover beats, and copy editors write headlines. Similarly, argued Google, news was broken down into separate units in its algorithm system. AFP, on the other hand, stressed the wholeness of journalism work. The news publisher argued that journalism is a whole process that involves practices and decision making that are highly professional and should be protected. Journalistic work, according to AFP, is presented to its audience as a package to reflect this process. AFP demonstrated in its expert report that the design of the news package, from headline writing to font selection and the size and placement of images, effectively shape the audience's attention, perception, and the overall experience of the news.[14] With Google News, AFP argued that journalistic work as a "whole" was not able to reach its audience. Through a series of eye-tracking studies, AFP demonstrated that after going through the combination of a headline, blurb, and image made publicly available on Google News, users were less likely to visit the publisher's news website or enjoy the whole package that journalism professionals hope to deliver. AFP therefore asserted that Google News harmed the professional and commercial value of the news.[15]

In the debate between AFP and Google, the news publisher defended journalism's traditional gatekeeping role. In this role, the selection, deselection, and arrangement of news are editorial decisions that determine what information the public should know and in what way. Google, on the other hand, took a technological view of news, which perceived news as pure facts that do not merit copyright protection. This technological view is related to how news is datafied in Google's algorithm systems, in which news needs to be transformed into quantifiable data that can be processed by machine (see chapter 4). During this datafication process, some journalistic logics are lost because they are elusive or unsolvable from an algorithmic point of view. At the core of the *AFP v. Google* lawsuit is the copyrightability issue of news. While it might be a technical question for Google, from a journalistic view, the copyrightability of news pertains to the legitimacy of journalism.

In 2007, the two-year litigation between AFP and Google News ended with a settlement. Though the details were not disclosed, the two parties agreed on using "innovative, new ways" to "dramatically improve the way" users experience news on the internet.[16] These "innovative, new ways," defined through the negotiation of the two parties, would contribute to the "Google way"—which apparently was not solely designed by Google. According to the settlement, Google agreed to use

DISPUTES SURROUNDING GOOGLE NEWS

AFP's content to "highlight original journalism," "giving credit to the newswire journalists who worked hard to break the news," and to "ensure that AFP's original journalism and breaking news are easily discoverable on Google services and in particular on Google News."[17] Observers viewed this settlement as something that marked a change from Google's "historical position" when the tech company believed that on the internet "it can grab whatever it wants without permission."[18]

BELGIUM

Shortly after the launch of Google News in Belgium in 2006, Copiepresse, an association representing the publishers of French- and German-language newspapers in Belgium, filed a descriptive distraint petition to the Brussels tribunal of first instance, claiming that Google News had breached its copyrights by counterfeiting.[19] The court granted the petition and appointed a judicial expert, Luc Golvers, to investigate Google News.[20] In August 2006, Copiepresse filed an official lawsuit against Google. Based on the Belgian Copyright and Related Rights Act of June 30, 1994, the court of appeal of Brussels ruled in September 2006 that Google had violated the publications' copyright. The ruling required Google to withdraw the press content from both Google.be and Google News Belgium and post the ruling on the homepage of these sites or pay the fine.[21]

In *Google Inc. v. Copiepresse*, the first thing the Belgian court had to decide is which law was applicable in this case. Google insisted that American law should prevail because the ownership, the location of the hardware and software, and the act called into question all were situated or had occurred in the United States. The Belgian court ruled, however, that Belgian law should be applied on the following grounds: (1) The affected news producers were Belgians; (2) Google used a Belgian domain name, google.be and news.google.be, which intentionally target the Belgian market; (3) Google worked with Belgian advertisers; and (4) the dissemination of the news content available on Google News Belgium occurred in Belgium. The ruling was a reminder that national boundaries persist even for those digital platforms considered "global superplayers."[22] These boundaries complicated the global media and technology landscape and contributed to the collision between local interests and digital platforms' global ambitions. Like AFP, Copiepresse also pursued legal means under the copyright framework, but unlike the French case, *Google Inc. v. Copiepresse* raised issues that heavily focused on the technological perspective.

First, caching was a major concern of Belgian publishers. Caching is a technique that Google uses to archive information. With this technology, Google is able to make information available to searchers even if the information is no longer accessible on the original website. In *Google Inc. v. Copiepresse*, Copiepresse argued that caching allowed Google to illegally reproduce Belgian publishers' content and breach their copyright. Google's defense was that caching was conducted by intelligent robots that came across the web content automatically. Since information on the web was publicly accessible, Google argued that the crawling should not be considered infringement. Google also maintained that it only transmitted the HTML files, not the actual news articles. It was the users, argued Google, who copied and downloaded the news articles, whereas Google only provided users with the "installations aimed at facilitating communication."[23] The disagreement about caching was not only between Copiepresse and Google but also among regulators. According to EU regulators, caching, as "an integral and essential part" of the technological process that is widely recognized and used by the tech industry to "enable transmission systems to function efficiently," was exempted from the European Copyright Directive.[24] However, the Brussels court ruled that Google's technical arguments were not founded, because the infringement relates to whether, rather than how, the copyrighted content was copied and communicated to the public by Google. The court pointed out that the public would not have had the access to the content that no longer existed on the original website had Google not made it available through caching.

Another argument that Google made was that Google News did not reproduce or communicate protected work to the public because it was a search engine that functioned on automated algorithms to generate search results. Search engines, argued Google, should be exempted from the reproduction right under Article 5.1 of the Copyright Directive because search engines engage in "temporary acts of reproduction . . . whose sole purpose is to enable . . . a transmission in a network between third parties by an intermediary."[25] As demonstrated in chapter 2, Google was ambiguous about whether Google News was a news search engine or a news aggregator—even though the website's name had changed from Google News Search to Google News. Google's arguments in this and other cases made one wonder if such ambiguousness was based on considerations intended to protect Google from potential legal risks. Luc Golvers, the judicial expert appointed to investigate Google News, concluded in his report that Google News functioned as an information portal, not as a search engine, because it did not merely host but also selected, classified, and ranked information based on its own algorithms. Golvers concluded that Google News was not a "passive intermediary" and therefore could not invoke the exception provided for under the Belgian copyright law.[26]

Another technical issue debated in *Google Inc. v. Copiepresse* was "implied consent." Google argued that technical standards—such as metatags and robots.txt files, which are robot exclusion protocols (REP) that allow websites to tell web crawlers not to collect information from a site—were "nearly universally accepted and are honored by all reputable search engines."[27] Since Belgian publishers did not use these technical standards, Google argued, they had given "implied consent" to Google to exploit their content. The court ruled that copyright protection requires "explicit permission," not implied consent. The technical means, the court said, cannot justify the assumption that anything that is not forbidden is permitted, even in a digital context. To support this decision, the court cited a long quotation from Carine Bernault, a professor at the University of Nantes in France, condemning the idea of "subjecting copyright to technology" to create "a situation of dependency": "These technological measures should therefore remain at the service of the social (judicial, if you wish) rules, of the rules society has chosen. It would not be acceptable that software programs would become some sort of normalization tool of the so-called information society, a technical 'law' that would be imposed surreptitiously!"[28] In 2008, Copiepresse and its member publishers proposed an alternative technical standard, known as ACAP (Automated Content Access Protocol), which was an extension of REP but would give publishers full control over their work about what crawlers can or cannot do with their content.[29] ACAP turned out to be an unsuccessful attempt, but it reflected Belgian publishers' demand for self-control through technical means.

With these concerns, Copiepresse demanded $77 million in compensation for losses caused by Google News's copyright infringement.[30] In 2006, the tribunal of first instance of Brussels held that Google News had led to the loss of advertising revenue for Belgian publishers and had allowed users to evade paying for news, which put publishers at risk of not being able to get the resources needed to pay their journalists properly.[31] The court also supported Copiepresse's argument that Google used its free news aggregation service as a "decoy" to attract traffic to Google's own platforms and gain advertising revenue.[32] The court of appeal of Brussels ruled: "Admittedly, the 'Google News' service is free of charge and, in Belgium, it does not contain any advertising; this fact does however not imply that the economic balance of the interests at stake would tilt in favor of Google, because it must be taken into account that this free service can only be provided thanks to the significant revenue Google generates as a result of the attractiveness of all its

DISPUTES SURROUNDING GOOGLE NEWS

services and the horizontal sliding of revenue which this interactivity facilitates."[33]

While there is no precise figure on how much monetary value Google News contributed to Google, in 2008, Google's vice president Marissa Mayer said at the Brainstorm Tech conference in Half Moon Bay, California, that Google News might not make money on its own but that it "funnels readers over to the main Google search engine, where they do searches that *do* produce ads" and suggested that Google News drove $100 million worth of benefit to the "Google ecosystem."[34] This statement put a controversial price tag on the financial impact that Google's news aggregation service had on news media, which later was used by some news publishers as a reference to claim their loss.

In September 2006, the tribunal of first instance of Brussels ruled that Google had violated the publications' copyright. Google appealed in 2007. In 2011, the court of appeal of Brussels issued a final judgment upholding the original decision to confirm Google's copyright violation. In 2012, the litigation between Copiepresse and Google was settled in an agreement in which Google agreed to partner with Belgian publishers on a broad range of business initiatives. Based on the agreement, Google would help publishers increase their revenue and audience engagement by optimizing their use of Google products, while publishers would advertise Google services on their media platforms.[35] It was reported that although Google said it did not pay to settle the dispute, the company actually paid €5 million to Belgian publishers and likely agreed to buy advertising from them as well.[36]

Compared to the French case, Copiepresse's resistance against the "Google way" focused more on technical and economic issues. While the AFP case was trying to make a copyright case, in *Copiepresse v. Google*, the Belgian news publisher made its economic demand stronger and more explicit, with charges targeting specific technical issues on which Google's technological specialization and business model relied. It is also noteworthy that the power dynamics between the journalistic way and the "Google way" started to shift after the Belgium case. In *Google Inc. v. Copiepresse*, Google accused Copiepresse of using its "dominant position" to restrict Google's access to the Belgian market and charged the intention of the news publisher as "first of all financial and protectionist."[37] In later cases, however, Google became the one who was accused of abusing the dominant position while news publishers considered themselves the victim of unfair competition. This change demonstrated the news industry's discursive approach to resistance and also reflected Google's fast expansion in the global news market, which led to the antitrust argument in the Italy case.

ITALY

In August 2009, the Italian Federation of Newspaper Publishers (Federazione Italiana Editori Giornali, or FIEG) filed an official complaint to the Competent Authority of Competition and Market (Autorità Garante della Concorrenza e del Mercato, or AGCM), Italy's antitrust watchdog, requesting an

DISPUTES SURROUNDING GOOGLE NEWS

investigation into Google News Italia about the lack of transparency in its operation.[38] The investigation began in August 2009 and was soon extended from Google News to Google Inc. in Italy and then to Google Ireland Limited in the following year.[39] AGCM ended the probe in January 2011, finding Google's proposals sufficient for removing the anticompetitive concerns raised in FIEG's complaint.[40] In 2016, Google and FIEG reached an agreement aiming at "strategic collaboration" through Google's investment of more than 12 million Euros.[41] Unlike the French and Belgian cases, which primarily depended on the legal framework of copyright, the dispute between FIEG and Google focused on the antitrust issue. Given that Google accounted for more than 90 percent of the online search market in Italy,[42] far beyond the 40 percent threshold set by Article 82 of the EC Treaty, the case was investigated under the "dominant market position" framework.[43]

According to FIEG, while publishers have the option to opt out of Google News, their absence on Google News would lead to their exclusion from Google Web Search. Italian publishers were concerned that given Google's over-90 percent market share in Italy, the link between Google News and Google Web Search could negatively affect the ranking, presentation, and accessibility of their online content. Without affecting its market domination, Google responded with a few technical proposals, including a separate crawler for Google News and a more sophisticated REP that gave publishers the option to opt out of Google News but remain available in Google Web Search. FIEG was also concerned about AdSense, an online advertising service in which Google plays an intermediary role between website owners and advertisers who seek online advertising space by matching website texts and display ads.[44] FIEG complained that Google couldn't justify its role connecting the buying and selling of online advertising space, nor did it share information with Italian news publishers about how advertising revenue acquired via AdSense was calculated and shared. In response, Google Ireland, Google's European headquarters, revised the terms and conditions of AdSense by providing more disclosure about the percentage of advertising revenue sharing. These surface-level adjustments allowed Google's core business interest to remain intact.

A technical issue that FIEG paid attention to was Google's deep-linking technology. Deep linking pinpointed specific news articles for users, rather than sending them to the homepage of a news site. Italian publishers considered the homepage the most prominent space on a news website, as this is the place for news media's branding message and homepage ads, which are usually the most profitable. Google defended its deep-linking technology by arguing that the premise of search engines is to save users time and effort by linking them to the most relevant information on the web. Directing users to the homepage rather than to specific news articles would harm the users' interest. This argument was supported by AGCM.

Overall, the Italian publishers weren't able to make a very strong antitrust case against Google. In its 2010 annual report to Italian Parliament, AGCM pointed out that "a real imbalance" between traditional news media and digital platforms had not been resolved, and the supranational nature of this imbalance complicated the relationships and the interests of

DISPUTES SURROUNDING GOOGLE NEWS

involved parties."[45] Google and FIEG later reached an agreement, in which Google agreed to invest 12 million euros over three years to support FIEG publishers through the use of Google tools, distribution solutions, and content protection.[46] Concerned about the temporary remedy without a solid legal basis, AGCM called on the Italian government for new regulations. In May 2017, following the Italian tax office's investigation, Google agreed to pay 306 million euros in back taxes.[47]

From *Agence France Presse v. Google Inc.* to *Google Inc. v. Copiepresse* and then to the dispute between FIEG and Google, news publishers' resistance against Google went deeper, zeroing in on the fundamentals of Google's technologies; business model; vertical integration across Google's own products, services, and platforms; and market domination. Google responded mostly through technological and economic means without altering its fundamental interests. For the most part, Google's defense and its proposed solutions involved its own technologies and monetary offers. It appeared that the tech giant would rather pay millions of dollars to settle these disputes than be pulled into the regulatory frameworks that the news industry advocated, whether about copyright or antitrust.

GERMANY

In 2012, a new law, the Ancillary Copyright Law for Press Publishers (Leistungsschutzrecht für Presseverleger), was drafted in Germany. The law particularly addressed search

DISPUTES SURROUNDING GOOGLE NEWS

engines and online news aggregators, prohibiting these platforms from using German publishers' news content without paying a fee. The law went into effect in 2013, but Google refused to abide by the law. In June 2014, VG Media, the collective that represented over 230 German publishers, sued Google for copyright violation under the Ancillary Copyright Law. In response, Google decided to display only links and headlines allowed by the law, without news snippets and images, for those German publishers who did not opt in to Google's news aggregation service.[48] Shortly afterward, all German publishers represented by VG Media gave Google permission to host their content for free, given the "major economic pressure" of losing traffic.[49] VG Media has filed several civil complaints against Google since then to enforce the law and collect payment.[50] In 2019, however, Europe's highest court ruled that German publishers could not claim their copyright compensation under the ancillary copyright law, not because Google did not violate German publishers' copyright but because German regulators did not follow the European Union's requirement to notify the European Commission about the new legislation (EU Directive 2015/1535 requires EU member states to notify the European Union of any draft technical regulation before its adoption).[51] VG Media continued to lobby the German government to implement the new EU copyright rules, which, according to the VG Media CEO, "favors the press publishers by conferring wider and (more) robust rights than the 2013 German law."[52]

It was reported that Germany's Ancillary Copyright Law was lobbied for by the big players in the German media industry.[53] The law was drafted as an addendum to Germany's Copyright Act of September 9, 1965, focusing on the rights of press publishers over their content.[54] The new law granted German press publishers a one-year exclusive right over their content after it was made publicly available online for commercial purposes. The law stipulated that the public accessibility of press products is permissible but not for "commercial providers of search engines or commercial providers of services that condition the content accordingly." The latter, according to the European Publishers Council, referred to news aggregators.[55] Google and opponents of the law questioned whether the law was necessary in the first place, given that technical tools, for example, metatags and robots.txt protocols, were available for publishers to opt out of Google News.[56] Publishers who supported the law insisted that a legal basis was urgently needed to differentiate undesirable and desired uses of their content.

After the law was passed, Google was able to use technical methods to bypass the payment obligation required by the law. In 2013, Google introduced a new confirmation system, which required publishers to submit verification information for inclusion in Google News.[57] Unlike the previous approach, in which Google allowed news publishers to opt out of its services by using robots.txt and metatags, the new confirmation system allowed Google to seek explicit rather than "implied" consent to use publishers' content. A technical tweak not only spared Google from potential legal obligations but also strengthened Google's control in its relationship with the news industry. Then, in October 2014, Google removed the snippets and images and made only headlines and links available (the law allowed free use of "single words or very small text excerpts") for German publishers that did not opt in.[58] One month later, after seeing the drop in online traffic, publishers represented by VG Media decided to give Google permission to use their content for free but criticized Google for "extortion."[59] Axel Springer, one of Europe's largest media companies and publisher of *Bild*, Germany's biggest mass-circulation newspaper, saw a 40 percent traffic drop from Google and an 80 percent drop from Google News during the turmoil.[60] Under the economic pressure and in fear of losing online relevance, Axel Springer decided to give its permission for Google to use its content for free. Axel Springer identified this decision as "the most successful failure," adding, "we now know very precisely just how far-reaching the consequences of the discrimination are, as well as the real effects of Google's market power and how Google punishes everyone who exercises a right that has been granted to them by the German Bundestag."[61]

Germany was the first country that passed new legislation to manage the disputes between Google and news organizations. The law was a product of German publishers' lobbying power, and it was used as the legal base for news organizations to sue Google. However, Google was able to bypass its requirements through technological means, diminishing the effectiveness of the legal intervention. Although the law was not necessarily effective or recognized by Europe's highest court, it set the precedent for later cases to tackle related disputes in the digital age.

SPAIN

In 2014, Spain reformed its copyright law, the Ley de Propiedad Intelectual (LPI), in which online news aggregators were required to pay Spanish news publishers for using their news content. The new law, which took effect on January 1, 2015, was referred to as the "Google Tax" or "Canon AEDE," a product of the lobbying of the Association of Spanish Daily Publishers—the Asociación de Editores de Diarios Españoles (AEDE)—which represents large news publishers in Spain. On December 16, 2014, two weeks before the official implementation of the new LPI, Google News shut down its service in Spain, Google's strongest reaction to such legislation in the European market.

In Spain's new law, Section 2 of Article 32 allowed online aggregators to use "nonsignificant fragments" of original content for information, public opinion, and entertainment purposes. In exchange, it entitled publishers to the right of fair compensation for such uses. The right, according to the new law, was inalienable. Spain's AEDE law was widely read as a piece of legislation that followed the precedent of the Ancillary Copyright Law in Germany, but it differed from the German law by its arbitrary nature. By setting up the inalienable right, Canon AEDE defined a "requirement" for publishers rather than a "privilege."[62] This mandatory right was also considered a lesson learned from the German case, in which since the compensation was not mandatory, Google was able to circumvent the law.[63] It's noteworthy that the Spanish law exempted search engines from the obligation under three conditions:

DISPUTES SURROUNDING GOOGLE NEWS

- The use of content was not for the search engine's own commercial purposes.
- The content was used to respond users' queries.
- A link to the original content is available.[64]

The clear distinction made between online aggregators and search engines was a unique characteristic of the Spanish case. Previous cases in the European Union had provided lessons for making such distinction. In the Belgian case, for example, Google argued that Google News was merely a search engine, and it used this argument as an attempt to invoke a copyright exception enjoyed by search engines. The German case also showed that while publishers resisted Google *news*, they did not want to be excluded from Google *search*, given its dominance on the search market and its power to determine websites' online visibility and revenue. In Spain, while the distinction was defined in Canon AEDE, it gave Google the opportunity to respond to the law without having to completely lose its influence in the Spanish market even after the Google News shutdown.

A few weeks before Canon AEDE came into effect on January 1, 2015, Richard Gingras, then the head of Google News, announced that Google was going to close Google News in Spain on December 16, 2014. Spanish publishers would be removed from Google News outside Spain as well.[65] On December 16, a visit to Google News Spain (news.google.es) only displayed a closure message.[66] Nevertheless, given the distinction between the news aggregator and the search engine addressed in Canon AEDE, after the shutdown, news from

Spanish publishers remained available on Google search through the news box and the "news" tab.[67] The news box was a segment embedded in Google web search results. When there were news stories relevant to a search query, these news stories would be included in Google web search results and returned to the searcher in a news box. The other option to see Spanish publishers' news on Google despite the shutdown was by using the "news" tab on the Google web search page right below the search window. These features were part of the "Google Universal Search," a strategy that Google uses to integrate search results from its various properties, such as news, maps, images, and videos, into Google web search results.[68] With the shutdown of Google News, Spain's news publishers would not be able to get compensation from Google, but since search engines were exempted from copyright obligation under Canon AEDE, showing news items in Google universal search still allowed Google to maintain its relevance in the Spanish market.

Studies on the impact that the Google News shutdown had on the Spanish media market revealed mixed results. Chartbeat, an American web analytics company, recorded a 10 to 15 percent traffic drop for fifty large Spanish news publishers within hours after Google News was shut down. AEDE, on the other hand, claimed that the association was not too worried about the shutdown because Google News contributed only about 5 percent of the overall traffic for its member publications.[69] Other analyses found that while external traffic, for example, traffic brought by the news aggregator, dropped sharply, internal traffic actually rose, suggesting that Spanish readers who were previously directed by Google News now were visiting news websites directly.[70] Another study found that the negative impact of Google News shutdown on Spanish publishers was not as strong as in Germany, and the study also pointed out that the traffic decline in the aftermath of the shutdown reflected the overall decrease of the rate of growth in Spain's internet penetration between 2014 and 2015.[71]

In Spain, the new law encountered challenges from groups such as the Asociación Española de Editoriales de Publicaciones Periódicas (AEEPP), a large association of Spanish periodicals, over concerns about market concentration, restriction of innovation, and legal uncertainty.[72] Supporters of the law countered that the passing of Canon AEDE marked the first time that a nation within the European Union "provided a voice for its domestic publishers by way of tangible regulations," which, according to these supporters, increased the incentive for Spanish publishers to innovate and to better compete against one another for more traffic.[73]

In the Spanish case, the news industry showed strong lobbying power that pushed the passing of a new law that was stricter than Germany's Ancillary Copyright Law. The law resulted in Google's strongest pushback in Europe. If the goal of the law was to help Spain's publishers get compensation from Google, the shutdown of Google News made it impossible; if the law aimed at regulatory influence, the goal was achieved partially, as Google was still able to maintain its relevance in the Spanish market through its search business.

In the cases examined here, the EU news publishers commonly pursued legal approaches to resist Google's influence on their news market. These disputes were often settled by Google's technological and financial power. New legislation was passed in Germany and Spain that required Google to pay news publishers, but the attempts seemed not very successful, with Google being able to find ways to bypass the regulatory efforts. Although with limited effectiveness, the legal frameworks the EU publishers used have become a frame of reference for news publishers elsewhere to challenge Google. But compared to their EU counterparts, the US news publishers took a different approach to resist the rise of the "Google way."

UNITED STATES

In the United States, as early as 2005, the Associated Press (AP), an American news agency headquartered in New York, pursued the licensing model for Google News to use its content.[74] Under this early licensing agreement, Google News could host the AP's news stories and pictures for an undisclosed amount of compensation.[75] A new agreement was signed in August 2007, in which Google agreed to introduce a new duplication detection feature to highlight original news stories and the publishers who produce them.[76] Before the 2007 agreement was to expire in January 2010, the negotiation between the two parties came to a standstill, which resulted in Google's decision in December 2009 to stop hosting the AP's news content on Google News.[77] The months-long impasse was resolved in August 2010 when Google and the AP agreed to extend the existing licensing agreement that permitted Google News to

DISPUTES SURROUNDING GOOGLE NEWS

host the AP content.[78] The length of the new deal was not disclosed.[79]

The AP had long used a business-to-business model to network member publishers through content syndication. Its revenue comes from content licensing and other services; these funds help the news agency hire reporters and maintain news bureaus worldwide to produce original news content, which is then syndicated to subscribing news outlets.[80] This business model, at the time when the AP and Google News were negotiating their early licensing agreement, had earned the news agency $700 million in revenue in 2006.[81] The AP accused Google News of keeping users on its own website rather than directing them to publishers who syndicate AP stories, making them less willing to pay for those stories.[82] AP also criticized Google's "self-referring network," which allowed Google to monetize news items across its own properties.[83] "And all that money has come to them, all 22 billion," said Tom Curley, then the president and CEO of AP. "Folks, they can share."[84] In response, Google worked to recruit more news agencies worldwide to its news service while also making sure that publishers that syndicated AP stories still agreed to be listed on Google News despite the dispute between the AP and Google.[85] In December 2009, Google News discontinued updating AP content on its website, sending the message that "it can live without the AP should it come to that."[86]

From the outset of the dispute, the AP used a commercial, rather than legal, approach to pursue contractual agreements with Google. Each agreement covered a relatively short term, for example, 2005–2007, 2007–2009, etc., and each round of negotiation aimed at specific and elevated demands. These strategies gave the AP the flexibility to adjust its negotiation position based on the development of Google News. The AP also strategically used the competitor effect. In addition to Google, AP negotiated with other search engine and internet companies for better deals and to enhance its leverage at the bargaining table with Google. After Microsoft introduced its own search engine, Bing.com, in June 2009, the AP worked with Microsoft for a partnership under conditions more favorable to it, including prioritizing original news sources in search results and providing real-time metrics for the AP to track and control the use of its content.[87] The AP also negotiated with Yahoo! and praised the company for having "always recognized the value and importance of original, authoritative news."[88] Unlike legal cases, details of commercial negotiations were often kept away from public knowledge.

The AP's CEO once made it clear that "we [the AP] are not suing them [Google]."[89] The AP was not unique in this. Litigations were rare in the United States when it came to the disputes between news publishers and digital aggregators. Why did the US news media pursue a different approach from their European counterparts? To answer this question, it is helpful to compare the copyright systems in the European Union and the United States and see how news is handled differently across these systems.[90]

Contemporary European copyright law developed from the Berne Convention, an international intellectual property treaty signed in 1886. Since this treaty was drafted in the pre-internet era, newer copyright systems were needed to respond to developments in the digital age. In 2002, the World Intellectual Property Organization (WIPO) Copyright Treaty went into effect to protect new types of intellectual property, such as computer programs and databases.[91] The WIPO required its member countries to update their copyright laws to comply with the new treaties.[92] It was against this backdrop that a series of legislative proposals were put forward to modernize EU copyright rules. This included the EU Copyright Directive (EUCD), which went into effect in 2001. EUCD aimed to harmonize copyright rules among EU members and avoid fragmented national legal approaches to ensure the proper functioning of an internal market in the European Union and the competitiveness of European industries.

While European countries shared a strong concern about digital platforms, the fragmentation of the internal market and legislative inconsistency were also the major concerns of the European Union. On March 26, 2019, the European Parliament approved the new Copyright Directive, which aimed to "harmonize legal protection for press publications in respect of online uses by information society service providers."[93] EU member states were given the deadline of June 2021 to implement the new copyright rules into their national legislation. Article 15 of the new EUCD grants EU press publications the unwaivable right to demand compensation from online use of their publications. News aggregators are one of the addressees of the new EUCD.

In July 2019, France became the first country to ratify the EUCD. Like what happened in the German case, Google wanted to bypass the payment obligation by removing news snippets, which are protected under the new EUCD, for French publishers who did not opt in. With the new EUCD, however, this approach resulted in a fine of 500 million euros (about $592 million) from France's competition authority, who charged Google for "failing to negotiate in good faith" over the compensation and threatened fines of another 900,000 euros (around $1 million) per day if Google refused to pay French publishers.[94] About a year after the fine and almost two decades after AFP first sued Google in 2005, Google pledged to negotiate fair licenses with French news publishers under the new EUCD.[95] At the same time, Google announced a $1 billion investment to pay publishers in Germany, Australia, Brazil, and other countries. Google's news aggregation service also returned to Spain in 2022.

So far, the new EUCD seems to be effective in resolving the disputes between EU publishers and Google, but it leaves some fundamental issues unaddressed. The first is about the nature of news. News was not traditionally protected under copyright law. As a commercial law, copyright law concerned the literary, scientific, and artistic domains and the creative works and innovations.[96] Article 2(8) of the Berne Convention noted that copyright protection would not apply to news and facts in press information.[97] When defining rightsholders, Article 2 of the old version of the EUCD in 2001 did not include press publishers either. The new EUCD changed this by incorporating news into copyright protection, but it also stipulated that the rights granted to press publishers should not extend to the "mere facts reported in the press publications." Where is the line between facts and nonfacts in news?

Is news privately owned intellectual property or a type of public service that the public should have free access to? These questions were left unanswered under the new EUCD.

Second, by imposing copyright obligations on online service providers, the new EUCD has adopted an opt-in model, which is a departure from the opt-out trend in the Berne Convention and the EUCD in 2001. The opt-in model assumes that content cannot be used without authorization unless publishers explicitly opt in to the given online service, while the opt-out model assumes the opposite: that content can be used without authorization unless publishers explicitly opt out of the given online service. Article 7 of the original Berne Convention held that news articles could be reproduced "unless the author or editor has expressly prohibited so."[98] Article 5(3) of the 2001 EUCD also allowed exceptions or limitations to the granted copyright if the use is "not expressly reserved." Under those provisions, online service providers, based on the opt-out approach, need to remove the infringing content only if the author or publisher clearly prohibits such use.[99] Under the new EUCD, however, news aggregators have to seek licenses from publishers that opt in. In a few cases discussed earlier in this chapter, Google defended the opt-out model by arguing that industry standards, such as meta tags and robot exclusion protocols, are widely adopted approaches that publishers can use to opt out. In this case, the new EUCD did not clearly give grounds for the shift from the opt-out model to opt-in model or effectively address the legitimacy of the technological ideology that tech companies used to justify the opt-out model. These unaddressed issues will carry the lingering problems between the tech and news industries into the AI era.

The United States, like many EU countries, is a member of the Berne Convention (since only 1988) and the WIPO, but there have long been notable differences between US and European views of copyright. Unlike the European Union, the United States has not enacted a law specifically addressing news aggregation, and it appears that only one federal court has ruled on whether aggregation practices are legal (*Associated Press v. Meltwater Holdings Inc.*, 931 F. Supp. 2d 537 2013). Various common laws and statutory approaches are relevant, however, to understand how the US legal system has approached practices involving news aggregation, such as the fair use doctrine, the "hot news" doctrine, and the Digital Millennium Copyright Act.

The US doctrine of fair use allows limited uses of copyrighted works without the copyright holder's permission. A few factors are used to assess whether a case qualifies as "fair use," including the nature of the use (commercial or nonprofit), the nature of the copyrighted work (expressive or factual), the amount and substantiality of the original work being used, the effect on the potential market for the original work, and the extent of the transformative use. News aggregators are likely to mount a successful defense on some or all of these fronts, especially regarding transformative use. Google has made the argument that the algorithmic processing of news made its use transformative to a great extent. Fair use is one of the main reasons that US news publishers don't want to sue Google, although the fair use doctrine may not guarantee a win in a copyright lawsuit for either a news aggregator or a news media company.[100]

In *International News Service v. Associated Press* (248 U.S. 215) in 1918, a case in which two US news agencies battled over whether the reuse of the news facts from published news stories violated the original news producer's copyright. INS, the defendant, argued that once news was published, it entered the public domain and could be freely used. The Supreme Court held that news facts are not copyrightable but defined a "quasi-property right" in breaking news (hot news), given that the "peculiar value of news is in the spreading of it while it is fresh." With the hot news doctrine, although news is protected while it is still "hot," courts have recognized a very narrow "hot news" exception with several elements to be met. News aggregators could challenge some or all of these elements by arguing that they aggregate both time-sensitive and non-time-sensitive news; that their practice is supported by their own technological and intellectual investment, and hence no free-riding; and that their news aggregation service is not in direct competition with news media but instead sends online traffic to news publishers, thereby incentivizing news publishers.

The Digital Millennium Copyright Act (DMCA), which the US Congress passed in 1998, made it illegal to circumvent technological measures used by copyright holders to prevent copying of their digital works. Meanwhile, the DMCA offers safe harbors to online platforms such as companies that provide internet connectivity and those that host or store material on the internet at the behest of their users.[101] Google

News could argue that its technologies qualify for DMCA protection.

In the US copyright system, when weighing the interests of copyright owners and users, the pendulum has swung back and forth to maintain a balance that ensures an incentive for the progress of the sciences, arts, and new knowledge, on the one hand, and further the First Amendment value to encourage free expression and promote the public's access to information, on the other hand.[102] Like the European Union, the copyrightability of news is not clarified in the US copyright system. As a member of the Berne Convention, the United States has limited copyright protection over news articles. Elements of news, such as headlines and short phrases, are traditionally not protected in the United States.[103] Under the fair use provision and the safe harbor protections granted in the DMCA, internet companies are more likely to enjoy copyright exemptions. There were precedent cases where the use in question involving technologies such as indexing and caching were ruled as fair use, for example *Field v. Google, Inc.* (2006) and *Kelly v. Arriba Soft Corp* (2003).

This comparison lays out the distinct copyright regulations in the European Union and the United States. The EU copyright system faces a complex internal and external environment, where the European Union as a "pan-European copyright legislator" needs to pursue consensus among its member countries and protect the European Union's internal market.[104] In the United States, the disputes are mostly an internal issue. Because of the risk in seeking legal actions under the existing copyright framework in the United States, American publishers

DISPUTES SURROUNDING GOOGLE NEWS

seldom pursued litigation but instead turned to legislative remedies, such as the aforementioned Journalism Competition and Preservation Act. In response, digital platforms have also increased their lobbying efforts. It has been reported that Google, Facebook, and Amazon combined spent more than $65 million in lobbying Congress in 2018.[105]

UNITED KINGDOM

Similar to the US case, in the United Kingdom, publishers tended to challenge Google through market means. Calling news aggregators "parasites" and "content kleptomaniacs," the tension between Google and News Corp culminated in 2010 when News International, News Corp's UK subsidiary, blocked Google and Google News from indexing content of its newspapers *The Times* and the *Sunday Times*. This decision was later reversed when these media outlets returned to Google News and Google search after seeing a 62 percent drop in online readership and a 90 percent plummet in page views.[106]

In its resistance against Google, Murdoch's media group used its discursive power to portray Google as a free-rider, warn of its "theft" of digital news content, and note its threat to quality journalism.[107] Murdoch's charges resonated. For many, harming "quality journalism" is to harm the fourth estate of democracy and the public good. Murdoch and News Corp's strategy banked on the supposition that Google might care more about its public perception than News Corp's content.[108] Google countered that by indexing news publishers' content, it sends traffic to news websites. In 2022, Google reported that globally it helped users find news sites more than 24 billion times each month.[109] Such traffic, Murdoch and his supporters pushed back, was the "least valuable" because it only brought users who "more often than not read one article and then leave the site," rather than loyal readers who have high advertising value. "We'd rather have fewer people coming to our website but paying," Murdoch said.[110]

Like its US counterpart, News Corp also approached Google's competitors, including Microsoft[111] and "second-tier" search engines, such as ask.com,[112] to gain more leverage when negotiating with Google. In addition, News Corp and its UK arm, News International, launched Project Alesia in 2009,[113] an attempt to create its own online news aggregation service, although the project failed shortly after. To respond to News Corp's challenges, in 2009 Google News revised its policy on subscription content. The previous "First Click Free" policy, which allowed users to access the first page of publishers' subscription content for no charge and for an unlimited time, was replaced by a new policy that limited the free access to paid news to five articles.[114]

Though hardcore conservatives, Murdoch and his News Corp have joined news publishers worldwide in calling for strong platform regulation and government intervention. They played a leading role in advocating collective action in the news industry to challenge Google and the like;[115] for example, they proposed an "algorithm review board" in 2018,[116] and in 2016, a consortium of major UK publishers was organized against Google and Facebook as their "common enemy."[117]

DISPUTES SURROUNDING GOOGLE NEWS

After years of resistance, in 2021, News Corp signed a three-year agreement with Google that granted News Corp "significant payments."[118]

In addition to the EU and the US/UK models examined here, disputes surrounding Google and its news services also broke out in other parts of the world, including Brazil, Indonesia, and South Africa. These dynamics also contribute to the complex global media-tech landscape.

BRAZIL

In light of the fact that news organizations in different parts of the world were pursuing favorable deals with Google, Brazilian news publishers approached Google in 2009 with a similar goal. A year later, the National Association of Newspapers in Brazil (Associacão Nacionāl de Jornais, or ANJ), an organization of 154 Brazilian newspapers representing about 90 percent of the daily circulation in the country, announced a project called "One line on Google," in which Google agreed to only display one line—the title—of ANJ publishers' news articles on Google News, discontinuing the use of snippets that showed a multiple-line summary of the news stories.

The broad background of the dispute was the growth of the Brazilian middle class, which led observers to believe that "if Google cannot get [Brazilian] publishers on board, it may be missing out on some of the Latin America boom opportunity."[119] According to the ANJ's report, Brazil saw continuous growth in newspaper circulation in the early 2000s until the

2008–2009 global financial crisis. When ANJ started its discussions with Google in 2011, Brazil's news industry was just seeing the first signs of recovery from the impact of the financial crisis, and Brazilian newspaper circulation grew 4.2 percent compared to the same period the year before. There was a mismatch, however, between the expansion of the newspaper industry and the overall decline of the industry's ad revenue.[120] To seek a better position in the digital market, the ANJ took note of what had happened outside Brazil and decided to seek a deal with Google.

But the "one line" project came to an end in just six months, after the ANJ discovered that the experiment "radically affected" publishers' ranking in Google search. Brazilian publishers' demand for revenue sharing was rejected by Google as well. Marcel Leonardi, the public policy head of Google Brazil at the time, responded that the Brazilian publishers' request "would be like a restaurant owner demanding money from taxi drivers who bring him the guests."[121] In 2011, ANJ publishers collectively withdrew from Google News. The dispute fell out of the public eye after that until 2020, when Google announced it would pay select publishers worldwide, including some in Brazil.[122] This happened in the wake of legislative changes in Brazil.

In 2020, a bill addressing digital media and disinformation entitled the Brazilian Law of Freedom, Responsibility, and Transparency on the Internet (Lei Brasileira de Liberdade, Responsabilidade e Transparência na Internet), aka the Fake News Bill, was approved by the Senate. When the draft legislation moved to the House, an article, which was believed to

DISPUTES SURROUNDING GOOGLE NEWS

be a "hushed addition," was added to the bill; it required platforms to remunerate news media when using their journalistic content.[123] "The valorization of professional journalism allows for the production of reliable information, which creates a framework to address disinformation," the bill's sponsor said in defense of the inclusion of the article.[124]

Based on its understanding of the divided journalism landscape in Brazil, Google warned the Brazilian news industry that with the new law, large media companies with competitive advantages would get more favorable deals than smaller ones.[125] There is a concentrated media market in Brazil, where mainstream media and traditional trade associations dominate the country's news environment.[126] The division between legacy media conglomerates and other media actors such as digital startups and independent journalism organizations was particularly pronounced when it came to the debate about whether Google should pay news publishers.[127] Google underscored this division to pressure Brazilian lawmakers. Nevertheless, inspired by the new Australian Media Act, another legislative proposal, HB1354/2021, was drafted in Brazil in 2021. The bill, addressed directly to Google and Facebook and aimed to challenge "the empire of large American corporations" on the web,[128] required these tech companies to pay a minimum of 50 percent of their gross revenue earned from the use of Brazilian news organizations' content. The Brazilian case unfolded in a unique socioeconomic context and media system. The country's burgeoning middle class increased its news industry's confidence to challenge Google, which dominated Brazil's search engine market with an over-92 percent

DISPUTES SURROUNDING GOOGLE NEWS

market share.[129] Meanwhile, the country has a divided media system where large Brazilian news media and journalism associations have strong power in lobbying the government, seeking legal protection, and mobilizing collective action. Google in this case had to leverage these local issues while also dealing with international influences, such as the ripple effect of the new Australian law. The Brazil case turned out to be an outcome of the interaction between the political and economic dynamics on the local and international markets.

Elsewhere in the world, news publishers and law and policy makers have been stepping up. In South Africa, the Competition Commission is reported to be investigating whether Google and other digital platforms' business constitutes unfair competition with news organizations. The investigation covers both search engines and news aggregators, among other digital services.[130] Following Australia and Canada's lead, in Indonesia, a new law, the Publisher Rights Decree, was signed in 2024, which requires tech companies to compensate news publishers through licensing arrangements, profit and data sharing, and algorithm design that favors quality journalism. The Indonesian president stressed that the new law was "initiated by media firms themselves, not the government."[131]

CHAPTER FLASHBACK AND DISCUSSION

As Google expanded its international reach, the company encountered resistance from news publishers across the globe. These disputes involved various means of resistance, from legal actions to commercial deals, discursive challenges, collective boycotts, and legislative lobbying. As discussed in the introduction, these are common approaches that established social institutions employ to resist emerging social sectors. Through these disputes, the issues in question covered technical, economic, and sociopolitical concerns of the traditional news industry. In many cases, the news industry depended on its lobbying power and close relationships with government and policy-making authorities to seek regulatory intervention. The news industry's lobbying power, together with their power in other domains, successfully waged a wave of resistance campaigns to challenge those tech superpowers. Entering the third decade of the twenty-first century, from the new EUCD to the Australian law, the global influence of these campaigns is being felt. The world is watching, and news publishers around the globe are taking notes from these cases, which set precedents for how established media actors defend their interests in the digital media ecosystem.

These disputes demonstrate that the main demand of the news industry focuses on economic measures, a demand often achieved through legal protection and other resistance strategies. The institutional pressure coming from the news industry and the regulatory community worldwide has pulled Google to strengthen its demand for autonomy. When pushing back the pressure of being integrated into the regulatory frameworks that the news industry advocated, Google's defense was made primarily through technological and financial means. In these interactions, the "Google way" was negotiated through resistance and counter-resistance. For Google, the "Google way" is metaphorically the taxi driver bringing guests to the restaurant owner, whereas for news companies, the "Google way" is to monetize their news content without profit sharing with traditional news media, who have been in the business for decades, investing money and professionalism to make news for a living. The distinction in perceiving the "Google way" changed the interrelationship of Google and the traditional news industry, which is further complicated in the global media-tech landscape by the interplay of local and international influences.

Chapter Four

DATAFICATION OF NEWS AND MEDIA DIVERSITY

GOOGLE'S TECHNOLOGICAL SPECIALIZATION AND ITS INFLUENCE

THE PREVIOUS chapters have demonstrated that Google's specialization in technology has largely defined the "Google way." The "Google way" has also been the source of Google's power in its relationship with the news industry. But given the technical and secretive nature of Google's key technologies, it's hard to investigate the company's technological specialization directly. This chapter addresses this challenge by looking into both the back-end decision making and front-end presentation related to Google's news-related technologies and algorithms. I first use patent analysis to examine the long-term trends of Google's technological innovations in the news area as well as the key factors and the inner workings of its algorithm systems when processing news. This analysis outlines the datafication process of news and the logics behind this process, which illustrates how the "Google way" differs starkly from the journalistic way of managing news. I then turn to the output end to examine what information was presented to users after the datafication process by studying Google's video search results in the context of the COVID-19 pandemic, a time when online video consumption surged. This analysis zooms out from Google News as a single platform of Google to other Google services in order to get a more comprehensive understanding of Google's influence in today's news environment, especially in the area of media diversity. The analysis shows that in a time of crisis, news media and their content still dominate on Google's video platform, although it's not a platform specifically dedicated to news, indicating the deep integration of news across Google services.

LONG-TERM TRENDS IN GOOGLE'S TECHNOLOGICAL INNOVATION

This section explores the "Google way" from a technological perspective, using patent analysis to first identify key areas of Google's news-related technological innovation and long-term trends. Issued by the US Patent and Trademark Office (USPTO), a patent is a legal document that describes an invention and its usage right in order to protect the property right of the patent owner who "invents or discovers any new and useful process, machine, manufacture, or composition of matter, or any new and useful improvement thereof."[1] Google claims that it holds more than fifty thousand patent assets worldwide,[2] and the company is among the largest patent holders in the technology realm.[3] Patent analysis has been traditionally used in the field of business and technology management to guide R&D planning and to investigate a company's technical strategies,[4] but the method has not been widely used by researchers of media and journalism studies. Patent files are semistructured documents that can reveal rich information about the addressed technology and innovation. One particular thing I paid attention to is the patent classification information.

Patent classification is a hierarchical system that organizes patent documents based on their subject matter. The USPTO currently uses the Cooperative Patent Classification (CPC) system, in which the classification hierarchy is specified into different levels, such as section, class, subclass, main group, and subgroup. At the section level, patents are classified into eight (A–H) categories, covering human necessities, operations and transport, chemistry and metallurgy, textiles, fixed constructions, mechanical engineering, physics, electricity, and emerging cross-sectional technologies. Then patents can be further classified into sublevels. The deeper the sub-level, the more specified information one can learn about the technological area the innovation addresses. The classification information therefore is very useful for understanding the technological areas that Google invests in.

In this section, I focus on Google's patents related to news. I collected 202 patent files from USPTO's database, using Google as the assignee and "news" as the keyword in the main areas of the patent files to query the database. For each patent file, classification information was extracted to analyze the key areas and long-term trends of Google's news-related technological innovations. This step allowed me to identify 383 classification categories that were assigned to the examined patents. The leading categories—the most frequently assigned ones—cover such areas as querying, crawling, indexing, personalization, ranking, document retrieval, data processing, website content management, online advertising, and social networking.[5] None of these technological areas sounds familiar to someone who was trained for the traditional news industry, an indicator of the distinction between the "Google way" and the traditional way of handling news.

When these leading classification categories are considered with the timeline of the patents, it can be seen that amid fluctuation, there are three overall peaks where the majority of the top classification categories increased across the news-related patents of Google, reflecting key points in Google's investment in its technological specialization in the news area. These peaks—one peak around 2006, an increase around 2009, and a significant surge around 2012—happened around landmark events in the history of Google's news business. Almost all top classification categories began in 2003, shortly after the 2002 launch of the beta version of Google News. Before that, news was not a top priority in Google's technology innovation. In 2006, Google News graduated from beta, which correlates with the overall peak of the top classification categories in that year. There is then a smaller peak around 2009, right before Google News's redesign in 2010, when most categories saw a mild increase. Another significant peak appears around 2012, when almost all categories went up greatly. This peak correlates with the tenth anniversary of Google News, when its engineers improved the technology across areas such as freshness, grouping, ranking, personalization, and infrastructure.[6]

Among the top ten classification categories, search engine technologies (such as querying, crawling, and indexing), personalization technologies, and ranking technologies have been the leading categories throughout the years, while social networking counters the overall trends in a few ways. First, the category was not as strong as other leading classification categories. Also, unlike other innovation areas, social networking had a very late start, in 2010, around the time when social networking–related features were first introduced on Google News. During this time, Google made several adjustments in response to the rise of social media platforms such as Facebook and Twitter. These attempts included Google Buzz, introduced in 2010 and shut down in 2011; Google Wave, launched in 2009 and ended in 2010; and Google+, launched in 2011 and discontinued for personal use in 2019. The countertrends revealed by the patent analysis align with Google's unsuccessful forays into social technology, which many have noted.[7]

Personalization stands out as a leading category that's particularly strong. Google has been experimenting with personalization on its news aggregation platform since the early days of Google News. Features that allowed users to customize the news page were introduced in 2005, and the personalization tool "News for you" became the "new heart" of the 2010 version of Google News after its redesign. The 2018 version of Google News continued to emphasize personalized news experience on the platform (see chapter 2). While search and ranking are traditionally considered Google's basic, core technology, personalization largely defines Google's technological specialization in the twenty-first century. Providing personalized news allows Google to tap into user data related to their preferences and behavior patterns. While there are mixed findings about whether personalization creates filter bubbles, this approach effectively undermines news media's gatekeeping and agenda-setting power by rearranging the news on offer based on users' preference, as opposed to news media's editorial decisions. Through a giving-the-users-what-they-like approach, personalization changes the relationships between news media, audience, and platform. These parties consist of an information supply chain, in which news media become the supplier and Google the intermediary. The news audience relies on the intermediary to get the news they prefer, losing the opportunity to make direct connection with news media as well as the journalistic logics involved in news making. Given the disputes between news organizations and Google that we discussed in the last chapter, it is surprising that in those cases personalization technologies and their effects were not addressed by either news publishers or regulators until recently, when generative AI gained traction (see chapter 5).[8] Instead, news publishers' concerns focused more on Google's technologies affecting the business side of news, such as advertising and subscription. In fact, these technologies, when long-term trends are considered, are in the classification categories that considerably dropped over time. The gap between Google's technological investment and the news industry's delayed and misplaced focus when assessing Google's influence on news afforded Google the time and opportunity to

DATAFICATION OF NEWS AND MEDIA DIVERSITY

solidify its technological power and advance its position in the digital news landscape.

ALGORITHMS AND DATAFICATION

GOOGLE ALGORITHMS AND WORKFLOW

Google runs on algorithms. Computer algorithms are "the logical series of steps for organizing and acting on a body of data to quickly achieve a desired outcome."[9] Today, almost all internet-based services rely heavily on algorithms of different kinds.[10] Algorithms are both technical and social, functioning as a "complex sociotechnical assemblage."[11] Since algorithms are designed in computer language and operated in the back end, they are often considered a "black box": Their processes and methods are opaque to outside observers.[12] Debates about how transparent algorithms should be have been longstanding. Some scholars call for algorithmic transparency, given the immense influence of algorithms in the digital age.[13] Others, particularly those in the tech industry, argue that a degree of secrecy is necessary to prevent algorithm holders from malicious attacks, gaming, and manipulation and to encourage healthy competition.[14] At the same time, algorithms are dynamic in nature and subject to influences from various sources, such as market feedback, organizational considerations, technological developments, and broader social, political influences. The algorithm system involves input, throughput, and output (I-T-O).[15] Information from user requests, available data sets, or big data in general serve as the input. Throughput is a process that uses codes to manage a specific task based on the input data. And output is the outcome of the process and can also serve as an additional input for subsequent algorithmic processes. In the I-T-O process, algorithms play an intermediary role to link user, data, and applications. The throughput part is usually in the black box, and the output and input ends can be observed. When observations about output and input are considered together, they can provide useful clues for understanding the throughput.

My patent analysis maps out the key steps of the algorithmic workflow in Google's news processing. It starts from data collection, which can be done through automatic crawling or data submission. Once different types of data are put into the system, predefined features are used to label the data. Labeled data will be classified into various categories, such as "news source," "genre," and "topic," and then levels of subcategories as needed. Classified data are stored in servers, repositories, or databases and can be processed within and across these systems. Using different models and criteria, classified data are then scored for varying purposes, for example, to determine the freshness, relevance, interest, and source quality related to the news. When ranking decisions are made, multiple scores are calculated using appropriate mathematical formulas to get a final score for each news item. Candidate news items are ranked based on their final scores and presented at the output end in ranking order. The actual workflow is much more complex than described here because these processes often overlap. Like a huge, intricate machine, the algorithm's interconnected components form a complex network in which software and hardware interact, meanings are defined, and different layers of decision making are intertwined.

While algorithms are computational methods for problem solving, they are not entirely machine driven. Human elements are involved in Google's algorithm design; for example, the criteria, metrics, and thresholds that are used to rank news are defined by humans. Human readers and evaluators are needed when reviewing, labeling, and evaluating news sources, articles, and web pages. In addition, users from the public are sometimes polled or recruited for user studies to help refine Google's algorithm. These human actors carry the prevailing social norms with them, which are woven into Google's machine way of handling news. There is another layer of human intervention that is introduced on top of the machine way of problem solving. As shown in chapter 2, the coming and going of many features on Google News's website are not driven by algorithmic but human decisions. In sections such as Local, Spotlight, Editors' Pick, and Fact Check, some news content may have little chance to stand out in Google's ranking algorithm without human intervention giving priority to such content. Many of the human decisions were made to respond to the pressure coming from the news industry, the regulatory community, and the global media-tech landscape. The addition of News Showcase and the removal of news snippets discussed in the previous chapters are some examples. These human decisions have been superimposed on algorithmic systems, making the datafication process not a pure technical undertaking but one influenced by social and institutional forces.[16] Indeed, the "Google way" has been an interplay of the machine way and the human way, reflecting the technical-social duality of algorithm.

THE DATAFICATION OF NEWS

In the I-T-O process, each step involves data. Without data, the algorithm does not exist. In this sense, algorithmic systems are processes of datafication in which aspects of the world are rendered into quantified data.[17] Data are not a given, a resource "out there" awaiting people to mine them, as suggested in the metaphor of data mining, but a "recorded abstraction of the world created and valorised by people using technology." When datafication becomes a business, that business needs a continuous data supply to sustain its development. What drives the data-driven economy is the idea of creating nonpassive data; in other words, "data driven" does not imply merely *collecting* first-order data from available sources but finding ways to actively and constantly *create* second-order data. This business model turns data into capital. In the data-driven business model, profit is not made primarily through individual sales but through data that can "continuously monetize" the relationship between a company and its customers. "The way to win in a data-driven business is to push prices as low as possible in order to build your customer base, enhance data flow, and cash in in the long-term."[18] During these processes, old values are changed while new values emerge to serve different purposes, whether it's about standardization, optimization, commodification, or control through surveillance.[19]

To sustain the data-driven business model, the consistency and quality of the data supply is critical. News happens to satisfy both. First, news is produced continuously by the news industry in an institutional way. In the digital age, the news cycle never stops. News as a continuous data supply is also a type of nonpassive data, which can be used as first-order data to create second-order data, also in a consistent fashion, through users' news consumption. When users search, click on, and share news, user data are yielded. In terms of the data's quality, news is a type of information that meets Google's E-A-T principle (Expertise, Authoritativeness, Trustworthiness), rating considerations that Google uses for content and search quality control. Considered together, news as a consistent and reliable data source that also meets the E-A-T principle is uniquely valuable for Google's algorithm system. This explains the important role of news in Google's data-driven business and why Google wouldn't let go of news in spite of all the "trouble" that Google's relationship with the news industry has produced. But how news is datafied in Google's algorithmic system, and how is qualified news transformed into quantified data in an analyzable form? The following section focuses on the input end of Google's news-related algorithm system, where different types of news data are fed into Google's algorithm system, from source and content data to machine-language data and user data.

The examination of Google's patent files illustrates that news sources are datafied through various metrics that are put in place to score source quality, including:[20]

- The number, average length, and importance of articles produced by a news source during a given time period, as well as the news work's originality, breadth (the range of topics the news source produces), writing style (spelling, grammar, and reading levels), and breaking news score (how quickly the news source can respond to breaking news)
- The news source's type, circulation statistics, analytics (such as the news website's click rate and traffic), website quality, staff size, history, and number of its news bureaus
- The news source's reputation, such as the number of Pulitzer prizes a news organization has won, and its international influence

While adopted from the journalistic field, these ideas are interpreted differently in Google's algorithm system. Some of these factors can be easily quantified, such as the number of news bureaus, a newspaper's circulation data, and the length of a news article, but others are not, such as importance and originality. When news elements are not quantitative in nature, algorithm designers have to find ways to translate them into something that can be algorithmically processed. Sometimes, much can be lost in translation. For journalists, the importance of a news item is often reflected in the idea of its "newsworthiness," which is judged by such factors as timeliness, impact, prominence of figures involved, proximity (geographic or psychological connections between the news and the audience), and unusualness.[21] Google's algorithm system, however, measures the importance of the news in a quantified way. Related news stories on the same subject are sorted in a cluster; importance score is then calculated based on the size of the cluster. The larger the cluster size, the higher the importance score.[22] This method assumes that news stories that are covered by more news sources are more important. This assumption makes sense in some cases but not in others. For example, nonmainstream news stories and those about underrepresented minority or marginalized groups might have a low importance score under such an assumption. The value of breaking news is also interpreted differently in Google's algorithm system. The breaking news score is determined through the calculation of the length of time between when the event occurred and when the related news was published. This method only addresses one element—timeliness—of what merits breaking news; journalistically, the social impact of breaking news is also an important consideration for news professionals deciding what to cover. Another example that reflects the difference between algorithmic and journalistic approaches is the originality of news. Journalists define original reporting as journalistic work that is not derived from syndicated news content produced by news agencies or news based on press releases or organized news conferences. In the journalistic sense, original reporting often involves pitching and firsthand reporting from the field, which values reporters' creativity, news sensitiveness, and the connection to the people and communities that they serve. In Google's algorithm system, however, originality is measured by comparing the named entities used in news stories within a cluster of related news articles. As explained in chapter 2, named entities are the terms used to label names of persons, places, events, etc. In a cluster of related news stories, for example, if a story has unique named entities (that is, ones that other stories do not contain), this story is considered more original and given a higher originality score. In these examples, only news aspects that can be algorithmically processed are adopted. Journalistic principles that cannot be quantified, such as accuracy, fairness, independence, ethnicity, and humanity, are not selected as ranking metrics, although they are critical to journalism. Without these journalistic norms and values, news is reduced to raw data.

In addition to news source–related information, data about news content, including texts, images, and audio and video components, are also input and processed by Google's algorithmic systems. Once collected, features are identified through various pattern recognition techniques, such as character recognition, facial recognition, and voice recognition. Temporal, geographic, and topical data are extracted across content types. These features cover some of the five Ws that are basic to news, for example, the "when," "where," "who," and "what," but the "why" (or "how") is hard to process algorithmically. Furthermore, related news stories are clustered, and they will be processed both individually and in aggregate. In a news cluster, each article's headline is parsed, and the number of keywords and their position in each article are calculated. The centroid of the cluster is calculated as well using mathematical models so that each article's relevance score can be computed in relation to the entire cluster.[23] In addition, news data can also be extracted from back-end machine language, such as HTML codes and metadata. Through back-end machine language, algorithm can parse information about the news website's layout, the position of the given news article on the webpage, and the characteristics of hyperlinks and other digital elements. All these factors have weight in Google's ranking algorithm. As discussed in previous chapters, news publishers can use back-end machine language to label their news as "fact check" or as "quality news" to request priority in Google's algorithm system, but Google determines how these features can be used. Through these processes, news content is transformed from social and cultural constructs into discrete bits of data. "Once we datafy things," as scholars realized, "we can transform their purpose and turn the information into new forms of value."[24] Not only does datafication radically change the journalistic way of defining news, but it also benefits Google in the legal field. As readers may remember from chapter 3, transformative use is one of the factors involved in determining fair use in the United States. Google's specialized technology enables the datafication process that allows Google to make arguments for its transformative use of news and to pursue exemption from some legal liabilities.

In Google's algorithm systems, another important input is user data, including the data of news users. User data are collected from a range of sources, including users' personal information associated with their Google account, such as name, email address, and demographic information; users' search history, including search queries, selections, preferences, and click data; users' social network data, including their contacts, relationships, and social media engagement, such as posting, sharing, endorsing, and commenting; and users' information stored by cookies, for example, device information, time spent on a certain webpage or app, and IP address. User data are collected and processed at both the individual and aggregate levels. At the individual level, a user's current interest is compared to this person's past interest to find long-term interest patterns so that the algorithm can predict the user's future interest. The algorithm also processes one individual user's data in connection with users who use the same kind of device, have the same location, or speak the same language, so that news relevance can be decided based on an individual user's interest as well as the broader communities' interest. Much of the user data are yielded when users constantly interact with something on Google's platforms. News as the source of continual data supply could serve this purpose when Google's news aggregation service and other Google platforms provide the infrastructure of "encouraging people to use the app or platform, that is, organising their habits so that life actions previously performed elsewhere (such as communicating with friends, sharing cultural products, hailing a taxi, etc.) become actions performed via the app."[25]

With the spread of the data-driven business model, data privacy is subject to stricter regulation worldwide. In May 2018, the General Data Protection Regulation (GDPR) went into effect in the European Union, which imposes obligations on data controllers and processors who use personal data.[26] The GDPR defines data protection as a fundamental right and urges data organizations to commit to data protection by design and by default. Under the GDPR, data companies should inform the data subjects about the nature, scope, context, risk, and purpose of the data processing in a clear and transparent way. It also grants data subjects the right to consent, access, rectify, and erase their data. In 2022, Google received fines totaling hundreds of millions of euros for GDPR violation, including €150 million from France's data protection authority and €10 million from Spain.[27] To respond to the rising data protection effort, Google offered a range of tools for its partner publishers to comply with GDPR, but some publishers complained that Google was trying to shift the obligation to them. Richard Gingras, the vice president of Google News, defended Google's approach: "They're not our users, they're their [the publishers'] users."[28]

GOOGLE, MEDIA DIVERSITY, AND THE PANDEMIC

Through the algorithmic processing of data related to news sources, news content, and news users, news is deeply datafied.[29] After going through this datafication process, what kind of information is presented to users on the output end? In the context of the COVID-19 pandemic, this section addresses this question using Google's video search as a case study. Findings from this analysis show that even for Google's video search, a service that is not specifically dedicated to news, content from news media still dominates the platform during times of global crisis. It can be argued that news business has been deeply integrated into Google's business, which in turn shapes the setup and future trajectory of the burgeoning online video sector, where the news industry has been increasing its presence. This section zooms out from discussions focusing on Google's news aggregation service and looks at Google services other than Google News to help us gain a more comprehensive picture of the tech giant's power and limitations in the twenty-first-century media-tech landscape. Tackling questions such as whose content gets to be presented to users through Google, what type, and how diverse, I hope to explore how Google's algorithm can shape users' information exposure and affect media diversity in the digital age.

Adopted from the pre-internet era, media diversity is a framework used to assess the media's role in serving a democratic society in areas such as ownership diversity, content diversity, and viewpoint diversity. In the digital era, the framework can also be used to investigate digital platforms' role as algorithmic gatekeepers. There have been ongoing debates about whether these digital platforms facilitate information access or produce filter bubbles and echo chambers, in other words, whether they benefit or harm media diversity. Such discussions, however, have been inadequate in the emerging online video sector.

Video content is an important information type serving the public's critical information needs, especially during times of crisis. For example, surges in television news watching were found during times of national or global crises such as the 9/11 attacks and the 1990–1991 Persian Gulf War.[30] Online, video content consumption grew remarkably since the first decade of the twenty-first century. In 2007, 57 percent of online adults in the United States used the internet to watch or download video.[31] That number grew to 78 percent in 2013 and 84 percent in 2020.[32] In Europe, online video subscription revenue reached €9.7 billion in 2020, up from 12 million in 2010.[33] Viewing time and subscriptions to online video has increased in Asia, Africa, and other parts of the world as well.[34] The demand for online video content was even stronger during the COVID-19 pandemic. Studies have found that TV news viewership, streaming, and online watching all grew greatly in the early days of the pandemic.[35] In the United States, users spent an average of eight hours a day streaming video content online during the lockdowns.[36] Many of these hours were spent on COVID-related online news watching.[37]

Google has been a leading actor on the global online video market, which was worth over US$7 billion as of 2021,[38] especially after the company acquired YouTube for US$1.6 billion in 2006. My patent analysis also shows that Google's video technologies and innovations have seen a strong growth since mid-2010s. Other tech companies also place high emphasis on the online video sector. Mark Zuckerberg, for example, has envisioned a video-focused Facebook.[39] These tech platforms' priority on video has spurred the investment in online video content in the media industry.[40] A survey from 2016 showed that 79 percent of the surveyed CEOs, editors, digital leaders, and other people who held senior positions in media companies in different parts of the world said they planned to invest more in online news video.[41] It's reported that video content is "not just a passing trend but a vital component" of news media companies' digital success.[42]

Google claimed that its video search was "the most comprehensive on the Web, containing millions of videos indexed and available for viewing."[43] Existing video studies related to Google often focus on YouTube, but studies find that the video content returned by Google search and YouTube are different in many ways; for example, there are many more video searches on Google than YouTube, and video producers on YouTube also seek traffic from Google search.[44] YouTube search results and Google video search results can be very different even with the same search queries.[45] The composition of the sources differs between the two platforms as well.[46] Google's top video results were also found to focus more on informational videos; YouTube is more entertainment focused.[47] In addition, since it is costly to maintain a dedicated YouTube channel, many local TV outlets have no YouTube presence.[48] These media outlets host their video content themselves and post the videos on their own websites, as opposed to having them on YouTube. These media organizations would rely on Google's video search for online visibility.

Through an analysis of 13,084 top Google video search results related to online video content published in the early days of the pandemic, I found that although Google's video search is not a platform exclusively for news, as in the case of Google News, here, news media sources across print, broadcast, and digital sectors still dominate over nonmedia sources, such as public health authorities, government offices, hospitals, and other individuals and organizations. Among the leading sources, that is, those that appeared in Google's top video search results the most, the vast majority of them are news media. The dominance of news sources in Google's video algorithm indicates that news has been well integrated into Google services beyond Google News. It also reflects Google's reliance on news as E-A-T information, especially during the COVID-19 pandemic, a global crisis not only about public health challenges but also an "infodemic," with "too much information including false or misleading information in digital and physical environments during a disease outbreak."[49]

When it comes to digital recommenders like Google, prediction is often a priority in their algorithm design, but scholars find that users welcome diversity in their information diet, and research attention to balancing diversity and prediction accuracy of algorithm systems has been growing.[50] Among Google data, when source diversity is considered, media sources are found largely concentrated on mainstream national media. Local media sources—as discussed earlier, many of them rely on Google for online visibility as they do not maintain a YouTube presence—also have a considerable share in Google's top video search results, but they concentrate on a few areas, such as California, North Carolina, New York, Florida, Pennsylvania, and Texas. While a study found that sources included in Google's video search are more diverse than other Western and non-Western search engines,[51] the source concentration echoes findings of previous studies about Google. For example, an algorithm audit of Google search with a focus on Google's top story box found that just twenty news sources accounted for more than half of the search results they examined. Legacy media such as CNN, the *New York Times*, and the *Washington*

Post were the sources that often appear in Google's top story box.[52] Google News search results were also found to have come from a small number of national publications, most of which were based in metro areas such as New York City, Washington, and Los Angeles.[53]

Google's algorithm can also shape the format-type diversity of the online video content presented on its video platform, which has profound implications for news players who want to enter this market. One particular style, articles with videos, stands out as the most popular format type returned by Google's video search. For this format type, videos were embedded in online articles. The text in the article usually provided background and context, explanation of the topic, and additional information, while the video content was complementary to the text. Other format types, such as YouTube videos and video-only web pages (non-YouTube) without accompanying articles, are also popular but have a much smaller share in the examined data. Compared to other search engines such as Bing, DuckDuckGo, and Yahoo!, which are dominated by YouTube videos,[54] Google's video search provides a platform for alternative video format types to be seen, especially for video producers who are unable to maintain an active YouTube channel, which is the case for many small and local producers.

The alternative format types also provide nonbroadcast actors who are not traditionally video content producers, such as print media, with a path to enter the online video market. At the same time, format-type diversity is limited, and the prioritization of the article-with-video style could produce another type of concentration, giving advantages to those who are professionally and financially able to produce both written and video content. Additionally, given Google's power in the search engine optimization field, the few format types that Google prioritizes could become templates for video producers who pursue higher search visibility and therefore limit the incentives to explore new format types for online video content.

Another media diversity factor that I investigated on Google's video platform is structural diversity, which addresses "the broader set of conditions that are beyond the scope of individual media outlets."[55] These broader issues, which create the environment in which digital platforms operate and function, can shape output diversity and policy choices. One social issue that was salient during the COVID-19 pandemic is that racial and ethnic minority groups were disproportionately affected by COVID-19 because of the social determinants of health, such as neighborhood environment, health care, job conditions, income, and education.[56] COVID-related disparities are considered "more of a social and economic phenomenon" rooted in structural inequalities. A *Washington Post* study found that compared to whites, African Americans, Hispanics, Asian Americans, and Native Americans were 37, 16, 53, and 26 percent more likely to die of COVID, respectively.[57] Many structural-social issues, according to this study, contributed to such disparities, such as the shortage of COVID testing in minority neighborhoods, the lack of data from communities of color, language barriers, housing issues, access to medical care and health insurance, and immigration policies. Some minority groups face unique challenges. For example, COVID-related health disparities among the Asian American community were largely unknown despite the disproportionately high COVID death rate in this group. Studies found that present-day racism (such as the anti-Asian hate during the COVID-19 pandemic) as well as historical racism (such as the model-minority stereotype that emerged in the 1960s depicting Asian Americans as a group that can do better than other minority groups and therefore "unworthy of resources") are profound reasons for the neglect and exclusion of this community. "The omission of Asian Americans from discussion of health disparities is itself a form of racism that has serious consequences," argued these researchers.[58]

Among the search results focusing on four racial and ethnic groups in the United States—African Americans, Hispanics, Asian Americans, and Native Americans,[59] I only found a small portion of minority sources, that is, sources run by and for minority groups. They concentrated on a handful of sources, although about one thousand ethnic media outlets exist in the United States as of 2000.[60] Studies found that ethnic media play an important role in the media ecosystem, as they reach about a quarter of the entire US adult population, and 45 percent of the surveyed ethnic adults, or 13 percent of the US adult population, prefer ethnic media to mainstream media to get their media information.[61] Given the disproportionate impact of COVID on minority groups, an opportunity to increase the visibility of ethnic media in order for the public to learn about the challenges facing these communities was missed. The very few and concentrated minority sources found on Google's video platform did not adequately respond to this information need. While previous chapters showed that Google has used nonalgorithmic intervention to accommodate news publishers' needs, such accommodation was seemingly not offered to minority sources. There is also a lack of representation of sources from areas where the given racial/ethnic group has the highest population ratio to the state's total population. The gap may be located on both the demand side and the supply side of the information environment. On the demand side, to what extent users would be interested in content outside their own neighborhoods or social groups is a factor for commercial digital services to weigh when designing their algorithm. On the supply side, the question is how many sources are able to consistently produce content so that they can be indexed by the platforms. Facebook, for example, complained that it could not find sufficient local news for its Today In, a feature launched in 2018 that aimed to promote local content to Facebook users.[62] This is especially the case for online video content, considering it requires more resources to produce, publish, and host, a challenge that is particularly tough for small, local newsrooms.

Industrial-level dynamics, such as cross-sector and cross-company relationships, also affect output diversity. For example, search engines were found to deprioritize their competitors' content, which influenced the diversity in their search results.[63] The interindustry pushes and pulls across the tech and news industries can result in tensions in some cases and collaborations in others.[64] Google's inclusion and removal of the AP's content, discussed in the previous chapter, is such an example. An examination of the Google-source relationship among the leading sources on Google's video platform reveals that most of the top sources have been involved in certain types of partnership with Google. These partnerships covered initiatives such as Google News Initiative, YouTube-related programs, and local news projects through a variety of Google products and services. As will be elaborated in the next chapter, Google has spent over a billion dollars in its global partnership network building. The prioritization of partner sources in Google's algorithm system tends to create an enclosed, centralized space across Google platforms. The centralized approach that rewards content and sources from Google's own network could discourage producers outside this partnership network or pressure them to join it. If partnership concentration and centralization became the underlying logic in algorithm design, independence and transparency at both the input and the output ends cannot be guaranteed.

CHAPTER FLASHBACK AND DISCUSSION

As the patent analysis in this chapter shows, Google's technological innovation focused on search, personalization, and ranking. These areas define Google's technological power and distinguish the "Google way" from conventional journalism in terms of how news is processed and perceived. The "Google way" involves the datafication of news, in which news aspects that can be processed by machine in quantitative ways are stripped off the news and fed into Google's algorithm systems, while those that cannot are lost. Datafication is sustained by a data-driven business model, under which news is reduced to first-order data that are used to produce profitable, second-order user data. By doing so, news becomes involved in a monetization loop where data becomes capital. The datafication process allows Google to radically change the meaning of news—news is no longer considered a sociocultural artifact that serves as the first draft of history but as machinized data items, and the news-audience relationship, being digitally commodified in the data economy, becomes less about the social interactions between members of the public and the information services they use to help them navigate the world. The machine way of datafying news is intertwined with human decision making, which helped Google maintain a sweet spot in the Google-news power relation. These dynamics, in a way that had both technologized the social and socialized the technological, contribute to a "Google way" that characterizes the tech-media hybridity.

The information that users see on Google platforms are the results of this Google way of datafying the news. Even on platforms outside Google News, news has been deeply integrated into Google business. In the context of the COVID-19 pandemic, a time of crisis that witnessed the surge of online video content consumption, news also played an important role on Google's video platform. The pandemic provided an opportunity to investigate Google's role in shaping media diversity in the digital era, but the analysis of Google's video search reveals a complicated picture—on the one hand, Google's algorithm provides non-YouTube videos and nontraditional video producers with a path to enter the online video landscape; on the other hand, concentrations were found in different areas, which produce a centralized space where styles, sources, and relationships prioritized by Google's algorithm are more likely to be seen.

There are ongoing debates about how proactive digital platforms should be in their commitment to media diversity. Should they proactively promote minority content, viewpoints, and sources to users? If so, would such a proactive approach harm user autonomy? These questions reflect different understanding about democracy, which can shape policy-making trends. In the liberal model of democracy, users' personal autonomy and freedom of expression can outweigh other interests, but this giving-users-what-they-want aspect can create "new concentrations of market or opinion power."[65] Compared to the liberal model of democracy, participatory democracy and deliberative democracy require a more proactive role for digital platforms in promoting media diversity, but concerns emerge in terms of where the lines between informing, educating, and manipulating should be drawn. In recent years, platform governance has been moving away from a self-regulation model toward government regulation or multistakeholder approaches. Proposals for creating socially sensitive and just algorithms have been put forward. These proposals range from technical approaches, such as the adoption of social media signals, to policy intervention, such as the involvement of trusted third parties to manage sensitive data. The regulatory climate shift in the global tech-media landscape sets the backdrop against which Google has undertaken a range of news initiatives worldwide to strengthen its institutional power, as will be elaborated in the next chapter.

Chapter Five

A GLOBAL NETWORK

GOOGLE'S SYSTEMATIC NEWS INITIATIVES

TWO DECADES have passed since Google first began in news. These two decades witnessed the digital transformation of the news industry and our society. In the global media and technology landscape, legal and policy debates have extended into the first few decades of the twenty-first century. After quieting down for a few years, persistent issues left over from early disputes surrounding Google and news publishers resurfaced and led to a push for regulatory changes around the world. Google's ambition in news, however, remains strong. Beyond Google News, Google had introduced a series of initiatives that aimed to grow its news-related business. These efforts were integrated into the umbrella Google News Initiative (GNI), which combines its older news-related projects such as Google News, Google Digital News Initiative, and Google News Lab with newer ones such as Google News Showcase, to "help journalism thrive in a digital age."[1] In March 2018,

A GLOBAL NETWORK

Google announced that GNI would invest $300 million over three years, aiming at "building a stronger future for news."[2] Compared to earlier, discrete news-related efforts, the launch of GNI signified that despite the tension between Google and the news industry, Google's ambition in news had not diminished. Instead, Google brought forth a more systematic and strategic plan to centralize its news enterprise and enhance its global influence. This chapter will demonstrate that through GNI, Google has been building a global news partnership network to strengthen its institutional power in order to withstand the pressures coming from the news industry and the regulatory community around the globe. These developments have profound implications for the Google-news relationship, the independence of journalism as an institution, and the future of the news industry. Based on the analysis of Google's development in the news area throughout this book, I then propose an N-D-N (normalization-differentiation-negotiation) framework to conceptualize the trends shaping the Google-news relationship over the past two decades and close by discussing where the relationship may go in the AI era.

To understand GNI's influence, this section provides an overview of GNI in three parts. The first part examines GNI's website and its manifestos—the discourses that technology companies use to outline "the goals and processes" and "clearly explain their unique contributions to an existing industry"[3]—to understand how GNI works, how it introduces itself to the public, and the implications of GNI's actions and objectives. Part 2 examines more than three hundred blog posts published on GNI's official blog from 2012 to 2021. These posts provide

A GLOBAL NETWORK

additional information not included on GNI's main website, illuminating how Google has changed its news focus over the years. The third part focuses on major news-related programs rolled out by Google, including the Digital News Initiative (DNI), a 150-million-euro investment of Google and a Europe-focused program that has a history longer than GNI itself; GNI Innovation Challenge, a program that funds projects worldwide addressing digital innovation ideas in newsrooms; and Google News Showcase, Google's new licensing program through which Google pays news publishers in different parts of the world to create and curate news content to be displayed on Google News. Through these initiatives, Google sets the agenda for the news industry to follow in terms of defining the industry's challenges and corresponding solutions. By doing so, Google's technologies, money, and values are spread into newsrooms worldwide via Google's global news partnership network.

AN OVERVIEW OF GNI

In early 2020, a visit to the GNI website would show that the rhetoric on the website centered on the theme of collaboration. The language Google used—such as "Gone are the days when news organizations—or tech companies—can 'go it alone,'" "The future of journalism depends on all of us working together," and "We believe in spreading knowledge to make life better for everyone. It's at the heart of Google's mission. It's the mission of publishers and journalists. Put simply, our

A GLOBAL NETWORK

futures are tied together"[4]—was distinct from when Google depicted itself as the reformer or salvation of journalism in crisis in the digital age or when Google likened its service to the taxi driver who brought guests to a restaurant, with news media being the absurd restaurant owner demanding money from the taxi driver for doing so. Indeed, observers saw GNI as Google's effort to "sweeten" its relationship with the news industry,[5] which many perceived to have been hurt by the disputes between news media and Google in different parts of the world, as discussed in chapter 3. Such a collaborative relationship has been maintained through a vast partnership network that Google has been building globally. As of 2022, Google has over seven thousand news partners in more than 130 countries and territories that reach various stakeholders in the news ecosystem, including traditional news organizations; digital native news media; nonprofits, news associations, and industry organizations as well as international organizations and networks that are well connected in the news industry; journalism research organizations and academic institutions; and journalism schools or programs run in universities.[6]

GNI's partnership takes various forms, including financial and technological support, research collaboration, education, and membership. GNI also offers training workshops and labs, fellowships and awards, competitions, grants, and events involving newsrooms of different sizes, from large to small and startups. These programs, covering the Americas, Europe, Asia, Africa, and Australia, introduce Google's own technologies, tools, and products to the journalism community worldwide for the alleged purpose of "advancing the practice of quality journalism," "strengthening publishers' business models, and building a global news community."[7] For example, Google Search, Google Maps, and Google Trends are introduced as fundamentals for newsgathering; Google Image, Google Earth, and Google Translate are tools for information verification; and YouTube, Google Sheets, and Google Data are resources for storytelling, visualization, and data journalism. If you want to "transform the business of news," Google tells news publishers, there's a range of Google tools, from Google Analytics to Google Ad Manager and Subscribe with Google, that can datafize audience behavior and monetize audience data.

Through its network building, GNI tends to normalize the news industry's economic concerns and provides it with technology-driven solutions. On the GNI website, it classified "the needs of news organizations" and "industry challenges" into categories such as distribution and audience engagement, revenue growth and monetization, digital business transformation through data and infrastructure management, and new digital ways of storytelling. For each category, GNI offered a wide range of Google products as solutions, from YouTube and Accelerated Mobile Pages (AMP) to Google Trends and Google Earth. Case studies about how news partners applied Google products in their journalism practices were mapped onto these categories as best practice to solve these challenges. These technological solutions are offered to newsrooms along with funds and grants. Through GNI, Google claims that it has become "one of the world's biggest financial supporters of journalism."[8] By defining industry challenges facing news media as techno-economic problems and offering Google's own technological and financial solutions, GNI builds up a partner network that centers the "Google way" in the name of "help[ing] journalism thrive in the digital age." These partnerships involve news publishers in a contractual relationship with Google, in which Google provides money and technology, while news organizations, once registered as a news partner, opt into Google's universe and become a Google-friendly actor in the media-tech landscape. The benefits are appealing—for example, as discussed in the last chapter, Google's algorithm system tends to prioritize its partners for better ranking and visibility, Google and its partners can share advertising revenue, and Google partners can obtain access to additional resources that Google may share. Scholars who interviewed newsroom members who are in senior roles in news organizations and those who are closely involved in high-level collaboration with digital platforms found that newsrooms seldom say no to such offers.[9]

When the partnership between Google and news media becomes a norm, especially at the institutional level, independence, an important principle of journalism, becomes subject to scrutiny. GNI has already played a role in setting the agenda for the news industry to define its struggles entering the digital age and pinpointing strategies to resolution. By sticking to Google's agenda, to what extent is the journalism community able to maintain an independent judgment about its strengths and weaknesses? And how would the "Google way," which consists of Google's technologies, money, and mindset, affect the future of journalism as an institution? These questions

A GLOBAL NETWORK

invite thoughtful contemplation as Google's partner network is expanding globally. The Society of Professional Journalists, the oldest organization representing journalists in the United States and itself a Google partner, lays out the code of ethics for its member journalists, in which it exhorts journalists to "act independently" as one of the principles of ethical journalism. According to the SPJ, conducting ethical journalism should avoid "real or perceived" conflicts of interest, and journalists should deny "favored treatment to advertisers, donors or any other special interests, and resist internal and external pressure to influence coverage."[10] In newsrooms, journalistic independence is often addressed as an ethical issue at the individual or organizational level to make sure journalists and their work are independent from political and economic influences. For example, news organizations typically maintain a separation between their editorial team and business team; newsrooms would advise their journalists not to get involved with political activities, not to take part in public demonstrations or social movements in favor of or opposed to a cause, not to accept freebies or gifts from sources or donate money to political or activist groups, and "if you cover a certain industry, say, drug companies or computer software makers, then you shouldn't own stock in those kinds of companies."[11] Reflections on how digital platforms as new stakeholders in the twenty-first-century news environment would affect journalistic independence at the *institutional* level, however, is lacking. Given this complex interrelationship, it's essential for journalism to stay focused on its core value and strengths, so it doesn't have to jump on the tech bandwagon whenever a new technology emerges, whether it's about SEO, audience analytics, or AI. However, small newsrooms are more vulnerable in these processes without the same resources or leverage as large news organizations do to resist the FOMO when powerful platforms like Google set the agenda.

GNI BLOG

Google's news initiatives are also recorded on GNI's official blog, another space where Google credits its technological and economic investment as proof of its support for the news industry, on the one hand, and seeks legitimacy through endorsement of its news partners in its expanding partner network, on the other. The largest cluster of GNI's blog posts revolves around Google's own technologies, which aimed at areas Google prioritized for newsrooms to pursue, from data analysis, visualization, and data journalism to revenue growth, digital advertising, subscription, and paywall. These Google tools are often introduced through examples about how they were applied by Google's news partners in areas such as fact checking, local news, diversity, digital business, and the COVID-19 pandemic. Since 2016, there was a growing number of posts about how Google technologies were applied to cover election news in different countries. In 2018, for example, election-related posts were much more common than other popular topics, such as fact checking and local news, indicating Google's effort, through its news partners, to further its economic and technological influence into the political realm. The blog posts also recorded GNI's expanding international coverage with news initiatives in Europe as the largest cluster, followed by those in Asia. The examination of the GNI blogs shows that Google's news initiatives have expanded to Africa, Australia, North America, and South America.

Going through the blog posts by year reveals the changing focus of GNI over time. Compared to the pre-2018 posts, which covered discrete technologies and events without a clear institutional goal, blog posts after GNI's launch in 2018 show that Google's news-related initiatives have strategically concentrated on areas in response to the dynamics of the journalism community. For example, fact checking–related posts reached its peak after the 2016 US elections and declined since then, with a small rise in the wake of the spread of COVID-related false information, along the timeline when these issues were intensely covered by news media. Posts about local journalism rose largely since 2018 and grew even more after 2019, when the Journalism Competition and Preservation Act, which aims to protect local journalism from big tech companies, was proposed. Another example is diversity-related issues, which did not appear on the GNI blog site until 2020, when there was a wave of racial reckoning in the news industry in the aftermath of a series of antiracism movements, from Black Lives Matter after George Floyd's death to Stop Asian Hate in the wake of the anti-Asian violence since the start of the COVID-19 pandemic. The examination of GNI's main website and blog site shows the two-way agenda shaping between Google and the news industry. On the one hand, Google, via technological and economic means, sets the agenda for the news industry, which influences how the news industry identifies its challenges and solutions. On the other hand, Google's news-related investment and its network building have been carried out in a more systematic way, strategically responding to the news industry's agenda. The pushes and pulls form the evolving power relations between Google and the news industry. These dynamics are also reflected in GNI's news programs, such as Google's Digital News Initiative (DNI), the most mentioned program on GNI blog site before 2019, which was replaced by the GNI Innovation Challenge program after 2019 and then Google News Showcase in 2021. Through these programs, Google transports its funding, technology, and values to newsrooms worldwide.

DIGITAL NEWS INITIATIVE

In the wake of the disputes between European news publishers and Google News, Google launched the Digital News Initiative in 2015, a program that aimed to "support high-quality journalism in Europe through technology and innovation." This initiative, according to Carlo D'Asaro Biondo, Google's president of strategic partnerships, Europe, was also a gesture to improve Google's relationship with the European news industry. When he announced the launch of the DNI in London, Biondo said, "I firmly believe that Google has always wanted to be a friend and partner to the news industry, but I also accept we've made some mistakes along the way."[12] The DNI Fund invested about 150 million euros from 2016 through 2019. In six rounds of competition, DNI funded 662 projects related to digital news innovation in thirty European

A GLOBAL NETWORK

countries. Google set the focus for each DNI competition, and the winning projects were selected by the Google Project Team and the DNI Fund Council, which consisted of representatives from Google, the European news industry, and academia. In round 1 in 2016, the ten topics addressed in the winning projects were multimedia, analytics and research, payment models, data journalism, AI technologies, visualization, user-generated content, niche editorial products, investigative journalism, and personalization.[13] Compared to the first round, round 2 projects showed evident growth in two categories: artificial intelligence and distribution and circulation. In 2017, the focus on artificial intelligence continued to grow in round 3. Fact checking, which was not among the top ten topics in rounds 1 and 2, stood out in round 3, making up almost a third of the applications. Immersive technologies, such as virtual reality and augmented reality, also increased largely in this round.[14] Round 4 saw a continued growth of AI technologies, which were applied in areas such as using machine learning technology for subscription and improving content visibility through personalization.[15] New technologies, from audio and mobile to AI, still dominated round 5 projects, announced in 2018.[16] In 2019, the round 6 winning projects were announced. In this round, Google asked large- and medium-size project applicants to focus on "one of the most pressing issues identified by the news ecosystem: the diversification of revenue streams."[17] To respond to this call, projects in that year concentrated on how to use Google's AI and machine learning technologies to drive subscriptions, create new payment models, and minimize churn (subscribers who leave the service during a given time period). Overall, finding ways to apply new technologies in different aspects of news making and exploring new, digital business opportunities are the two lasting themes throughout DNI. Since the winning projects were selected based on Google's criteria, funding allocation pointed newsrooms to areas that Google encouraged and in which it invested.

GNI INNOVATION CHALLENGE

After the Europe-based DNI, Google invested $30 million in GNI Innovation Challenge, a program aiming at expanding Google's global network to other parts of the world, including (using Google's geographic categories) Asian Pacific, Latin America, North America, and Middle East, Turkey & Africa. The program was initially launched in Asia Pacific, with a focus on increasing "revenue from readers" through subscriptions, membership programs, contributions, and other digital products and services.[18] The second-round Asia Pacific Innovation Challenge continued to focus on opening up new business opportunities through audience engagement. Google advised applicants to submit proposals about "engaged users," those that are more likely to "return more often to a news website," "visit more pages during a session," "sign up for an email newsletter," and "are also more likely to convert to paid subscribers."[19] These ideas about "engaged audience" and "reader revenue," while not different from traditional commercial media's understanding of audience as ad consumers, datafy and further commodify the news audience, which departs from the journalistic mission that values the news audience as citizens and community members. Through Google programs, ideas like these were encouraged and rewarded. Value systems associated with these ideas are spread in the journalism community around the world. Elsewhere, there were two rounds of GNI Innovation Challenge in Latin America as well as in Middle East, Turkey, and Africa between 2019 and 2021. These programs solicited proposals about digital subscription growth, online active users, and digital ad revenue, which were considered "digital news objectives" that applicants should address in their proposals.[20] In North America, three rounds of GNI Innovation Challenge were launched since 2019. Priorities were given to similar digital areas, with a particular focus on local news media.

Since the launch of GNI Innovation Challenge, 227 projects were selected and funded, covering forty-seven countries and areas. Google reported that among the 227 projects, 75 percent of them saw "a measurable increase" in audience growth and engagement, and more than half of the recipients had "a measurable increase" in monetization.[21] Applications for the program were reviewed by a project team, who then recommended a shortlist for a jury to vote on. The project teams in different regions consisted of members who, one assumes, shared Google's interests, serving as senior employees, executives of Google, or Google partners. As a global program, GNI Innovation Challenge produced homogeneity in news industries worldwide by spreading its prioritization of technologies and ideas related to datafication and digital business models.

GOOGLE NEWS SHOWCASE

After 2020, another GNI global program, Google News Showcase, was heavily promoted on the GNI blog site. News Showcase, a "product and licensing program,"[22] is Google's "single biggest investment in news partnerships" to date.[23] The program was launched in October 2020, when the company invested $1 billion to pay news publishers in the aftermath of the elevated regulatory pressure in Australia, Europe, and other parts of the world (see chapter 3).

Through News Showcase, Google pays news publishers that opt in to this program to create and curate news content on Google's platforms. Google provides templates, particularly, panels in formats such as "rundown," "timeline," and "bullets," for these news publishers to choose from and asks publishers to organize the news into these panels. Google's news partners can also add related articles to the panels and extend access for a certain number of free news items that would otherwise be behind their paywall. If users are interested in a publisher's content, they can follow the publisher through News Showcase. In areas of the world where News Showcase is available, a large matrix of news panels across various newsrooms appears on the Google News mobile app under the Newsstand tab and on the Google News desktop version via news.google.com/showcase. News displayed in News Showcase panels is hand-picked by participating news publishers, making the program look like an upgraded version of the early "Editors' picks." If readers recall the discussions in chapter 2, "Editors' picks" was a feature that allowed news organizations to submit their own, preferred news items to be shown on Google News. But this time, Google pays news publishers to do this as a response to recent legislation around the world that requires big tech platforms to compensate news organizations (details in chapter 3). Participating news media receive monthly payments from Google with a three-year contract.

There are many concerns about Google News Showcase and other GNI programs, especially regarding these programs' impact on small newsrooms. Google programs like these are welcomed by some small newsrooms, as they rely on Google for financial support, visibility, and traffic in the digital environment, but the financial bond turns these news publishers into paid labor that produces news content for Google's platforms. As of 2023, Google News Showcase has signed over 2,200 news partners worldwide, the majority of whom are local publishers. In addition to aforementioned concerns about the impact on journalistic independence, some critics pointed out that the three-daily-story quota required by News Showcase put pressure on short-staffed small newsrooms to rush to produce low-quality news or even clickbait journalism, others are worried that Google's terms would harm the slow journalism model some newsrooms are exploring, and still others showed resistance to big tech companies' involvement in community journalism in any form.[24] "I can also see no reason to assume that support for journalism from big tech is a panacea," said a media writer for organizations focusing on public interest journalism. "We only need to look to Australia's recent legislation to make Facebook and Google pay publishers [the majority of this money went to Murdoch] to see the problems with this relationship."²⁵ While more than 90 percent of the participating publishers in the News Showcase program are local or community news organizations, with many of them being small or independent newsrooms,²⁶ it has come to light that it was the large players, such as News Corp, who had more negotiation power and took away much larger payments from Google.²⁷ It was reported that some US newsrooms felt offended by Google's offers, which were as little as $200,000 a year; others took a wait-and-see approach, hoping that proposals like the Journalism Competition and Preservation Act bring legal changes.²⁸

Through these programs under GNI, Google invests in a vast global partnership network that organizes newsrooms, big or small, within the Google universe. With such a global network in place, Google lays down the infrastructure for its institutional power to grow globally, no matter how individual technologies may evolve. Such institutional power helps Google gain more legitimacy and exert influence beyond the technological and economic domains in the global media and technology landscape.

N-D-N

Google's news ambition reached a milestone when 2022 marked the twentieth anniversary of Google News. Amid uncertainties in the Google-news relationship and the global platform governance landscape, there was no big celebration

A GLOBAL NETWORK

on GNI's website apart from a short paragraph in a blog post that talked about the new look of Google News. In the post, Brad Bender, Google's VP of product management, and Olivia Ma, GNI's director, described Google News as an effort that "broke new ground in news aggregation." Google executives stressed Google's goal of creating "the new ways people look for and consume news."[29] The "new way" mentioned in this post was reminiscent of the "Google way" that the company had hailed when it first introduced its news aggregation service two decades ago. Looking back at the trajectory of Google's news ambition over the past twenty-plus years, it reveals that Google has never given a clear answer on what the "Google way" is. Instead, the "Google way" has been a fluid, evolving idea, transformed by the changing relationship between Google and news. To sum up the analysis in this book, I next propose an N-D-N (normalization-differentiation-negotiation) framework, drawing on concepts related to normalization and differentiation discussed in the introduction, that is, legitimacy, specialization, resistance, and autonomy, and also using institutionalization as a complementary perspective, to conceptualize the long-term trends that shape the "Google way" through pushes and pulls over the course of more than two decades.

NORMALIZATION STAGE

During the evolution of the "Google way," normalization primarily defined the early years of Google's news endeavor, when it was incorporating news business into Google business. At this stage, Google was seeking ways to grow its legitimacy in the digital information ecosystem. The company was still in the process of defining its specialization and experimenting with different models of organizing the web. Google's search algorithm was not strong enough to completely replace the directory model. By adopting the directory model, Google also adopted an editorial approach to managing information on the web. Back then, however, Google did not pay particular attention to news in its search business, assuming it was no different from any other type of information on the web. But when people searched "New York Twin Towers" after the 9/11 attacks, Google's search returned information irrelevant to the attacks, because news sources had been "crawled" a month earlier (see chapter 1). After witnessing the huge news demand on the web created by 9/11, Google realized that news was its own particular type of information, with both social and economic value—and with a uniquely timely nature. Google also seized on traditional news media's technological limitations, which had caused the news paralysis on 9/11, seeing it as an opportunity to provide alternatives made possible by its own technological specialization. During that national emergency, Google joined many other internet actors to practice online news aggregation by adopting the news media's role of informing the public. On its search platform, Google provided access to information and resources that it aggregated to meet the public's critical information needs even without users' search queries. As a young company, the lack of legitimacy, low level of specialization, and an unprecedented national emergency led Google to explore its identity beyond that of a pure search

A GLOBAL NETWORK

engine. These circumstances also shielded Google from resistance when adopting certain functionalities and practices of the traditional news industry. These were conditions necessary for normalization to happen. The normalization stage that characterized the early history of Google's news endeavor set the tone for Google's relationship with the traditional news industry—on the occasions when tensions escalated between platforms and news publishers, Google's approach tended to be less intense compared to other platform companies.

After 9/11, Google formalized its news ambition in 2002 with the rollout of Google News. To start up its news aggregation service, Google integrated news into its business more deeply; for example, before 9/11, Google had only irregularly scanned limited numbers of news sites. Thereafter, the new news aggregation service automatically crawled thousands of news sources worldwide at a much higher frequency. Google also integrated common journalistic practices into its website structure and design. Journalistic ideas were also adopted into Google's news-related algorithmic systems. In many ways, normalizing the news helped Google gain legitimacy to sustain the company as a newcomer in both the tech and media communities. In 2004, two years after Google launched its news aggregation service, Google's founders wrote the IPO letter to the company's shareholders. In the letter, they used ideas adopted from journalism several times to justify Google's business, viewing independence and objectivity as the "most important" and "most fundamental" values in Google's success.[30] When explaining Google's motto "Don't be evil," Google founders made connections to traditional news media, stating that what Google was doing was "similar to a well-run newspaper."[31] Google was not a news company after all. The "Google way" of experiencing news brought new ideas and practices into the news environment, such as automation, cross-source multiple perspectives, and news debundling and rebundling. Despite the differences that the "Google way" introduced, normalization dominated at this stage, when Google's specialization was still forming and its demand for autonomy in relation to the news industry was not a top priority; rather, Google depended on the news industry in many ways to legitimize its news business.

Differentiation Stage

As Google's power and influence kept growing, the dominance of normalization gave way to differentiation in Google's development vis-à-vis the news industry. This stage featured a high degree of specialization, strong resistance, and an urgent demand for autonomy. Internally, Google's technological specialization was strengthened through a few waves of investment in news-related technology innovations. The higher level of specialization increased Google's legitimacy and made its news aggregation service more popular. With Google's technology specialization, news is datafied by its algorithm systems, where news as sociocultural artifact is converted into quantitative, machine-processable data points. During this process, news is also reduced into first-order data to generate profitable user data. The datafication of news and news users radically differentiates the "Google way" from how journalists make sense of and treat the news.

During this period, institutional resistance against Google's power rose in the global news community. Resistance came in different forms, from legal actions and commercial negotiations to discursive challenges, collective boycott, and legislative lobbying. The traditional news industry employed existing legal, moral, and discursive frameworks and demonstrated strong institutional power that allowed them to effectively bring an industrial issue, namely, the news industry's struggle with the rise of tech platforms in the digital era, into the public arena, which contributed to the seismic shift in the regulatory landscape. In these disputes, news publishers challenged Google's specialized technologies, standards, and algorithms, as well as Google's business model and competition position supported by its cross-platform integration. The external pressure from the news industry made Google's demand for autonomy more urgent than it had been during the early years of its history. In these disputes, Google's defense primarily relied on its technological specialization to either settle the disputes in some cases, make arguments about its transformative use of news to claim fair use in others, or bypass the laws to avoid liabilities.

During this period, the news industry continued to exert its institutional influence in different media markets. From Germany and Spain to Australia and Canada, news publishers used their lobbying power to push for the passage of new laws that would require Google to compensate news publishers. In the United States, where regulatory intervention in the tech sector has often been a token gesture,[32] news media have strongly influenced the public discourse about tech platforms' responsibilities and impacts. Around the globe, the rising call for platform governance and the recent reforms in copyright, antitrust, privacy, and data protection regulations demonstrate a power contest in the tech-media landscape, in which one side is the traditional media industry, representing an established social institution that has the power to mobilize other social sectors to defend the economic and political order of the status quo; the other side is a new power, whose accumulation of economic and technological influence has allowed it to differentiate itself from this old order. This power contest was the main feature of the differentiation stage, where news media insisted that the "Google way" monetized news but without news organizations being the beneficiaries, whereas from Google's point of view, the "Google way" is a highly specialized process of datafication that does not fall into conventional regulatory categories and therefore should not be regulated under such frameworks.

Negotiation Stage

In Europe, the frontline of the Google-publisher disputes, the years between Google News's shutdown in Spain and the passing of the new EUCD seemed to be less eventful than the previous years. In fact, Google had been exercising its techno-economic power to deal with news publishers and regulators in the region. During those years, for example, Google invested €150 million DNI funds in the area. In the

A GLOBAL NETWORK

aftermath of the new EUCD in Europe as well as the passage of new laws in other parts of the world, Google successively launched a series of news-related initiatives, spending over a billion dollars to compensate news publishers. Despite these financial investments, Danielle Coffey, the president and chief executive of the News/Media Alliance, pointed out that what the news industry sought was not just "benevolence" compensation but "legally founded right to payment . . . no matter the medium, distributor, or new emerging technology."[33] This is the fundamental demand of the news as an institution. For Google, its response to such demand has been made through technological and economic means. While the company claims that the value of news to Google "is not economic—it's societal," Google tends to rely on the economic defense when pushing back against news publishers' charge that Google monetizes the news without compensating the news media. "Nearly all of our revenue comes not from news queries, but from queries with commercial intent," Google claimed.[34] When explaining how Google supports journalism, Google frames itself as "one of the world's biggest financial supporters" of journalism. This type of narrative has prevailed in Google's defense: "We don't make money from Google News," "We pay for content," and "Google generates traffic and revenue for news publishers."[35] Google's economic and technological argument alone, however, would not be sufficient to withstand the news industry's challenge when the latter was able to mobilize other social institutions using its institutional power. Google's situation reflects the lack of institutionalization of the tech sector, a key reason that differentiation gave way to negotiation as the main trend at this stage.

As discussed in the introduction, institutionalization involves three pillars: the regulative, the normative, and the cultural-cognitive.[36] While large tech companies have strong regulative power to create rules that define the infrastructure of the digital world, this power has been limited in economic and technological domains and has not extended into the normative realm, which addresses the "prescriptive, evaluative, and obligatory dimension" of society, stressing what social actors "should do,"[37] nor does it reach through the cultural-cognitive realm, which concerns ideas, knowledge systems, and shared symbolic frameworks that define reality. In the cultural-cognitive domain, the discourses Google constructed do not hold very well, especially in comparison to those of the news industry, an institution that is particularly strong in the cultural-cognitive domain. For example, "Don't be evil," the motto that Google used to define its company culture, was dropped from the company's code of conduct in 2018.[38] Google's discursive emphasis has been instead put on "open access" or "universal access" for a "more informed world." The shift resulted in a lack of consistency in the cultural-cognitive domain. The discourse is also challenged by the news industry, which has effectively argued that open access is not free access and that quality journalism costs money. For the public, Google also has the burden of legitimizing its role as the executor of the universal access to information. Policy scholars believe that "underlying any field is a set of collective frames that define the aims, the relationships and the rules."³⁹ Google in particular and the tech industry in general have yet to construct such collective frames that represent the tech sector's shared aims, functions, and behavioral practices to compete with those that legitimize the news industry.

Another weaker area for the tech sector is the normative pillar. Scholars point to public interest as a normative principle that is currently absent in the tech industry's development.⁴⁰ One of the main concerns relates to "a public-interest vacuum at the institutional level," given that tech companies tend to apply an individualist approach when it comes to the public interest commitment; that is, while these companies provide "an enabling environment" for users to exercise their rights and freedoms, they transfer public interest responsibilities to individual users to take care of their own choices and actions, whether it's about liking or reposting a social media post, deciding which search results to click on, or making personalized information choices.⁴¹ In other cases, the tech companies' public interest commitment is not proactive but a response to outside pressures on specific issues. For example, when public criticism rose regarding the spread of false information on tech platforms or when antiracism and social justice movements called for diversity and justice as digital gatekeepers' responsibility, tech companies would adjust toward these dynamics, but such actions are rather reactive. Scholars also pointed out that unlike traditional media that adopt the public interest principle in both restrictive and affirmative ways, platform companies tend to focus on what they should not do rather than what they should.⁴² Given the individualist, nonproactive, and

A GLOBAL NETWORK

restrictive approach the tech industry has adopted, the public interest model has yet to be registered as the "institutional imperative" in the field.[43]

Given its lack of institutional power, in the past few years, Google's narrative has transformed from Google's being the savior of the news industry in trouble to the major financial supporter of journalism and then to a collaborative tone, as demonstrated on the GNI website, drawing a picture of the future of journalism with Google in it. The shifts signify the transition to a negotiation stage in Google's relationship with the news industry. With the collaboration mindset, the "Google way" focuses more on network building that leverages Google's resources to recruit global news partners, a strategy that helps grow Google's institutional influence. With Google's investment in network building, there would still be resistance, but less at the institutional level. Collaboration at this stage shapes a Google-friendly environment that could help Google gain more legitimacy and protect its autonomy from being severely challenged so that the company can get through the global regulatory climate change that calls for stricter platform governance. Institutionalization is not a linear process, nor a given. It has been, for example, disrupted by the backlash against the establishment that challenges the core pillars of major institutions, from political parties to educational and media systems, as shown in recent elections in different parts of the world. In the 2024 US presidential election, less-institutionalized media and tech actors, such as podcasters, social media influencers, and high-impact individuals in Silicon Valley, played an important role in shaping the election outcomes. These dynamics constitute the broader context for Google to adjust its strategies when managing the Google-news relationship in these testing times.

THE "GOOGLE WAY" AND THE TECH-NEWS RELATIONSHIP IN THE AI ERA

November 2022 became another landmark in the history of technology development when OpenAI's ChatGPT, a generative AI tool, quickly became a phenomenon worldwide and opened a new chapter of the AI era. It only took ChatGPT two months after its release to become "the fastest-growing consumer application in history," reaching 100 million monthly active users, compared to nine months for TikTok and two and a half years for Instagram.[44] Before that, Google had been working on AI technologies for years. Since the mid-2010s, the application of artificial intelligence technology has been a growing priority in Google's news-related initiatives. Initially, the effort was limited to early AI technologies, such as machine learning and its application in the throughput phase. Newsrooms were encouraged to use machine learning technology to analyze data in order to find new ways to help with their subscriptions, content moderation, and personalization. For the most part, Google's AI technology had not been exploited on the output end, as generative AI does. It was ChatGPT's birth and its quick rise to prominence that prompted Google to declare a "code red"—"For Google, this was akin to pulling the fire alarm."[45]

To catch up in the AI race, Google rolled out a range of AI initiatives. One AI tool on which news media keep a close eye is Google's own generative AI feature used by its search engine, called AI Overviews. Introduced in May 2024, AI Overviews can automatically produce comprehensive answers about topics that users search. These AI-generated answers are summaries based on data scraped across the web, including, but not exclusively, content from news sites. With this AI tool, Google states that searchers can get "quick answers" without having to "piece together all the information you need."[46] While Google claimed that AI-generated summaries would not be made available for current event news, that promise did not ease news publishers' worries that generative AI is moving toward replacing them and their content.[47]

Despite the uneasiness in the news industry, some news companies are embracing AI. In the United States, by the end of 2023, news publishers that have reached a deal with OpenAI included the Associated Press, the *Atlantic*, News Corp (the parent company of the *Wall Street Journal*), BuzzFeed, the *Financial Times*, Vox Media, and the digital publishing giant Dotdash Meredith, which owns *People* magazine and other brands. Outside the United States, the Germany-based Axel Springer (the parent company of *Business Insider* and *Politico*) was the first publisher to partner with OpenAI. With such contractual agreements, OpenAI can use these publishers' content to train its AI models; in exchange, news publishers will have access to OpenAI's AI tools and products.[48] While Google hasn't signed similar contracts since its release of AI Overviews, news companies such as the *Atlantic* have expressed willingness to collaborate with Google in its AI initiatives. As Nicholas Thompson, the chief executive of the *Atlantic*, said, "We know traffic will go down as Google makes this transition, but I think that being part of the new product will help us minimize how much it goes down." The idea that motivates these media companies' decisions is that AI is the future and that "you can't opt out of the future," as Roger Lynch, the chief executive of Condé Nast, the media company that owns the *New Yorker*, *Vogue*, and other publications, said.[49]

Along with the more open attitudes about AI are varying forms of reluctance to adopt the new technology. For example, studies find a high degree of restrictions, especially since mid-2023, used by website administrators to block AI crawlers from scraping and using their data. Scholars found that news websites tend to be more likely to employ restrictions—using REP (Robots Exclusion Protocol) and/or terms of service—than other web sources to prohibit AI crawlers. News websites' AI restrictions were found in different parts of the world. A study examining these news websites' blocking mechanisms found that over the course of 2023, none of these news websites chose to unblock AI crawlers or removed their AI restrictions.[50] At the same time, these studies found that fewer news sites were blocking Google's AI crawler than OpenAI's, reflecting that news organizations are still very much reliant on Google for online visibility.

Another possible reason not mentioned in these studies is that Google's years of effort in building its global news partnership network has paid off. Through this network, Google has an infrastructure ready to reach its news partners worldwide;

it can also test and distribute its new products and ideas among partners and hopefully keep negative responses at bay. When a new technology like AI emerges, this kind of relationship building can help buffer resistance from the news industry and maintain a more collaborative relationship, which would secure more legitimacy for Google's AI advancement in the news world. In fact, when the *New York Times* sued OpenAI and Microsoft in 2023 over their AI technologies, the *Times* cited its history with Google as a model of "working productively with large technology platforms,"[51] suggesting that Google's model might be something that news media can look to pursue in the AI era.

Since the release of ChatGPT, the strongest pushback from the US news industry is the *New York Times*' lawsuit against OpenAI and Microsoft. The *Times* responded quickly to ChatGPT's rapid rise to prominence. Just a few months after ChatGPT's introduction, the *Times* reached out to OpenAI and Microsoft to negotiate commercial terms for these companies to use the *Times*' content in their AI systems. Failing to reach a resolution, the *Times* sued OpenAI and Microsoft in December 2023, one year after ChatGPT was rolled out. The *Times*' complaint focused on issues about copyright infringement and unfair competition. The arguments are not much different from those involved in the disputes surrounding Google and news publishers in the pre-AI era discussed in chapter 3. The *Times* addressed these issues by attacking both the input and the output ends of the defendants' AI systems. On the input end, the *Times* argued that OpenAI and Microsoft had used the *Times*' copyrighted content as their training data without permission or compensation. The *Times* stressed that its content was a key source that's largely used in these companies' main datasets to train their AI models, and that as "high-quality content," the *Times*' work was "more important and valuable for training the GPT models as compared to content taken from other, lower-quality sources."[52] The *Times* also accused the defendants of reproducing and distributing its content and producing same or similar content on the output end. The AI-generated content, the *Times* argued, directly competes with *Times* content. According to the *Times*, generative AI "substitute[s] for The Times and steal[s] audiences away from it," affecting the newspaper's traffic, subscription, and referral revenues.[53] Compared to the cases discussed in chapter 3, these arguments and narratives would sound familiar to Google.

The *New York Times* claims that millions of *Times*-owned works across News, Cooking, Wirecutter, and the Athletic were used in GPT training data. The *Times*' complaint also reveals that content from reputable news media like the *New York Times* represents "high value," "high quality," and frequently sampled training data for GPT models. For example, according to the *Times*, the company's website, NYTimes.com, is the fifth top domain in an internal training dataset for ChatGPT-2. It's also the "most highly represented proprietary source" in Common Crawl, the main dataset to train ChatGPT-3, in which the top domains also include other news sources such as latimes.com, theguardian.com, washingtonpost.com, npr.org, and more.[54] Other studies also found that news is a main component of the head distribution of domains that represent "the largest, most actively maintained, and critical domains for AI Training."⁵⁵

In seeking a dismissal, OpenAI defended its "non-consumptive," transformative use of the *Times*' copyright material, which, according to OpenAI, is protected by fair use, another familiar argument that Google made to defend its use of news content in the pre-AI age. OpenAI believed that its AI products are transformative technologies that "leverage existing works *internally* . . . to new and useful ends."⁵⁶ OpenAI backed up its fair use defense with prior court decisions ruled to protect "useful innovations like home video recording, internet search, book search tools, reuse of software APIs, and many others."⁵⁷ It argued that the foundational principle of the copyright law is "not to grant authors 'absolute control' over all uses of their work"; instead, the basic purpose of fair use is to "keep [the] copyright monopoly within [these] lawful bounds."⁵⁸ As discussed in chapter 3, precedents in the US legal system within and without the AI context were likely to prioritize innovation and competition over regulation, one reason that US news publishers, unlike their counterparts in the European Union, tended not to pursue legal actions against Google in the last wave of the press-platform tension. Although the *New York Times* was the first major American news organization to challenge AI technology through litigation, most of the arguments and counterarguments involved in the case are not necessarily new to Google. With its past experience, Google may be more prepared than before to cope with AI-related challenges coming from the news industry.

Despite errors and backlash, Google's AI Overviews is forging ahead. From a technological perspective, the "Google way" in the AI era, just like how OpenAI defended itself in the lawsuit with the *Times*, is expected to be another "new, different, and innovative" way of experiencing news in the AI age.[59] What the "Google way" and many other "new, different, innovative" ways bring along is an information ecosystem that is increasingly intertwined, in which news media have to compete with numerous proprietary and nonproprietary information sources who produce facts, knowledge, language, and human experience that can be fed into the large language models to train the AI systems. When Google updated its information quality principle from E-A-T (expertise, authoritativeness, and trustworthiness) to E-E-A-T (the extra E is for experience), it is that extra E for experience that news media really need to think hard about and work hard on in the age of AI. Questions such as how journalism should build authentic connection with the people and communities they serve, how journalistic work can enrich and uplift humanity, how to revise the elitist approach in journalistic processes, how to better serve the underrepresented and give voice to the voiceless, and how to search answers to these questions across individual, routine, organizational, institutional, and social system levels are pressing issues for the news industry to reflect upon and take action on at the dawn of the AI era.[60]

The "Google way" in the AI age is certainly subject to a complex and evolving global environment. In countries and areas that currently lead in AI development, each can contribute to influence the next steps of the AI industry. For example, the European Union has positioned itself as the "global standard setter" by pioneering AI regulation.[61] The position continues European authorities' role as "the world's most assertive watchdog of the technology industry" in the pre-AI era[62] with the objective of safeguarding Europe's internal market from non-European platforms (see chapter 3). At the end of 2023, the European Union reached an agreement on a new law, the AI Act, as "the world's first comprehensive AI law"[63] to regulate AI-related issues ranging from data use to misinformation, automating jobs, national security, and the application of facial recognition technology. The law will apply to AI companies that do business in Europe and will have influence on the global regulatory community. China, following the United States, is currently the second-leading country in terms of the AI market size[64] and total AI investment over the past five years as of May 2024.[65] Globally, China also produces the most research papers on AI and has the most AI-related patents.[66] China sees AI technology as a key force of the fourth industrial revolution, which will produce "new types of productivity" and contribute to the rejuvenation of the nation after the "unprecedented change of the world over the past century." China believes that compared to the previous industrial revolutions, it now enjoys strong economic growth and comprehensive national power, which prepares the country for playing a bigger role in the next round of scientific and technological innovation.[67] In the United States, China's AI ambition is believed to be part of the country's strategic plan to surpass the United States for AI leadership in the world.[68] As the global AI race is heating up, the US National Security Commission on Artificial Intelligence asserted, "AI is going to reorganize the world. America must lead the charge."[69] In response, OpenAI, amid its legal troubles, plans to base its lobbying effort on the idea that US AI companies are a "bulwark" against China.[70] With the regulatory pressure from Europe and competition from China, the world is watching how US policy makers will manage the growth of its AI sector and where priorities will be placed when dealing with relationships across different sectors and between incumbent and emerging stakeholders of the twenty-first-century world order.

The development of the AI technologies is another milestone in the tech-news relationship. When the relationship is examined through the N-D-N framework, Google seems to be in a place where its technological specialization remains high, especially as it gets more involved in the AI race. At the same time, after years of normalization, differentiation, and negotiation, Google has gained more legitimacy in the news area, especially through its global network building, which at the institutional level would help the company offset news media's resistance to Google's AI effort. Furthermore, prior lessons learned from the pre-AI era, when Google went through ups and downs in its relationship with the news industry, prepared Google to cope with AI-related disputes from concerned news publishers, especially given that news organizations have not raised any fundamentally different arguments so far to challenge the involvement of AI technologies in the news environment. As indicated in the *New York Times* lawsuit against

OpenAI and Microsoft, the news media's main demand was still about compensation and still relied mainly on legal frameworks of copyright and fair competition. While technologies and the logics these technologies represent have evolved, the demand and the approaches pursued are not substantially different from those when news publishers challenged news aggregators and search engines in the pre-AI era. It's understandable for news media to first focus on financial security when new technologies disrupt the status quo, but in the long term the news industry as an institution will need to seek paradigmatic solutions.

In the United States, Google is facing an uncertain time: Its antitrust case is pending at the changeover between the two administrations. The 2024 US presidential election surfaced both new media power and new tech power, which integrated in an unprecedented way, and such power has proven to be a strong shaping force beyond the technological and economic domains and across national borders. In turn, Google and other US-based, global-facing corporate superpowers will continue to evolve under both domestic and international influences. In the AI era, the "Google way" remains a window through which we can see how these influences play out. Both domestically and globally, it seems that the tech sector, in a move similar to the traditional media industry, has sought to strengthen its political and economic position in today's world order by engaging closely with other stakeholders, whether the political community or the public, as demonstrated during and after the 2024 election cycle in the United States. During this process, it has deepened the tech-media hybridity that was forged through decades of pushes and pulls between the two sectors. In the postelection era, such hybridity reflects the not fully developed institutionalization of the tech sector, on the one hand, and it may indicate the rise of deinstitutionalization, on the other.

NOTES

INTRODUCTION

1. News Corp, "News Corp and Google Agree to Global Partnership on News," Newscorp.com, February 17, 2021, https://newscorp.com/2021/02/17/news-corp-and-google-agree-to-global-partnership-on-news/.
2. Mike Isaac, Daisuke Wakabayashi, Damien Cave, and Edmund Lee, "Facebook Blocks News in Australia, Diverging with Google on Proposed Law," *New York Times*, February 17, 2021, https://www.nytimes.com/2021/02/17/technology/facebook-google-australia-news.html.
3. Nick Statt, "Facebook Strikes News Corp Deal to License News from Australian Media Outlets," *The Verge*, March 15, 2021, https://www.theverge.com/2021/3/15/22332658/facebook-news-corp-rupert-murdoch-deal-australia-sky-news.
4. James Vincent, "This Is What Google Says Search Will Look Like Under EU Copyright Laws," *The Verge*, January 17, 2019, https://www.theverge.com/2019/1/17/18186879/google-eu-copyright-laws-search-news-link-tax.
5. Philipp Schindler, "The Google News Initiative: Building a Stronger Future for News," *Google* (blog), March 20, 2018, https://blog.google/outreach-initiatives/google-news-initiative/announcing-google-news-initiative/.

INTRODUCTION

6. Edward Helmore, "Google Made $4.7bn from News Sites in 2018, Study Claims," *Guardian*, June 10, 2019, https://www.theguardian.com/technology/2019/jun/10/google-news-revenue-2018-new-study.
7. Bobbie Johnson, "Murdoch Could Block Google Searches Entirely," *Guardian*, November 9, 2009, https://www.theguardian.com/media/2009/nov/09/murdoch-google.
8. Christopher W. Anderson, "What Aggregators Do: Towards a Networked Concept of Journalistic Expertise in the Digital Age," *Journalism* 14, no. 8 (2013): 1008–23.
9. Marcus Baram, "Facebook Finally Admits It's a Giant Media Company—Almost," *Fast Company*, January 11, 2017, https://www.fastcompany.com/3067148/facebook-finally-admits-its-a-giant-media-company-almost; Philip Napoli and Robyn Caplan, "Why Media Companies Insist They're Not Media Companies, Why They're Wrong, and Why It Matters," *First Monday* 22, no. 5 (2017), https://doi.org/10.5210/fm.v22i5.7051; Philip Napoli, "Social Media and the Public Interest: Governance of News Platforms in the Realm of Individual and Algorithmic Gatekeepers," *Telecommunications Policy* 39, no. 9 (2015): 751–60.
10. Adam Schweigert, "Towards a Better Definition of Curation in Journalism," *Adam Schweigert* (blog), June 14, 2012, https://adamschweigert.com/towards-a-better-definition-of-curation-in-journalism/.
11. Mark Coddington, *Aggregating the News: Secondhand News and the Erosion of Journalistic Authority* (Columbia University Press, 2019).
12. Jane Sasseen, Kenny Olmstead, and Amy Mitchell, "Digital: By the Numbers," Pew Research Center, March 18, 2013, http://www.stateofthemedia.org/2013/digital-as-mobile-grows-rapidly-the-pressures-on-news-intensify/digital-by-the-numbers/.
13. Sasseen, Olmstead, and Mitchell, "Digital"; Angela M. Lee and Hsiang Iris Chyi, "The Rise of Online News Aggregators: Consumption and Competition," *International Journal on Media Management* 17, no. 1 (2015): 3–24.
14. Laura H. Owen, "News Apps Are Making a Comeback. More Young Americans Are Paying for News. 2017 Is Weird," *Nieman Lab*, June 21, 2017, http://www.niemanlab.org/2017/06/news-apps-are-making-a-comeback-more-young-americans-are-paying-for-news-2017-is-weird/.
15. Piet Bakker, "Aggregation, Content Farms, and Huffinization: The Rise of Low-Pay and No-Pay Journalism," *Journalism Practice* 6, no. 5–6 (2012): 627–37.

INTRODUCTION

16. Jemima Kiss, "My Taptu App Takes the Visual News Aggregator to Mobile," *Guardian*, November 9, 2010, https://www.theguardian.com/technology/pda/2010/nov/09/taptu-app-aggregator.
17. Kimberley Isbell, "The Rise of the News Aggregator: Legal Implications and Best Practices," Citizen Media Law Project, 2010, https://papers.ssrn.com/sol3/papers.cfm?abstract_id=1670339.
18. Ian C. Campbell, "News Corp Gives Up on Its 'Knewz' Aggregator After 18 Months," *The Verge*, July 9, 2021, https://www.theverge.com/2021/7/9/22570164/knewz-news-corp-aggregation-google-facebook.
19. CNN, "CNN Acquires Canopy to Accelerate the Development of Its Forthcoming Digital News and Information Platform," CNN press release, April 7, 2020, https://cnnpressroom.blogs.cnn.com/2020/04/07/cnn-acquires-canopy/.
20. Sara Fischer, "News Aggregation Apps Take on Big Tech," *Axios*, August 23, 2019, https://www.axios.com/2019/08/23/news-aggregation-apps-big-tech-knewz-news-corp.
21. Lee and Chyi, "The Rise of Online News Aggregators."
22. Sasseen, Olmstead, Mitchell, "Digital."
23. Bakker, "Aggregation, Content Farms, and Huffinization."
24. Sean Silverthorne, "Tracks of My Tears: Reconstructing Digital Music," *Working Knowledge* (blog), November 30, 2009, https://www.library.hbs.edu/working-knowledge/tracks-of-my-tears-reconstructing-digital-music.
25. Helmore, "Google Made $4.7bn."
26. Lauren Stier, "Making Google News Work on Every Phone, Everywhere." *Google* (blog), September 10, 2018, https://www.blog.google/products/news/making-google-news-work-every-phone-everywhere/; Google, "Everyone Benefits from Access to Information and Creativity Online," Google.com, 2019, https://www.google.com/intl/en/togetherforcopyright/.
27. Statcounter, "Search Engine Market Share Worldwide," Statcounter GlobalStats, 2023, https://gs.statcounter.com/search-engine-market-share.
28. Safiya Umoja Noble, "Algorithms of Oppression," in *Algorithms of Oppression* (New York University Press, 2018).
29. Kohei Watanabe, "The Western Perspective in Yahoo! News and Google News: Quantitative Analysis of Geographic Coverage of Online News," *International Communication Gazette* 75, no. 2 (2013): 141–56.
30. Min Jiang, "The Business and Politics of Search Engines: A Comparative Study of Baidu and Google's Search Results of Internet Events in China," *New Media & Society* 16, no. 2 (2014): 212–33.

INTRODUCTION

31. Laura A. Granka, "The Politics of Search: A Decade Retrospective." *Information Society* 26, no. 5 (2010): 364–74.
32. Eric Goldman, "Search Engine Bias and the Demise of Search Engine Utopianism," *Yale Journal of Law & Technology* 8 (2005): 188. Junghoo Cho, Sourashis Roy, and Robert E. Adams, "Page Quality: In Search of an Unbiased Web Ranking," in *Proceedings of the 2005 ACM SIGMOD International Conference on Management of Data* (2005), 551–62.
33. Kevin Potts, *Web Design and Marketing Solutions for Business Websites* (Apress, 2007).
34. Pamela J. Shoemaker and Timothy Vos, *Gatekeeping Theory* (Routledge, 2009).
35. Lesley Chiou and Catherine Tucker, "Copyright, Digitization, and Aggregation," 2011, https://ide.mit.edu/wp-content/uploads/2016/04/2011.12_Chiou_Tucker_Copyright-Digitization-and-Aggregation_309.pdf?x61816; Joan Calzada and Ricard Gil, "What Do News Aggregators Do? Evidence from Google News in Spain and Germany," *Marketing Science* 39, no. 1 (2020): 134–67.
36. Doh-Shin Jeon and Nikrooz Nasr, "News Aggregators and Competition Among Newspapers on the Internet," *American Economic Journal: Microeconomics* 8, no. 4 (2016): 91–114.
37. Roland Schroeder and Moritz Kralemann, "Journalism Ex Machina—Google News Germany and Its News Selection Processes," *Journalism Studies* 6, no. 2 (2005): 245–47; Watanabe, "The Western Perspective."
38. Matt Carlson, "Order Versus Access: News Search Engines and the Challenge to Traditional Journalistic Roles," *Media, Culture & Society* 29, no. 6 (2007): 1014–30.
39. Susan Athey, Markus Mobius, and Jeno Pál, "The Impact of Aggregators on Internet News Consumption," Working Paper 28746, National Bureau of Economic Research, 2021.
40. Athey, Mobius, and Pál, "The Impact."
41. Athey, Mobius, and Pál, "The Impact."
42. Calzada and Gil, "What Do News Aggregators Do?"
43. Emily Bell, "Facebook Is Eating the World," *Columbia Journalism Review*, March 7, 2016, https://www.cjr.org/analysis/facebook_and_media.php; "Emily Bell: Journalism in the Age of Trump and the Real-Time Social Web," *The Conversation*, June 14, 2017, https://theconversation.com/emily-bell-journalism-in-the-age-of-trump-and-the-real-time-social-web-74627; Emily Bell, Taylor Owen, Peter Brown, Codi Hauka, and

INTRODUCTION

Nushin Rashidian, "The Platform Press: How Silicon Valley Reengineered Journalism," Columbia Academic Commons, May 26, 2017, https://academiccommons.columbia.edu/catalog/ac:15dv4ins27.

44. Nushin Rashidian, Pete Brown, Elizabeth Hansen, Emily Bell, Jonathan Albright, and Abigail Hartstone, "Friend and Foe: The Platform Press at the Heart of Journalism," *Columbia Journalism Review*, June 14, 2018, https://www.cjr.org/tow_center_reports/the-platform-press-at-the-heart-of-journalism.php.

45. Nushin Rashidian, George Civeris, Pete Brown, Emily Bell, and Abigail Hartstone, "Platforms and Publishers: The End of an Era," *Columbia Journalism Review*, November 22, 2019, https://www.cjr.org/tow_center_reports/platforms-and-publishers-end-of-an-era.php.

46. Michael Margolis and David Resnick, *Politics as Usual: The Cyberspace "Revolution"* (Sage, 2000), 1.

47. Carl May and Tracy Finch, "Implementing, Embedding, and Integrating Practices: An Outline of Normalization Process Theory," *Sociology* 43, no. 3 (2009): 535–54.

48. Jitendra V. Singh, David J. Tucker, and Robert J. House, "Organizational Legitimacy and the Liability of Newness," *Administrative Science Quarterly* (1986): 171–93.

49. Arthur L. Stinchcombe, *Constructing Social Theories* (University of Chicago Press, 1987); Cathryn Johnson, Timothy J. Dowd, and Cecilia L. Ridgeway, "Legitimacy as a Social Process," *Annual Review of Sociology* 32 (2006): 53–78.

50. Logan Molyneux and Rachel R. Mourão, "Political Journalists' Normalization of Twitter: Interaction and New Affordances," *Journalism Studies* 20, no. 2 (2019): 248–66; Qun Wang and Vikki Katz, "Ethnic Digital Media as Agenda Setters and Agenda Marketers: The Case of WXC and the *Jimmy Kimmel Live!* Controversy," in *Ethnic Media in the Digital Age*, ed. Sherry S. Yu and Matthew D. Matsaganispp (Routledge, 2018), 23–32; Edson Tandoc Jr. and Tim P. Vos, "The Journalist Is Marketing the News: Social Media in the Gatekeeping Process," *Journalism Practice* 10, no. 8 (2016): 950–66; Mark Coddington, "Normalizing the Hyperlink: How Bloggers, Professional Journalists, and Institutions Shape Linking Values," *Digital Journalism* 2, no. 2 (2014): 140–55.

51. Lev Manovich, *Software Takes Command*, vol. 5 (A&C Black, 2013).

52. Carlos A. Scolari, "Media Evolution," in *Mediated Communication* (De Gruyter. 2018), 161.

INTRODUCTION

53. Manovich, *Software Takes Command*, 267, 268.
54. Corinna Peil and Sergio Sparviero, "Media Convergence Meets Deconvergence," in *Media Convergence and Deconvergence* (Palgrave Macmillan, 2017), 3; Graham Meikle and Sherman Young, *Media Convergence: Networked Digital Media in Everyday Life* (Macmillan International Higher Education, 2011), 2.
55. Pablo J. Boczkowski, *Digitizing the News: Innovation in Online Newspapers* (MIT Press, 2005).
56. Steve Outing, "Where's the Money?," *Editor & Publisher* 12, no. 7, 81, 341 (1996).
57. David Domingo and Chris Paterson, *Making Online News*, vol. 2: *Newsroom Ethnographies in the Second Decade of Internet Journalism* (Peter Lang, 2011).
58. Pablo J. Boczkowski and José A. Ferris, "Multiple Media, Convergent Processes, and Divergent Products: Organizational Innovation in Digital Media Production at a European Firm," *Annals of the American Academy of Political and Social Science* 597, no. 1 (2005): 32–47.
59. Jane B. Singer, "The Political J-Blogger: 'Normalizing' a New Media Form to Fit Old Norms and Practices," *Journalism* 6, no. 2 (2005): 173–98.
60. Henry Jenkins and Mark Deuze, "Convergence Culture," *Convergence* 14, no. 1 (2008): 5–12; Sue Robinson, "'Journalism as Process': The Organizational Implications of Participatory Online News," *Journalism & Communication Monographs* 13, no. 3 (2011): 137–210.
61. Leslie-Jean Thornton and Susan M. Keith, "From Convergence to Webvergence: Tracking the Evolution of Broadcast-Print Partnerships Through the Lens of Change Theory," *Journalism & Mass Communication Quarterly* 86, no. 2 (2009): 257–76.
62. Bell, Owen, Brown, Hauka, and Rashidian, "The Platform Press."
63. Philip Napoli, "Evolutionary Theories of Media Institutions and Their Responses to New Technologies," in *Communication Theory: A Reader*, ed. Linda Costigan Lederman (Kendall/Hunt, 1998), 315–29.
64. Rashidian et al., "Friend and Foe."
65. Mark Coddington, "Clarifying Journalism's Quantitative Turn: A Typology for Evaluating Data Journalism, Computational Journalism, and Computer-Assisted Reporting," *Digital Journalism* 3, no. 3 (2015): 331–48.
66. Simon Rogers, "Turning Official Figures Into Understandable Graphics, at the Press of a Button," *Inside the Guardian* (blog), December 18, 2008, https://www.theguardian.com/help/insideguardian/2008/dec/18/unemploy

INTRODUCTION

mentdata; Sylvain Parasie and Eric Dagiral, "Data-Driven Journalism and the Public Good: 'Computer-Assisted Reporters' and 'Programmer-Journalists' in Chicago," *New Media & Society* 15, no. 6 (2013): 853–71.

67. Nonny De la Peña, Peggy Weil, Joan Llobera, Bernhard Spanlang, Doron Friedman, Maria V. Sanchez-Vives, and Mel Slater, "Immersive Journalism: Immersive Virtual Reality for the First-Person Experience of News," *Presence* 19, no. 4 (2010): 291–301.
68. Nytimes.com (n.d.), http://www.nytimes.com/marketing/nytvr/.
69. BBC News Labs, "In Our Toolkit: BBC News Botbuilder," 2018, http://bbcnewslabs.co.uk/2018/06/07/botbuilder/; Lucia Moses, "For News Publishers, Smart Speakers Are the Hot New Platform," *Digiday*, July 23, 2018, https://digiday.com/media/news-publishers-smart-speakers-hot-new-platform/.
70. Jeffrey C. Alexander and Paul Burbank Colomy, *Differentiation Theory: Problems and Prospects* (Columbia University Press, 1990); Daniel C. Hallin, "Field Theory, Differentiation Theory, and Comparative Media Research," in *Bourdieu and the Journalistic Field*, ed. Rodney Benson and Eric Neveu (Polity, 2005), 224–43.
71. Napoli, "Evolutionary Theories"; Tim P. Vos and Frank Michael Russell, "Theorizing Journalism's Institutional Relationships: An Elaboration of Gatekeeping Theory," *Journalism Studies* 20, no. 16 (2019): 2331–48.
72. Napoli, "Evolutionary Theories."
73. Napoli, "Evolutionary Theories."
74. Vos and Russell, "Theorizing Journalism's Institutional Relationships," 2334.
75. Vos and Russell, "Theorizing Journalism's Institutional Relationships," 2335.
76. Christopher W. Anderson, "What Aggregators Do: Towards a Networked Concept of Journalistic Expertise in the Digital Age"; Chris Paterson, "Convergence in the News Wholesalers: Trends in International News Agencies," in *Making Online News: Newsroom Ethnography in the Second Decade of Internet Journalism*, ed. David Domingo and Chris A. Paterson (Peter Lang, 2011), 129–40.
77. David Domingo and Chris A. Paterson, eds., *Making Online News: The Ethnography of New Media Production*, vol. 1 (Peter Lang, 2008).
78. Domingo and Paterson, eds., *Making Online News*, 72, 89.
79. Sue Robinson, "'Journalism as Process'"; Qun Wang, "Participatory Journalism in the Chinese Context: Understanding Journalism as

Process in China's Participatory Culture," *Journalism* 18, no. 4 (2017): 501–17.
80. Suzanne Vranica and Jack Marshall, "Plummeting Newspaper Ad Revenue Sparks New Wave of Changes," *Wall Street Journal*, October 20, 2016, https://www.wsj.com/articles/plummeting-newspaper-ad-revenue-sparks-new-wave-of-changes-1476955801.
81. Rashidian et al., "Friend and Foe."
82. Rashidian et al., "Friend and Foe."
83. Rashidian et al., "Friend and Foe."
84. Ylan Mui, "Congress Takes on Big Tech in Hearing on Anti-competitive Behavior Among Digital Giants," *CNBC*, June 10, 2019, https://www.cnbc.com/2019/06/10/congressional-hearingtakes-on-antitrust-behavior-among-digital-giants.html.
85. Scott W. Richard, "Lords of the Dance: Professionals as Institutional Agents," *Organization Studies* 29, no. 2 (2008): 219–38.
86. Qun Wang, "Dimensional Field Theory: The Adoption of Audience Metrics in theJournalistic Field and Cross-Field Influences," *Digital Journalism* 6, no. 4 (2018): 472–91.
87. Jean-Christophe Plantin, Carl Lagoze, Paul N. Edwards, and Christian Sandvig, "Infrastructure Studies Meet Platform Studies in the Age of Google and Facebook," *New Media & Society* 20, no. 1 (2018): 293–310.
88. Sara Salinas, "Amazon's Ad Business Will Steal Market Share from Google This Year, Says eMarketer," *CNBC*, February 20, 2019, https://www.cnbc.com/2019/02/20/amazon-advertisingbusiness-stealing-market-share-from-google.html.
89. Kari Paul, "Zuckerberg Defends Facebook as Bastion of 'Free Expression' in Speech," *Guardian*, October 17, 2019, https://www.theguardian.com/technology/2019/oct/17/mark-zuckerberg-facebook-free-expression-speech.
90. Tarleton Gillespie, "The politics of 'platforms,'" *New Media & Society* 12, no. 3 (2010): 348.
91. Tarleton Gillespie, "Governance of and by Platforms," in *SAGE Handbook of Social Media*, ed. Jean Burgess, Thomas Poell, and Alice E. Marwick (Sage, 2017), 254–78.
92. Sam Gill, "Should Platforms be Regulated? A New Survey Says Yes," *Medium*, August 15, 2018, https://medium.com/trust-media-and-democracy/should-platforms-be-regulated-a-newsurvey-says-yes-2f3f4d0d1f00.

1. WHY WAS GOOGLE INTERESTED IN NEWS?

93. Mark C. Suchman, "Managing Legitimacy: Strategic and Institutional Approaches," *Academy of Management Review* 20, no. 3 (1995): 571–610.
94. Vos and Russell, "Theorizing Journalism's Institutional Relationships," 2334.

1. WHY WAS GOOGLE INTERESTED IN NEWS IN THE FIRST PLACE? 9/11, A TURNING POINT

1. Danny Sullivan, "The Yahoo Directory—Once the Internet's Most Important Search Engine—Is to Close," *Searchengineland.com*, September 26, 2014, https://searchengineland.com/yahoo-directory-close-204370.
2. "The History of SEO," https://www.thehistoryofseo.com/The-Industry/Short_History_of_Early_Search_Engines.aspx.
3. Sullivan, "The Yahoo Directory."
4. Chris Sherman, "Humans Do It Better: Inside the Open Directory Project," *Online* 24, no. 4 (2000): 43–48.
5. Sherman, "Humans Do It Better," para. 2.
6. Dmoz, "Organize the Web," dmoz.org, https://dmoztools.net/.
7. "About the Google Directory," Google, https://web.archive.org/web/20000511160233/http://directory.google.com/dirhelp.html#whenuse.
8. Elizabeth Van Couvering, "Navigational Media: The Political Economy of Online Traffic," in *The Political Economics of Media: The Transformation of the Global Media Industries*, ed. Dal Yong Jin and Dwayne Winseck (Bloomsbury Academic, 2011), 183–200.
9. Lawrence Page, Sergey Brin, Rajeev Motwani, and Terry Winograd, "The PageRank Citation Ranking: Bringing Order to the Web," Stanford InfoLab, 1999, http://ilpubs.stanford.edu:8090/422/1/1999-66.pdf.
10. Sullivan, "The Yahoo Directory."
11. Google, "About the Google Directory."
12. Google, "About the Google Directory."
13. Van Couvering, "Navigational Media," 7.
14. "Why Use Google," Google, https://web.archive.org/web/20000511135541/http://www.google.com/why_use.html.
15. Richard W. Wiggins, "The Effects of September 11 on the Leading Search Engine," *First Monday* 7, no. 10 (2001).
16. "How Do I Submit a Link to Full Coverage," Yahoo! News Help, 2000, https://web.archive.org/web/20000815053533/http://help.yahoo.com/help/us/news/news-17.html.

1. WHY WAS GOOGLE INTERESTED IN NEWS?

17. Google, "About the Google Directory."
18. "September 11th Attacks," n.d., https://historyday911.weebly.com/largest-attack-on-us-soil.html.
19. Alec H. Bemis, "Remains of the Day," *LA Weekly*, September 12, 2001, https://www.laweekly.com/news/remains-of-the-day-2133806.
20. Catharine P. Taylor, "Web Hits Rise," *Adage.com*, September 17, 2001, https://adage.com/article/news/web-hits-rise/53814.
21. Bemis, "Remains of the Day," para. 4.
22. "Evolution of Search," Google, YouTube video, November 27, 2011, https://youtu.be/mTBShTwCnD4.
23. Paul N. Rappoport, "The Internet and the Demand for News," *Prometheus* 20, no. 3 (2002): 255–62.
24. Taylor, "Web Hits Rise."
25. "Google Search Statistics from 9/11/01," Google, 2001, https://archive.google.com/press/zeitgeist/9-11-search.html.
26. Nostradamus published a book in 1555 containing 942 quatrains that allegedly predict famous future events, including the 9/11 attacks.
27. Barbara Kay Olson was an American lawyer and television commentator. She was a passenger on American Airlines Flight 77 when it crashed into the Pentagon during the September 11 attacks. She had delayed a trip to California on September 10 so that she could be in town with her husband on his birthday on September 11.
28. Google, "Google Search."
29. Rappoport, "The Internet," 256.
30. Wiggins, "The Effects of September 11 on the Leading Search Engine."
31. Wiggins, "The Effects of September 11 on the Leading Search Engine."
32. Wiggins, "The Effects of September 11 on the Leading Search Engine."
33. "One Year Later: September 11 and the Internet," Pew Research Center, 2002, http://www.pewinternet.org/2002/09/05/one-year-later-september-11-and-the-internet/.
34. Alex Halavais, "The Rise of Do-It-Yourself Journalism After September 11," Pew Research Center, September 5, 2002, http://www.pewinternet.org/2002/09/05/one-year-later-september-11-and-the-internet/.
35. Leander Kahney, "Who Said the Web Fell Apart?," *Wired*, September 12, 2001, https://www.wired.com/2001/09/who-said-the-web-fell-apart/.
36. "World Trade Towers and Pentagon Attacked," Slashdot.org, 2001, https://slashdot.org/story/01/09/11/1314258/world-trade-towers-and-pentagon-attacked.

1. WHY WAS GOOGLE INTERESTED IN NEWS?

37. Halavais, "The Rise of Do-It-Yourself Journalism," 3–4, emphasis added.
38. Robin Miller, "From Niche Site to News Portal: How Slashdot Survived the Attack," *Online Journalism Review* 14 (2001).
39. Miller, "From Niche Site to News Portal."
40. Rappoport, "The Internet."
41. Halavais, "The Rise of Do-It-Yourself Journalism."
42. Walt Crawford, "Turn On the Radio," *EContent* 25, no. 2 (2002): 44–45.
43. David Mikkelson, "Palestinians Dancing in the Street," Snopes.com, September 23, 2001, https://www.snopes.com/fact-check/false-footaging/.
44. Halavais, "The Rise of Do-It-Yourself Journalism."
45. Staci D. Kramer, "Google News Creator Watches Portal Quiet Critics with 'Best News' Webby," Ojr.org, September 25, 2003, http://www.ojr.org/ojr/kramer/1064449044.php.
46. Matt Carlson, "Order Versus Access: News Search Engines and the Challenge to Traditional Journalistic Roles," *Media, Culture & Society* 29, no. 6 (2007): 1014–30.
47. Mark Glaser, "Google News to Publishers: Let's Make Love Not War," Mediashift.org, February 4, 2010, http://mediashift.org/2010/02/google-news-to-publishers-lets-make-love-not-war035/, emphasis mine.
48. Glaser, "Google News to Publishers."
49. Megan Garber, "Google News Founder Krishna Bharat: For News Consumers, 'the Whole Experience Is What Counts,'" *Nieman Lab*, April 8, 2011, http://www.niemanlab.org/2011/04/google-news-founder-krishna-bharat-for-news-consumers-the-whole-experience-is-what-counts/.
50. Garber, "Google News Founder Krishna Bharat."
51. Kramer, "Google News Creator Watches Portal Quiet Critics."
52. Maggie Shiels, "Building Google News for Everyone—a Retrospective," Google (blog), **September 18, 2018**, https://www.blog.google/products/news/building-google-news-everyone-retrospective/.
53. Keith H. Hammonds, "How Google Grows . . . and grows . . . and grows," *Fast Company*, March 31, 2003, https://www.fastcompany.com/46495/how-google-growsand-growsand-grows.
54. Wiggins, "The Effects of September 11 on the Leading Search Engine."
55. Matt Carlson, "Facebook in the News: Social Media, Journalism, and Public Responsibility Following the 2016 Trending Topics Controversy," *Digital Journalism* 6, no. 1 (2018): 4–20; Mike Isaac, "Facebook 'Trending' List Skewed by Individual Judgment, Not Institutional Bias," *New York*

1. WHY WAS GOOGLE INTERESTED IN NEWS?

Times, May 20, 2016, https://www.nytimes.com/2016/05/21/technology/facebook-trending-list-skewed-by-individual-judgment-not-institutional-bias.html.
56. Rappoport, "The Internet," 255.

2. THE GOOGLE NEWS HOMEPAGE OVER TWENTY YEARS: WHAT IS THE "GOOGLE WAY"?

1. "A Novel Approach to News," Google News (BETA), 2002, https://web.archive.org/web/20021013214112/http://news.google.com/help/about_news_search.html.
2. Google "crawl rate" refers to how often the Googlebot visits a website to index its content. As discussed in the last chapter, the low crawl frequency before 9/11 led to search results irrelevant to the attacks when users searched for 9/11-related information. Google's spider had last crawled a month ago before 9/11. Today, its crawl rate can scan websites several times per second.
3. Lynne Cooke, "A Visual Convergence of Print, Television, and the Internet: Charting 40 Years of Design Change in News Presentation," *New Media & Society* 7, no. 1 (2005): 40.
4. Frederick O'Brien, "What Newspapers Can Teach Us About Web Design," *Smashing Magazine*, November 8, 2019, https://www.smashingmagazine.com/2019/11/newspapers-teach-web-design/.
5. Google, "A Novel Approach to News."
6. Google, "A Novel Approach to News."
7. Google, "A Novel Approach to News."
8. Mario R. García, "*USA Today* Turns 30: Part 1," Garciamedia.com, September 9, 2012, https://www.garciamedia.com/blog/usa_today_turns_30-part_1-looking_into_the_attic_for_those_early_sketches/.
9. "Ambiguous named entities" refer to those that can be denoted by the same proper name; for example, George Washington could be the first president of the United States or the inventor. Razvan Bunescu and Marius Pasca, "Using Encyclopedic Knowledge for Named Entity Disambiguation," *Proceedings of the 11th Conference of the European Chapter of the Association for Computational Linguistics (EACL-06)* (2006): 9–16.
10. Bill Slawski, "Extracting Knowledge Base Facts for Entities from Sources Such as Wikipedia Titles and Infoboxes," Seobythesea.com,

2. THE GOOGLE NEWS HOMEPAGE OVER TWENTY YEARS

August 31, 2014, https://www.seobythesea.com/2014/08/extracting-facts-for-entities-from-sources/.
11. Philip M. Napoli, "Requiem for the Long Tail: Towards a Political Economy of Content Aggregation and Fragmentation," *International Journal of Media & Cultural Politics* 12, no. 3 (2016): 341–56.
12. José Van Dijck, "Seeing the Forest for the Trees: Visualizing Platformization and Its Governance," *New Media & Society* 23, no. 9 (2021): 2801–19.
13. Chris Beckmann, "Google News Changes Reflect Your Feedback," *Google* (blog), July 15, 2010, https://news.googleblog.com/2010/07/google-news-changes-reflect-your.html.
14. Yogita Mehta, "Google News Highlights Unique Content with Editors' Picks," *Google News* (blog), August 4, 2011, https://news.googleblog.com/2011/08/google-news-highlights-unique-content.html.
15. Peter Dolan and Jiahui Liu, *U.S. Patent No. 8,229,873 B1*, US Patent and Trademark Office, July 24, 2012.
16. Richard Gingras, "Labeling Fact-Check Articles in Google News," *Google* (blog), October 13, 2016, https://blog.google/outreach-initiatives/google-news-initiative/labeling-fact-check-articles-google-news/.
17. Pew Research Center, "For Local News, Americans Embrace Digital but Still Want Strong Community Connection," March 26, 2019, https://www.journalism.org/2019/03/26/for-local-news-americans-embrace-digital-but-still-want-strong-community-connection/.
18. David Chavern, "It's Time to Rein In the Tech Platforms' Anticompetitive Behavior," News Media Alliance, August 21, 2008, https://www.newsmediaalliance.org/ceo-time-to-rein-in-platforms/.
19. "Exploring a New, More Dynamic Way of Reading News with Living Stories," *Google* (blog), December 8, 2009, http://googleblog.blogspot.com:80/2009/12/exploring-new-more-dynamic-way-of.html.
20. Zachary M. Seward, "Google News Shines a Spotlight on 'In-Depth' Journalism," *Nieman Lab*, September 3, 2009, https://www.niemanlab.org/2009/09/google-news-shines-a-spotlight-on-in-depth-journalism/; Mac Slocum, "What Qualifies as a Spotlight Story on Google News? Here's a Few Clues," *Nieman Lab*, January 6, 2010, http://www.niemanlab.org/2010/01/what-qualifies-as-a-spotlight-story-on-google-news-heres-a-few-clues/.
21. Seward, "Google News Shines a Spotlight on 'In-Depth' Journalism."
22. Mehta, "Google News Highlights Unique Content with Editors' Picks."

2. THE GOOGLE NEWS HOMEPAGE OVER TWENTY YEARS

23. Megan Garber, "Google News Experiments with Human Control, Promotes a New Serendipity with Editors' Picks," *Nieman Lab*, June 10, 2010, http://www.niemanlab.org/2010/06/google-news-experiments-with-human-control-promotes-a-new-serendipity-with-editors-pick/.
24. Amar Toor, "Google News Launches Fact Check Feature Ahead of Election Day," *The Verge*, October 14, 2016, http://www.theverge.com/2016/10/14/13283200/google-news-fact-check-election.
25. ClaimReview, introduced by schema.org, is a "fact-checking review of claims made (or reported) in some creative work (referenced via itemReviewed)" that can enable a "summarized version" of fact-checked content (e.g., "Claim: The world is flat. Claimed by: Flat World Society") to be displayed on Google. Schema.org is "a collaborative, community activity with a mission to create, maintain, and promote schemas for structured data on the Internet, on web pages, in email messages, and beyond." Google is one of its founders.
26. Gingras, "Labeling Fact-Check Articles in Google News."
27. Anand Paka, "Redesigning Google News for Everyone," *Google* (blog), June 27, 2017, https://www.blog.google/outreach-initiatives/google-news-initiative/redesigning-google-news-everyone/.
28. Justin Kosslyn and Cong Yu, "Fact Check Now Available in Google Search and News Around the World," *Google* (blog), April 7, 2017, https://www.blog.google/products/search/fact-check-now-available-google-search-and-news-around-world/.
29. Lucian Parfeni, "Google News Gets a Most Shared Section," Softpedia.com, December 1, 2010, https://news.softpedia.com/news/Google-News-Gets-a-Most-Shared-Section-169797.shtml.
30. Chris Welch, "Google Begins Shutting Down Its Failed Google+ Social Network," *The Verge*, April 2, 2019, https://www.theverge.com/2019/4/2/18290637/google-plus-shutdown-consumer-personal-account-delete.
31. Ben Smith, "Project Strobe: Protecting Your Data, Improving Our Third-Party APIs, and Sunsetting Consumer Google+," *Google* (blog), October 8, 2018, https://www.blog.google/technology/safety-security/project-strobe/.
32. Paka, "Redesigning Google News."
33. "What Does Each Label Mean?," https://support.google.com/news/publisher-center/answer/9606542?sjid=13946638176335596969-NA.

2. THE GOOGLE NEWS HOMEPAGE OVER TWENTY YEARS

34. Paka, "Redesigning Google News."
35. Yngve Benestad Hågvar, "Labelling Journalism: The Discourse of Sectional Paratexts in Print and Online Newspapers," *Nordicom Review* 33, no. 2 (2012): 27–42.
36. Paka, "Redesigning Google News."
37. Tystan Upstill, "The New Google News: AI Meets Human Intelligence," *Google* (blog), May 8, 2018, https://www.blog.google/products/news/new-google-news-ai-meets-human-intelligence/.
38. Altan Coner, "Personalization and Customization in Financial Portals," *Journal of American Academy of Business* 2, no. 2 (2003): 498–504; S. Shyam Sundar and Sampada S. Marathe, "Personalization Versus Customization: The Importance of Agency, Privacy, and Power Usage," *Human Communication Research* 36, no. 3 (2010): 298–322.
39. Philipp Lenssen, "Google News Adds Most Popular, Recommended," Blogoscoped.com, January 21, 2006, http://blogoscoped.com/archive/2006-01-21-n38.html. Emphasis added.
40. Kevin Stolt, "Extra! Extra! Google News Redesigned to Be More Customizable and Shareable," *Google* (blog), June 30, 2010, https://googleblog.blogspot.com/2010/06/extra-extra-google-news-redesigned-to.html.
41. Mario Haim, Andreas Graefe, and Hans-Bernd Brosius, "Burst of the Filter Bubble? Effects of Personalization on the Diversity of Google News," *Digital Journalism* 6, no. 3 (2018): 330–43; Jennifer Duke, "Facebook, Google to Be Probed Over Role in Creating 'Filter Bubbles,'" Smh.com.au, February 26, 2018, https://www.smh.com.au/business/companies/facebook-google-to-be-probed-over-role-in-creating-filter-bubbles-20180226-p4z1pj.html.
42. Anna Schjøtt Hansen and Jannie Møller Hartley, "Designing What's News: An Ethnography of a Personalization Algorithm and the Data-Driven (Re)assembling of the News," *Digital Journalism* 11, no. 6 (2023): 924–42.
43. Upstill, "The New Google News."
44. Greg Sterling, "Google Gives Publishers New Content 'Showcase' on News, Search, Discover," *Search Engine Land*, October 1, 2020, https://searchengineland.com/google-gives-publishers-new-content-showcase-on-news-search-discover-341393.
45. "Google Privacy & Terms," https://policies.google.com/?hl=en-US.
46. Lenssen, "Google News Adds Most Popular, Recommended."

2. THE GOOGLE NEWS HOMEPAGE OVER TWENTY YEARS

47. James Vincent, "Google News Gets More Personal with Desktop Redesign," *The Verge*, June 22, 2022, https://www.theverge.com/2022/6/22/23178163/google-news-desktop-redesign-personal-local-content.
48. Alexandra Bruell, "Google to Launch Long-Delayed News Showcase Product in U.S. This Summer," *Wall Street Journal*, June 8, 2023, https://www.wsj.com/articles/google-to-launch-long-delayed-news-showcase-product-in-u-s-this-summer-4aec324d.
49. Trân Nguyễn, "California Bill Requiring Big Tech to Pay for News Gains Momentum," Associated Press, June 1, 2023, https://apnews.com/article/google-meta-big-tech-journalism-fee-california-lawmakers-ec3a926252f59e589e5d48b067c7904e.
50. Liam Reilly, "Google Agrees to First-in-the-Nation Deal to Fund California Newsrooms, but Journalists Are Calling It a Disaster," CNN, August 22, 2024, https://www.cnn.com/2024/08/21/media/google-california-pay-newsrooms-journalists-content-deal/index.html.
51. Sterling, "Google Gives Publishers New Content 'Showcase.'"
52. Sara Fischer, "Google to Launch News Showcase Product in U.S.," *Axios*, June 8, 2023, https://www.axios.com/2023/06/08/google-news-showcase-us.
53. Brad Bender and Olivia Ma, "Read All About It: A New Look for Google News," *Google* (blog), June 22, 2022, https://blog.google/products/news/google-news-anniversary-local-reporting-funding/.
54. Daniel Trielli and Nicholas Diakopoulos, "Search as News Curator: The Role of Google in Shaping Attention to News Information," *Proceedings of the 2019 CHI Conference on Human Factors in Computing Systems* (2019): 1–15; Efrat Nechushtai and Seth C. Lewis, "What Kind of News Gatekeepers Do We Want Machines to Be? Filter Bubbles, Fragmentation, and the Normative Dimensions of Algorithmic Recommendations," *Computers in Human Behavior* 90 (2019): 298–307.
55. Andrew Goffey, "Algorithm," in *Software Studies: A Lexicon*, ed. Matthew Fuller (MIT Press, 2008), 15–20. 19.

3. DISPUTES SURROUNDING GOOGLE NEWS: A GLOBAL MEDIA-TECH LANDSCAPE

1. Daniel Van Boom and Queenie Wong, "Australia Passes Law Forcing Google and Facebook to Pay News Publications," *CNET*, February 24,

3. DISPUTES SURROUNDING GOOGLE NEWS

    2021, https://www.cnet.com/tech/mobile/australia-passes-law-forcing-google-and-facebook-to-pay-news-publications/.
2. Alex Hern, "News Corp Agrees Deal with Google Over Payments for Journalism," *Guardian*, February 17, 2021, https://www.theguardian.com/media/2021/feb/17/news-corp-agrees-deal-with-google-over-payments-for-journalism.
3. Ismail Shakil, "Canada Introduces Legislation to Compel Facebook, Google to Pay for News," Reuters, April 5, 2022, https://www.reuters.com/world/americas/canada-lays-out-details-proposed-law-compel-facebook-google-pay-news-2022-04-05/.
4. Eric Auchard, "AFP, Google News Settle Lawsuit Over Google News," Reuters, April 7, 2007, https://www.reuters.com/article/us-google-afp/afp-google-news-settle-lawsuit-over-google-news-idUSN0728115420070407.
5. Eric Pfanner, "French Publishers Forge Deal with Google, Breaking Ranks with Europe," *New York Times*, February 17, 2013, https://www.nytimes.com/2013/02/18/technology/a-first-step-on-continent-for-google-on-use-of-content.html. Chris Welch, "Google Ends Standoff with French Publishers, Commits to €60 Million 'Innovation' Fund," *The Verge*, February 1, 2013, https://www.theverge.com/2013/2/1/3941854/google-ends-standoff-french-news-sites-digital-publishing-innovation-fund.
6. "Berne Convention for the Protection of Literary and Artistic Works," WIPO, 1979, https://www.wipo.int/wipolex/en/treaties/textdetails/12214.
7. Michael Schudson, *Discovering the News: A Social History of American Newspapers* (Basic Books, 1981).
8. Rodney Benson, *Shaping Immigration News: A French-American Comparison* (Cambridge University Press, 2013).
9. Susan Keith, "Searching for News Headlines: Connections Between Unresolved Hyperlinking Issues and a New Battle Over Copyright Online," in *Die wachsende Macht von Suchmaschinen im Internet/The Power of Search Engines*, ed. Marcel Machill and Markus Beiler (Herbert von Halem, 2007), 202–19.
10. *Agence France-Presse v. Google, Inc.* 1:05CV00546-GK, Google's Reply to AFP's Opposition to Partial Summary Judgment Dismissing Count II (Headlines) for Lack of Protectable Subject Matter (2005).
11. *Agence France-Presse v. Google, Inc.*
12. *Agence France-Presse v. Google, Inc.* 1:05CV00546-GK, In the US District Court for the District of Columbia (2007).

3. DISPUTES SURROUNDING GOOGLE NEWS

13. *Agence France-Presse v. Google, Inc.* 1:05CV00546-GK, Report (2006).
14. *Agence France-Presse v. Google, Inc.* 2005.
15. *Agence France-Presse v. Google, Inc.* 2006.
16. Danny Sullivan, "AFP & Google Settle Over Google News Copyright Case," Searchengineland.com, April 6, 2007, https://searchengineland.com/afp-google-settle-over-google-news-copyright-case-10926.
17. Sullivan, "AFP & Google Settle Over Google News Copyright Case."
18. Juan Carlos Perez, "AFP-Google Settlement Leaves Open Questions," Infoworld.com, April 6, 2007, https://www.infoworld.com/article/2662703/techology-business/afp-google-settlement-leaves-open-questions.html.
19. *Google Inc. v. Copiepresse,* 2011, https://www.copiepresse.be/pdf/Copiepresse%20-%20ruling%20appeal%20Google_5May2011.pdf.
20. Graham Smith, "Copiepresse v Google—the Belgian Judgment Dissected,"Twobirds.com, March 13, 2007, http://www.twobirds.com/en/news/articles/2007/copiepresse-v-google.
21. Rachel Whetstone, "About the Google News Case in Belgium," *Google* (blog), September 2006, https://googleblog.blogspot.com/2006/09/about-google-news-case-in-belgium.html.
22. Helle Sjøvaag, "Media Diversity and the Global Superplayers: Operationalising Pluralism for a Digital Media Market," *Journal of Media Business Studies* 13, no. 3 (2016): 170–86.
23. *Google Inc. v. Copiepresse,* 15.
24. Directive 2001/29/EC of the European Parliament and of the Council of 22 May 2001 on the harmonisation of certain aspects of copyright and related rights in the information society, The European Parliament and the Council of the European Union, Article 33.
25. Directive 2001/29/EC.
26. The court of appeal of Brussels, no.: 2007/AR/1730, 2011, 41.
27. Rachel Whetstone, "About the Google News Case in Belgium," *Google* (blog), September 2006, https://googleblog.blogspot.com/2006/09/about-google-news-case-in-belgium.html.
28. The court of appeal of Brussels, 36.
29. Groklaw, "An Update on the Copiepresse/Google Dispute—ACAP Enters the Picture," Groklaw.net, October 16, 2008, http://www.groklaw.net/articlebasic.php?story=20081016024354825.
30. Mikael Ricknäs, "Belgian Newspapers Ask Google for $77.5 Million in Damages," *PC World,* May 28, 2008, https://www.pcworld.com/article/146380/article.html.

3. DISPUTES SURROUNDING GOOGLE NEWS

31. Court of first instance of Brussels, 2006/9099/4, Ref. no. 39513, August 3, 2006.
32. Copiepresse, "Introduction," copiepresse.be, 2011.
33. The court of appeal of Brussels, 42.
34. Jon Fortt, "What's Google News Worth? $100 Million," *Fortune*, July 23, 2008, http://fortune.com/2008/07/22/whats-google-news-worth-100-million/.
35. Thierry Geerts, "Partnering with Belgian News Publishers," *Google* (blog), December 12, 2012, https://europe.googleblog.com/2012/12/partnering-with-belgian-news-publishers.html.
36. Sam Byford, "Google Finally Settles with Belgian Publishers Over Content Scraping Lawsuit," *The Verge*, December 13, 2012, https://www.theverge.com/2012/12/13/3764692/google-copyright-lawsuit-settlement-belgium.
37. The court of appeal of Brussels, 45.
38. "Antitrust Watchdog Probes Google Italy," Associated Press, August 27, 2009, https://phys.org/news/2009-08-antitrust-watchdog-probes-google-italy.html#nRlv.
39. Peter Sayer, "Google Faces Broad Antitrust Investigation in Italy," *PC World*, September 2009, https://www.pcworld.com/article/171460/article.html; AGCM, "AGCM Annual Report," 2011, http://www.agcm.it/en/component/joomdoc/annual-reports/AnnualReport2010_Catrical.pdf/download.html.
40. Eric Pfanner, "A Google Worry Recedes, for Now, as Italy Ends Investigation Into News Service," *New York Times*, January 17, 2011, https://www.nytimes.com/2011/01/18/technology/18iht-google18.html .
41. "FIEG-Google Deal to Boost Media Sector (2)," Ansa.it, June 7, 2016, http://www.ansa.it/english/news/science_tecnology/2016/06/07/fieg-google-deal-to-boost-media-sector-2_fd3880f1-19b9-4a88-a49a-42b29e602eco.html.
42. Sabrina Cohen, Giada Zampano, and Peppi Kiviniemi, "Italy Opens Antitrust Probe of Local Google News Service," *Wall Street Journal*, August 28, 2009, https://www.wsj.com/articles/SB125137301333663261.
43. MEMO/08/761, "Antitrust: Guidance on Commission enforcement priorities in applying Article 82 to exclusionary conduct by dominant firms—frequently asked questions," European Commission, 2008, https://ec.europa.eu/commission/presscorner/detail/en/MEMO_08_761 .

3. DISPUTES SURROUNDING GOOGLE NEWS

44. "How AdSense Works," Google.com, https://support.google.com/adsense/answer/6242051?hl=en.
45. "AGCM Annual Report," Agcm.it, 2011, http://www.agcm.it/en/componente/joomdoc/annual-reports/AnnualReport2010_Catrical.pdf/download.html.
46. ANSA, "FIEG-Google Deal to Boost Media Sector (2)."
47. "Google to Pay $334 Million to Settle Italian Tax Dispute," Reuters, May 4, 2017, https://www.reuters.com/article/us-google-italy-tax-idUSKBN1801CP.
48. AFP, "Google Removes News Snippets in Germany Legal Fight," Phys.org, October 1, 2014, https://phys.org/news/2014-10-google-news-snippets-germany-legal.html.
49. D. B. Hebbard, "German Publishers 'Bow to Pressure,' Will Allow Google to Display Search Result Snippets," Talingnewmedia.com, October 23, 2014.
50. "German Publishers Have Filed Complaint Against Google: VG Media," Reuters, January 5, 2016, https://www.reuters.com/article/us-google-media-germany/german-publishers-have-filed-complaint-against-google-vg-media-idUSKBN0UJ1KF20160105.
51. Foo Y. Chee and Klaus Lauer, "Google Wins legal Battle with German Publishers Over Fee Demands," Reuters, September 12, 2019, https://www.reuters.com/article/us-google-germany-publishers-idUSKCN1VX0R2.
52. Lauer Chee, "Google Wins Legal Battle."
53. Greg Sterling, "Germany Wants to Force Google to Pay License Fees for Links," Searchengineland.com, August 22, 2012, https://searchengineland.com/germany-wants-to-force-google-to-pay-license-fees-for-links-131288.
54. Federal Law Gazette, "Law on Copyright and Related Rights," 2013, https://www.gesetze-im-internet.de/englisch_urhg/englisch_urhg.html.
55. "Europe's Publishers Welcome New German Law to Force Content Aggregators and Search Engines to Recognise Copyright," European Publishers Council, March 1, 2013, http://www.editorandpublisher.com/news/europe-s-publishers-welcome-new-german-law-to-force-content-aggregators-and-search-engines-to-recognise-copyright/.
56. Kay Oberbeck, "A Law to the Detriment of All," August 21, 2012, https://plus.google.com/+KayOberbeck.

3. DISPUTES SURROUNDING GOOGLE NEWS

57. Gerrit Rabenstein, "Google News Remains an Open Platform for All German Publishers," *Google Germany* (blog), June 21, 2013, https://germany.googleblog.com/2013/06/google-news-bleibt-offene-plattform-fuer-verlage.html.
58. Axel Springer, "Axel Springer Concludes Its Data Documentation: Major Losses Resulting from Downgraded Search Notices on Google," Axelspringer.com, November 5, 2014, https://www.axelspringer.com/en/presse/Axel-Springer-concludes-its-data-documentation-Major-losses-resulting-from-downgraded-search-notices-on-Google_22070687.html.
59. Hebbard, "German Publishers 'Bow to Pressure.'"
60. A. Becker, "German publishers vs. Google," *DW*, October 30, 2014, https://www.dw.com/en/german-publishers-vs-google/a-18030444.
61. Axel Springer, "Axel Springer Concludes Its Data Documentation."
62. Christopher Gagne, "Canon AEDE: Publishers' Protections from Digital Reproductions of Works by Search Engines Under European Copyright Law," *Temp. Int'l & Comp. LJ* 29 (2015): 203.
63. Mike Masnick, "Study of Spain's 'Google Tax' on News Shows How Much Damage It Has Done," *Techdirt*, July 29, 2015, https://www.techdirt.com/2015/07/29/study-spains-google-tax-news-shows-how-much-damage-it-has-done/.
64. BOE-A-2014-11404, "Ley 21/2014, de 4 de noviembre, por la que se modifica el texto refundido de la Ley de Propiedad Intelectual, aprobado por Real Decreto Legislativo 1/1996, de 12 de abril, y la Ley 1/2000, de 7 de enero, de Enjuiciamiento Civil," 2014, https://www.boe.es/buscar/doc.php?id=BOE-A-2014-11404.
65. Richard Gingras, "Helping Local News Thrive," *Google* (blog), February 24, 2014, https://news.googleblog.com/2014/02/helping-local-news-thrive.html.
66. Greg Sterling, "Google News Still Available in Spain Despite Closure Deadline," Searchengineland.com, December 16, 2014, https://searchengineland.com/google-news-still-available-spain-despite-closure-deadline-210990.
67. Sterling, "Google News Still Available in Spain Despite Closure Deadline."
68. Vanessa Fox, "Taking Advantage of Universal Search," *Google* (blog), May 17, 2007, https://webmasters.googleblog.com/2007/05/taking-advantage-of-universal-search.html.

3. DISPUTES SURROUNDING GOOGLE NEWS

69. Marcus Wohlsen, "Spain's Google News Shutdown Is a Silly Victory for Publishers," *Wired*, December 16, 2014, https://www.wired.com/2014/12/google-news-shutdown-spain-empty-victory-publishers/.
70. Mathew Ingram, "External Traffic to Spanish News Sites Plummets After Google Move," Gigaom.com, December 16, 2014, https://gigaom.com/2014/12/16/traffic-to-spanish-news-publishers-plummets-after-google-move/.
71. Míchel Olmedo and José Luis Caballero, "A Battle Without Winners, as Spain Examines Early Results of Its 'Google Tax,'" Ecija.com, 2015, https://ecija.com/sala-de-prensa/a-battle-without-winners-as-spain-examines-early-results-of-its-google-tax-2/.
72. AEEPP, "Economic Report on the Impact of the New Article 32.2 of the LPI," Aeepp.com, July 9, 2015, https://www.aeepp.com/noticia/2272/actividades/informe-economico-del-impacto-del-nuevo-articulo-32.2-de-la-lpi-nera-para-la-aeepp.html .
73. Gagne, "Canon AEDE," 233.
74. Rafat Ali, "Google News Starts Publishing Full Stories; AP, AFP, PA and Canadian Press; Still No Ads," Gigaom.com, August 31, 2007, https://gigaom.com/2007/08/31/419-google-starts-publishing-full-stories-on-its-news-section-ap-afp-pa-and/.
75. Caroline McCarthy, "Google Reveals Payment Deal with AP," *CNET*, August 4, 2006, https://www.cnet.com/uk/news/google-reveals-payment-deal-with-ap/.
76. Josh Cohen, "Original Stories, from the Source," *Google* (blog), August 31, 2007, https://news.googleblog.com/2007/08/original-stories-from-source.html.
77. Joseph Tartakoff, "Google News Stops Hosting New AP Content," Gigaom.com, January 8, 2010, https://gigaom.com/2010/01/08/419-google-stops-hosting-new-ap-content/.
78. Josh Cohen, "Extending the Associated Press as Hosted News Partner," *Google* (blog), August 30, 2010, https://news.googleblog.com/2010/08/extending-associated-press-as-hosted.html.
79. Tom Krazit, "Google, AP Reach Deal for Google News Content," *CNET*, August 30, 2010, https://www.cnet.com/news/google-ap-reach-deal-for-google-news-content/.
80. "AP by the Numbers," https://www.ap.org/about/annual-report/2018/ap-by-the-numbers.
81. Staci Kramer, "AP's Curley, Google's Mayer Talk Aggregation—Carefully; AP-Google Deal?," Gigaom.com, April 25, 2006. https://gigaom.com

3. DISPUTES SURROUNDING GOOGLE NEWS

/2006/04/25/nab-aps-curley-googles-mayer-talk-aggregation-carefully-ap-google-deal/.
82. Thomas Claburn, "Google News Becomes a Publisher," *Information Week*, August 31, 2007, https://www.informationweek.com/google-news-becomes-a-publisher/d/d-id/1058737.
83. Zachary Seward, "What the Associated Press Is Saying to Google, Microsoft, and Yahoo," *Nieman Lab*, October 9, 2009, http://www.niemanlab.org/2009/10/what-the-associated-press-is-saying-to-google-microsoft-and-yahoo/.
84. Seward, "What the Associated Press Is Saying."
85. Danny Sullivan, "Where's AP in Google News? Apparently in Limbo, as Contract Running Out," Searchengineland.com, January 8, 2010, https://searchengineland.com/wheres-ap-in-google-news-33164.
86. Tom Krazit, "AP, Yahoo Strike Content Deal; AP, Google Still Talking," *CNET*, February 2010, https://www.cnet.com/news/ap-yahoo-strike-content-deal-ap-google-still-talking/.
87. Zachary Seward, "What the Associated Press Is Saying to Google, Microsoft, and Yahoo," *Nieman Lab*, October 9, 2009, http://www.niemanlab.org/2009/10/what-the-associated-press-is-saying-to-google-microsoft-and-yahoo/.
88. Juan Carlos Perez, "AP Renews Licensing Deal with Yahoo, Not Yet with Google," *Computer World*, February 1, 2010, https://www.pcworld.com/article/516644/article-4786.html.
89. Kramer, "AP's Curley, Google's Mayer Talk Aggregation—Carefully."
90. The following section draws on discussions in Qun Wang and Susan Keith, "News Aggregators and Copyright in the European Union and the United States in the Digital Age: Evolution, Comparisons, and Implications," *First Monday* 26, no. 9 (2021).
91. "Summary of the WIPO Copyright Treaty (WCT)," World Intellectual Property Organization, 1996, https://www.wipo.int/treaties/en/ip/wct/summary_wct.html.
92. Stephen E. Blythe, "The US Digital Millennium Copyright Act and the EU Copyright Directive: Comparative Impact on Fair Use Rights." *Tul. J. Tech. & Intell. Prop.* 8 (2006): 111.
93. European Parliament, "Copyright in the Digital Single Market," March 26, 2019, http://www.europarl.europa.eu/doceo/document/TA-8-2019-0231_EN.pdf.

3. DISPUTES SURROUNDING GOOGLE NEWS

94. "France Fines Google $592M in a Dispute Over Paying News Publishers for Content," NPR, July 13, 2021, https://www.npr.org/2021/07/13/1015596060/france-fines-google-592m-in-a-dispute-over-paying-news-publishers-for-content.
95. Sam Schechner, "Google Pledges to Negotiate Fair Licenses with French News Publishers," *Wall Street Journal*, June 21, 2022, https://www.wsj.com/articles/google-pledges-to-negotiate-fair-licenses-with-french-news-publishers-11655807346.
96. "Berne Convention for the Protection of Literary and Artistic Works (as amended on September 28, 1979)," World Intellectual Property Organization, 1979, https://wipolex.wipo.int/en/treaties/textdetails/12214.
97. "Berne Convention."
98. Original texts in "The Berne Convention for the Protection of Literary and Artistic Works from 1886 to 1986," World Intellectual Property Organization, 1986, https://www.wipo.int/edocs/pubdocs/en/copyright/877/wipo_pub_877.pdf.
99. Directive 2001/29/EC of the European Parliament and of the Council of 22 May 2001 on the harmonisation of certain aspects of copyright and related rights in the information society, The European Parliament and the Council of the European Union.
100. Raquel Xalabarder, "Google News and Copyright," in *Google and the Law*, ed. Aurelio Lopez-Tarruella (TMC Asser, 2012), 113–67.
101. Hannibal Travis, "Opting Out of the Internet in the United States and the European Union: Copyright, Safe Harbors, and International Law," *Notre Dame Law Review* 84 (2008): 331.
102. Neil Netanel, *Copyright: What Everyone Needs to Know* (Oxford University Press, 2018).
103. Xalabarder, "Google News and Copyright."
104. P. Bernt Hugenholtz, "Copyright and Freedom of Expression in Europe," in *Expanding the Boundaries of Intellectual Property: Innovation Policy for the Knowledge Society*, ed. Rochelle Cooper Dreyfuss, Diane Leenheer Zimmerman, and Harry First (Oxford University Press, 2001), 363.
105. Alfred Ng, "Google, Facebook and Amazon Spending More Than Ever Lobbying Congress," *CNET*, January 23, 2019, https://www.cnet.com/news/google-facebook-amazon-spending-more-than-ever-lobbying-congress/.

3. DISPUTES SURROUNDING GOOGLE NEWS

106. Erick Schonfeld, "The Times UK Lost 4 Million Readers to Its Paywall Experiment," Techcrunch.com, November 2, 2010, https://techcrunch.com/2010/11/02/times-paywall-4-million-readers/.
107. David Sarno, "Murdoch Accuses Google of News 'Theft,'" *Los Angeles Times*, December 2, 2009, https://www.latimes.com/archives/la-xpm-2009-dec-02-la-fi-news-google2-2009dec02-story.html.
108. Kara Swisher, "What's Really Behind the Rope-a-Dope with Google and Microsoft? Here Are Five Possibilities!," November 24, 2009, http://kara.allthingsd.com/20091124/whats-really-behind-the-rupe-a-dope-with-google-and-microsoft-here-are-five-possibilities/.
109. Sabrina Geremia, "Our Concerns with Bill C-18, the Online News Act," *Google* (blog), May 16, 2022, https://blog.google/intl/en-ca/our-concerns-with-bill-c-18-the-online-news-act/.
110. Interview with David Speers, Sky News Australia, 2009, https://www.youtube.com/watch?v=M7GkJqRv3BI.
111. Kara Swisher, "What's Really Behind the Rope-a-Dope."
112. Carl Franzen, "What Lies Behind Murdoch's Move to Block Google?," *The Atlantic*, November 9, 2009, https://www.theatlantic.com/entertainment/archive/2009/11/what-lies-behind-murdoch-s-move-to-block-google/347627/.
113. Kara Swisher, "Project Alesia: News Corp.'s Roman Battle Cry—Does That Cast Googlers as the Gauls?," December 23, 2009, https://allthingsd.com/20091223/project-alesia-news-corp-s-roman-battle-cry-does-that-cast-googlers-as-the-gauls/.
114. David Goldman, "Worst Year for Jobs Since '45," CNN, January 9, 2009, https://money.cnn.com/2009/01/09/news/economy/jobs_december/.
115. Emma Barnett, "Rupert Murdoch Has Warned That His Paywall Plans Could Be Delayed," *Telegraph*, November 13, 2009, https://www.telegraph.co.uk/finance/newsbysector/mediatechnologyandtelecoms/digital-media/6559694/Rupert-Murdoch-to-remove-News-Corps-content-from-Google-in-months.html.
116. Jason Schwartz, "Murdoch Embraces Liberal Approach to Curb Facebook, Google," *Politico*, May 18, 2018, https://www.politico.com/story/2018/05/18/rupert-murdoch-facebook-google-news-social-media-algorithm-596738.
117. Robert Elder, "Publishers in the UK Are Uniting Against Google and Facebook," *Business Insider*, August 9, 2016, http://www.businessinsider.com/uk-publishers-unite-to-take-on-google-and-facebook-2016-8.

3. DISPUTES SURROUNDING GOOGLE NEWS

118. Alex Hern, "News Corp Agrees Deal with Google Over Payments for Journalism," *Guardian*, February 17, 2021, https://www.theguardian.com/media/2021/feb/17/news-corp-agrees-deal-with-google-over-payments-for-journalism.
119. Natalia Mazotte, "Newspapers in Brazil Say Their Boycott Turned Google News 'Deficient,' Reiterate Request for Payment," *LatAm Journalism Review*, October 22, 2012, https://latamjournalismreview.org/articles/newspapers-in-brazil-say-their-boycott-turned-google-news-deficient-reiterate-request-for-payment/.
120. "Relatórios de atividades e de liberdade de imprensa," Associacão Nacionāl de Jornais, 2011, https://web.archive.org/web/20111125131215/http://www.anj.org.br/programas-e-acoes/relatorios/relatorios-de-atividades/RELATORIO%20DE%20ATIVIDADES%202010-2011.pdf.
121. Jan D. Walter, "Brazil's Papers Without Google News," *DW*, October 24, 2012, https://www.dw.com/en/brazils-papers-without-google-news/a-16326960.
122. Brad Bender, "A New Licensing Program to Support the News Industry," *Google* (blog), June 25, 2020, https://www.blog.google/outreach-initiatives/google-news-initiative/licensing-program-support-news-industry-/?_ga=2.236282177.1122694280.1593072794-752983740.1593072794.
123. Natalia Viana, "Should Google Pay for News in Brazil? It's Complicated," *Nieman Lab*, June 2, 2022, https://www.niemanlab.org/2022/06/should-google-pay-for-news-in-brazil-its-complicated/.
124. Júlio Lubianco, "Big Tech Companies Unite Against Payment for News Content in Brazil; Journalists Are Divided," *LatAm Journalism Review*, March 30, 2022, https://latamjournalismreview.org/articles/big-techs-payment-news-brazil/.
125. Fabio Coelho, "O PL 2630 pode impactar a internet que você conhece," Google, March 11, 2022, https://services.google.com/fh/files/blogs/gcarta2630.pdf.
126. Viana, "Should Google Pay for News in Brazil?"
127. Abraji, "Abraji assina manifesto pela supressão de artigo do PL das Fake News," May 11, 2021, https://abraji.org.br/noticias/abraji-assina-manifesto-pela-supressao-de-artigo-do-pl-das-fake-news.
128. Lubianco, "Big Tech Companies Unite Against Payment for News Content in Brazil."
129. Isabela Fraga, "Brazilian Newspapers Leave Google News En Masse," Knight Center for Journalism, October 18, 2012, https://web.archive.org

4. DATAFICATION OF NEWS AND MEDIA DIVERSITY

/web/20121023213333/https://knightcenter.utexas.edu/blog/00-11803-brazilian-newspapers-leave-google-news-en-masse.
130. "South Africa to Probe Meta, Google Competition with News Publishers," Reuters, October 17, 2023, https://www.reuters.com/world/africa/south-africa-probe-meta-google-competition-with-news-publishers-2023-10-17/.
131. Putra Muskita, "Indonesia to Require Google, Meta to Compensate News Publishers," *Tech in Asia*, February 20, 2024, https://www.techinasia.com/indonesia-require-google-meta-compensate-news-publishers.

4. DATAFICATION OF NEWS AND MEDIA DIVERSITY: GOOGLE'S TECHNOLOGICAL SPECIALIZATION AND ITS INFLUENCE

1. "Inventions Patentable," USPTO, https://www.uspto.gov/web/offices/pac/mpep/s2104.html.
2. Google, "Patent Programs," https://www.google.com/patents/licensing/.
3. John Koetsier, "Samsung Beats IBM, Apple, Intel, Google for 2022 Patent Crown; 56% of U.S. Patents Go to Foreign Firms," *Forbes*, January 14, 2023, https://www.forbes.com/sites/johnkoetsier/2023/01/14/samsung-beats-ibm-apple-intel-google-for-2022-patent-crown-56-of-us-patents-go-to-foreign-firms/.
4. Mary Ellen Mogee, "Using Patent Data for Technology Analysis and Planning," *Research-Technology Management* 34, no. 4 (1991): 43–49. Gabjo Kim and Jinwoo Bae, "A Novel Approach to Forecast Promising Technology Through Patent Analysis," *Technological Forecasting and Social Change* 117 (2017): 228–37. R. Kruppert, "Dispute the Patent, Short the Stock: Empirical Analysis of a New Hedge Fund Strategy," *International Review of Law and Economics* 50 (2017): 25–35. Michael A. DeVito, "From Editors to Algorithms: A Values-Based Approach to Understanding Story Selection in the Facebook News Feed," *Digital Journalism* 5, no. 6 (2017): 753–73; Frederic Filloux, "Google News: The Secret Sauce," *Guardian*, February 25, 2013, https://www.theguardian.com/technology/2013/feb/25/1.
5. For methodological details, see Qun Wang, "Normalization and Differentiation in Google News: A Multi-Method Analysis of the World's Largest News Aggregator," PhD diss., Rutgers University, publication no. 27672379, ProQuest Dissertations Publishing.

4. DATAFICATION OF NEWS AND MEDIA DIVERSITY

6. Krishna Bharat, "Google News Turns 10," *Google* (blog), September 12, 2012, https://news.googleblog.com/2012/09/google-news-turns-10.html.
7. Nick Bastone, "Eric Schmidt Takes the Blame for Google's Social Networking Failures: 'I Suspect We Didn't Fully Understand How to Do It,'" *Business Insider*, November 7, 2018, https://www.businessinsider.com/eric-schmidt-takes-responsibility-for-google-social-networking-problems-2018-11.
8. Michael M. Grynbaum and Ryan Mac, "The Times Sues OpenAI and Microsoft Over A. I. Use of Copyrighted Work," *New York Times*, December 27, 2023, https://www.nytimes.com/2023/12/27/business/media/new-york-times-open-ai-microsoft-lawsuit.html.
9. Tarleton Gillespie, "Algorithm," in *Digital Keywords: A Vocabulary of Information Society and Culture*, ed. Benjamin Peters (Princeton University Press, 2016), 18–30.
10. Michael Latzer, Katharina Hollnbuchner, Natascha Just, and Florian Saurwein, "The Economics of Algorithmic Selection on the Internet," in *Handbook on the Economics of the Internet* (Edward Elgar, 2016), 395–425.
11. Gillespie, "Algorithm," 24.
12. Nicholas Diakopoulos, "Algorithmic Accountability Reporting: On the Investigation of Black Boxes," Tow Center for Digital Journalism, 2014, http://towcenter.org/wp-content/uploads/2014/02/78524_Tow-Center-Report-WEB-1.pdf.
13. Nicholas Diakopoulos and Michael Koliska, "Algorithmic Transparency in the News Media," *Digital Journalism* 5, no. 7 (2017): 809–28.
14. Laura A. Granka, "The Politics of Search: A Decade Retrospective," *Information Society* 26, no. 5 (2010): 364–74. Nelson Granados and Alok Gupta, "Transparency Strategy: Competing with Information in a Digital World," *MIS Quarterly* (2013): 637–41.
15. Lazter et al., "The Economics of Algorithmic Selection on the Internet."
16. José Van Dijck, "Datafication, Dataism and Dataveillance: Big Data Between Scientific Paradigm and Ideology," *Surveillance & Society* 12, no. 2 (2014): 197–208.
17. Kenneth Cukier and Viktor Mayer-Schoenberger, "The Rise of Big Data: How It's Changing the Way We Think About the World," *Foreign Affairs* 92 (2013): 28.
18. Jathan Sadowski, "When Data Is Capital: Datafication, Accumulation, and Extraction," *Big Data & Society* 6, no. 1 (2019).

4. DATAFICATION OF NEWS AND MEDIA DIVERSITY

19. Ulises A. Mejias and Nick Couldry, "Datafication," *Internet Policy Review* 8, no. 4 (2019).
20. Michael Curtiss, Krishna Bharat, and Michael Schmitt, "Systems and Methods for Improving the Ranking of News Articles," US 10,459,926 B2, October 29, 2012.
21. John R. Bender, Lucinda Davenport, Michael W. Drager, and Fred Fedler, *Writing and Reporting for the Media* (Oxford University Press, 2019).
22. Curtiss, Bharat, and Schmitt, "Systems and Methods for Improving the Ranking of News Articles."
23. Krishna Bharat, Michael Curtiss, and Michael Schmitt, "Method and Apparatus for Clustering News Online Content Based on Content Freshness and Quality of Content Source," US 9,361,369 B1, June 7, 2016.
24. Cukier and Mayer-Schoenberger, "The Rise of Big Data," 35.
25. Mejias and Couldry, "Datafication," 3.
26. CNIL, "General Data Protection Regulation: A Guide to Assist Processors," 2017, https://www.cnil.fr/en/general-data-protection-regulation-guide-assist-processors.
27. Juta Gurinaviciute, "Lessons to Take Away from €4.5 Billion in GDPR Fines," *Forbes*, July 3, 2024, https://www.forbes.com/councils/forbestechcouncil/2024/07/02/lessons-to-take-away-from-45-billion-in-gdpr-fines/.
28. David Skok, "In Conversation with Richard Gingras, VP of Google News," *Medium*, May 10, 2018, https://medium.com/@dskok/in-conversation-with-richard-gingras-vp-of-google-news-ab2cdb53ee12.
29. This section draws on Qun Wang, "A Complicated Picture: Media Diversity in the Case of Google's Video Search During the Pandemic," *Internet Policy Review* 12, no. 4 (2023).
30. Scott L. Althaus, "American News Consumption During Times of National Crisis," *PS: Political Science and Politics* 35, no. 3 (2002): 517–21.
31. "Online Video Proliferates as Viewers Share What They Find Online; 57% of Online Adults Watch or Download Video," Pew Research Center, July 25, 2007, https://www.pewresearch.org/internet/2007/07/25/online-video-proliferates-as-viewers-share-what-they-find-online-57-of-online-adults-watch-or-download-video/.
32. "Online Video 2013," Pew Research Center, October 10, 2013, http://www.lifelongfaith.com/uploads/5/1/6/4/5164069/online_video_use_2013_-_pew_research.pdf; Laura Ceci, "Online Video Usage in the United States—Statistics and Facts," *Statista*, July 12, 2021, https://www.statista.com/topics/1137/online-video/#dossierKeyfigures.

4. DATAFICATION OF NEWS AND MEDIA DIVERSITY

33. "European Online Video Subscription Growth," *Informitv*, February 9, 2021, https://informitv.com/2021/02/09/european-online-video-subscription-growth/.
34. David Bloom, "Online Video Increases Worldwide Even as U.S. and Europe Streaming Slows," *Forbes*, May 18, 2022, https://www.forbes.com/sites/dbloom/2022/05/18/online-video-viewing-growth-flattens-in-us-europe-but-big-screens-roku-rule/.
35. Brad Adgate, "Nielsen: How the Pandemic Changed At-Home Media Consumption," *Forbes*, August 21, 2020, https://www.forbes.com/sites/bradadgate/2020/08/21/nielsen-how-the-pandemic-changed-at-home-media-consumption/.
36. Allison Sadlier, "Americans Are Streaming 8 Hours a Day During Coronavirus Lockdown," *New York Post*, April 14, 2020, https://nypost.com/2020/04/14/average-american-streaming-content-8-hours-a-day-during-covid-19-according-to-new-research/.
37. Alison Weissbrot, "Daytime Is Streaming Time: TV Viewing Habits in the Time of COVID-19," *Ad Exchanger*, April 9, 2020, https://www.adexchanger.com/tv-and-video/daytime-is-streaming-time-tv-viewing-habits-in-the-time-of-covid-19/.
38. "Global Online Video Platforms Market Drives over 80% of Total Internet Traffic," Skyquest Technology, August 2, 2022, https://www.globenewswire.com/en/news-release/2022/08/02/2490661/0/en/Global-Online-Video-Platforms-Market-Drives-over-80-of-Total-Internet-Traffic-Skyquest-Technology.html.
39. Zach Miners, "Facebook Will Be Mostly Video in 5 Years, Zuckerberg Says," *PC World*, November 6, 2014, https://www.pcworld.com/article/2844852/facebook-will-be-mostly-video-in-5-years-zuckerberg-says.html.
40. Antonis Kalogeropoulos and Rasmus Kleis Nielsen, "Investing in Online Video News: A Cross-National Analysis of News Organizations' Enterprising Approach to Digital Media," *Journalism Studies* 19, no. 15 (2018): 2207–24.
41. Antonis Kalogeropoulos and Federica Cherubini, "The Future of Online News Video," Digital News Project, 2016, https://www.digitalnewsreport.org/publications/2016/future-online-news-video/.
42. Dawn DeGuzman, "The Power of Video in News Media: How Increased Audience Engagement Drives Success," AP, September 23, 2024. https://www.ap.org/news-highlights/insights/2024/the-power-of

4. DATAFICATION OF NEWS AND MEDIA DIVERSITY

-video-in-news-media-how-increased-audience-engagement-drives-success/.
43. Alex Chitu, "Google Frames a Video Search Engine," *Google Operating System* (blog), June 13, 2007, https://googlesystem.blogspot.com/2007/06/google-videos-new-frame.html.
44. Greg Jarboe, "YouTube Algorithm: 7 Key Findings You Must Know," *Search Engine Journal*, March 13, 2019, https://www.searchenginejournal.com/youtube-algorithm-findings/296291/.
45. Eric Enge, "Ranking Videos on Google and YouTube: Study Shows How They Differ," *Perficient*, July 19, 2017, https://blogs.perficient.com/2017/07/19/ranking-videos-on-google-and-youtube-study-shows-how-they-differ/.
46. Isabelle Krebs, Philipp Bachmann, Gabriele Siegert, Rafael Schwab, and Raphael Willi, "Non-journalistic Competitors of News Media Brands on Google and YouTube: From Solid Competition to a Liquid Media Market," *Journal of Media Business Studies* 18, no. 1 (2021): 27–44.
47. Amanda DiSilvestro, "Google Videos vs. YouTube: Which Is the Best Video Search Engine?," *Search Engine Watch*, October 31, 2017, https://www.searchenginewatch.com/2017/10/31/google-videos-vs-youtube-which-is-the-best-video-search-engine/.
48. Amy Mitchell, Jesse Holcomb, Kenneth Olmstead, and Nancy Vogt, "Developments in Online News Video Content," Pew Research Center, March 26, 2014, https://www.pewresearch.org/journalism/2014/03/26/developments-in-online-news-video-content/.
49. World Health Organization, "Infodemic," https://www.who.int/health-topics/infodemic/understanding-the-infodemic-and-misinformation-in-the-fight-against-covid-19.
50. Tao Zhou, Zoltán Kuscsik, Jian-Guo Liu, Matúš Medo, Joseph Rushton Wakeling, and Yi-Cheng Zhang, "Solving the Apparent Diversity-Accuracy Dilemma of Recommender Systems," *Proceedings of the National Academy of Sciences* 107, no. 10 (2010): 4511–15.
51. Aleksandra Urman, Mykola Makhortykh, and Roberto Ulloa, "Auditing Source Diversity Bias in Video Search Results Using Virtual Agents," *Companion Proceedings of the Web Conference 2021* (2021): 232–36.
52. Trielli and Diakopoulos, "Search as News Curator."
53. Efrat Nechushtai and Seth C. Lewis, "What Kind of News Gatekeepers Do We Want Machines to Be? Filter Bubbles, Fragmentation, and the

Normative Dimensions of Algorithmic Recommendations," *Computers in Human Behavior* 90 (2019): 298–307.
54. Urman et al., "Auditing Source Diversity Bias."
55. Helle Sjøvaag, "Media Diversity and the Global Superplayers: Operationalising Pluralism for a Digital Media Market," 2016, 5.
56. Centers for Disease Control and Prevention, "Introduction to COVID-19 Racial and Ethnic Health Disparities," https://www.cdc.gov/coronavirus/2019-ncov/community/health-equity/racial-ethnic-disparities/index.html.
57. Dan Keating, Ariana Eunjung Cha, and Gabriel Florit, "'I Just Pray God Will Help Me': Racial, Ethnic Minorities Reel from Higher Covid-19 Death Rates," Washington Post, November 20, 2020, https://www.washingtonpost.com/graphics/2020/health/covid-race-mortality-rate/.
58. Brandon W. Yan, Andrea L. Hwang, Fiona Ng, Janet N. Chu, Janice Y. Tsoh, and Tung T. Nguyen, "Death Toll of COVID-19 on Asian Americans: Disparities Revealed," *Journal of General Internal Medicine* 36, no. 11 (2021): 3545–49.
59. "Standards for Maintaining, Collecting, and Presenting Federal Data on Race and Ethnicity," US Department of the Interior, https://www.doi.gov/pmb/eeo/directives/race-data.
60. UNC, "Journalistic Mission: The Challenges and Opportunities for Ethnic Media," 2020, https://www.usnewsdeserts.com/reports/news-deserts-and-ghost-newspapers-will-local-news-survive/the-news-landscape-of-the-future-transformed-and-renewed/journalistic-mission-the-challenges-and-opportunities-for-ethnic-media/.
61. "The Ethnic Media in America: The Giant Hidden in Plain Sight," New California Media, 2005, https://legacy.npr.org/documents/2005/jul/ncmfreport.pdf.
62. Chris Holt, "Facebook Can't Find Enough Local News for Its Local News Service," *Engadget*, March 18, 2019, https://www.engadget.com/2019-03-18-facebook-local-news-availability-today-in-journalism-project.html.
63. Min Jiang, "The Business and Politics of Search Engines: A Comparative Study of Baidu and Google's Search Results of Internet Events in China," *New Media & Society* 16, no. 2 (2014): 212–33; Urman et al., "Auditing Source Diversity Bias"; Sam Schechner, Kirsten Grind, and John West, "Searching for Video? Google Pushes YouTube Over Rivals,"

5. A GLOBAL NETWORK

Wall Street Journal, July 14, 2020, https://www.wsj.com/articles/google-steers-users-to-youtube-over-rivals-11594745232.

64. Qun Wang, "Differentiation and De-differentiation: The Evolving Power Dynamics Between News Industry and Tech Industry," *Journalism & Mass Communication Quarterly* 97, no. 2 (2020): 509–27.
65. Natali Helberger, "On the Democratic Role of News Recommenders," Digital Journalism 7, no. 8 (2019): 1000.

5. A GLOBAL NETWORK: GOOGLE'S SYSTEMATIC NEWS INITIATIVES

1. Steve Grove, "Our Next Steps in the Google News Initiative," *Medium,* March 20, 2018, https://medium.com/@grove/our-next-steps-in-the-google-news-initiative-ec5b7fe4dcb8.
2. Philipp Schindler, "The Google News Initiative: Building a Stronger Future for News," *Google* (blog), March 20, 2018, https://blog.google/outreach-initiatives/google-news-initiative/announcing-google-news-initiative/.
3. Matt Carlson and Nikki Usher, "News Startups as Agents of Innovation: For-profit Digital News Startup Manifestos as Metajournalistic Discourse," *Digital Journalism* 4, no. 5 (2016): 567, 565.
4. Google News Initiative, "About," https://newsinitiative.withgoogle.com/about/.
5. Shan Wang, "Google Announces a $300M 'Google News Initiative,'" *Nieman Lab,* March 20, 2018, http://www.niemanlab.org/2018/03/google-announces-a-300m-google-news-initiative-though-this-isnt-about-giving-out-grants-directly-to-newsrooms-like-it-does-in-europe/.
6. "How Google Supports Journalism and the News Industry," *Google* (blog), https://blog.google/supportingnews/#overview.
7. Google News Initiative, "About."
8. "How Google Supports Journalism and the News Industry," *Google* (blog).
9. Rasmus Kleis Nielsen and Sarah Anne Ganter, "Dealing with Digital Intermediaries: A Case Study of the Relations Between Publishers and Platforms," *New Media & Society* 20, no. 4 (2018): 1600–17.
10. "SPJ Code of Ethics," Society of Professional Journalists, September 6, 2014, https://www.spj.org/ethicscode.asp.

5. A GLOBAL NETWORK

11. Tony Rogers, "6 Ways Reporters Can Avoid Conflicts of Interest," *ThoughtCo*, February 13, 2019, https://www.thoughtco.com/avoid-conflicts-of-interest-2073885.
12. Al Verney, "Let's Work Together to Support Quality Journalism," *Google Europe* (blog), April 28, 2015, https://europe.googleblog.com/2015/04/lets-work-together-to-support-quality.html.
13. Google Digital News Initiative, "Stimulate Engage Innovate: Digital News Initiative Innovation Fund," *Google* (blog), 2017, https://newsinitiative.withgoogle.com/dnifund/insights/2016-2017-dni-innovation-fund-report-available-now-download/.
14. Ludovic Blecher, "More Than EUR 21 Million in Funding from Round 3 of the Digital News Initiative Fund," *Google* (blog), July 6, 2017, https://www.blog.google/around-the-globe/google-europe/21-million-funding-round-3-digital-news-initiative-fund/.
15. DNI, "Announcing Successful Recipients of Round 4 Funding," *Google* (blog), 2017, https://digitalnewsinitiative.com/news/announcing-successful-recipients-round-4-funding/.
16. Ludovic Blecher, "Digital News Innovation Fund: More Than €21m of Funding to Reach €115m to Date for Innovation in News," *Google* (blog), July 24, 2018, https://www.blog.google/around-the-globe/google-europe/digital-news-innovation-fund-more-21m-funding-reach-115m-date-innovation-news/.
17. Ludovic Blecher, "Digital News Innovation Fund: Three Years in, and 662 Total Projects Supported," *Google* (blog), March 21, 2019, https://www.blog.google/around-the-globe/google-europe/digital-news-innovation-fund-three-years-and-662-total-projects-supported/.
18. Kate Beddoe, "Google News Initiative Kicks Off Asia-Pacific Innovation Challenge," *Google* (blog), November 20, 2018, https://blog.google/outreach-initiatives/google-news-initiative/asia-pacific-challenge/.
19. Innovation Challenges, "FAQs," Google, https://web.archive.org/web/20210410220913/https://newsinitiative.withgoogle.com/innovation-challenges/how-to-apply/apac/#eligible-projects.
20. Innovation Challenges, "Eligible Projects," Google, https://web.archive.org/web/20210517102728/https://newsinitiative.withgoogle.com/innovation-challenges/how-to-apply/latam/.
21. Chrissy Towle, "These 25 Publishers Want to Know Their Communities," *Google* (blog), November 16, 2021, https://blog.google/outreach-initiatives/google-news-initiative/innovation-challenge-publishers/.

5. A GLOBAL NETWORK

22. Alex Cox, "Dive Deeper Into Local News with News Showcase," *Google* (blog), February 9, 2022, https://blog.google/products/news/local-news-showcase-product-updates/.
23. Joe Golder, "Google's News Showcase Teaches Executives What Not to Do," *Forbes*, October 25, 2021, https://www.forbes.com/sites/zengernews/2021/10/25/googles-news-showcase-teaches-executives-what-not-to-do/.
24. Jacob Granger, "Google News Showcase: Is It Viable for the Smallest of Newsrooms?," journalism.co.uk, July 7, 2022, https://www.journalism.co.uk/news/google-news-showcase-is-it-viable-for-the-smallest-of-news rooms-/s2/a944419/.
25. Granger, "Google News Showcase."
26. Brad Bender, "Google News Showcase, One Year in," *Google* (blog), November 16, 2021, https://blog.google/products/news/news-showcase-one-year-/.
27. Golder, "Google's News Showcase Teaches Executives What Not to Do"; William Turvill, "Why US Publishers Aren't Signing Up to Google News Showcase," *Press Gazette*, December 16, 2021, https://pressgazette.co.uk/google-news-showcase-us-launch/.
28. Turvill, "Why US Publishers Aren't Signing Up to Google News Showcase."
29. Brad Bender and Olivia Ma, "Read All About It: A New Look for Google News," *Google* (blog), June 22, 2022, https://blog.google/products/news/google-news-anniversary-local-reporting-funding/.
30. Larry Page and Sergey Brin, "2004 Founders' IPO Letter," Google.com, 2004, https://abc.xyz/investor/founders-letters/2004-ipo-letter/.
31. Page and Brin, "2004 Founders' Letter."
32. Philip M. Napoli, "The Symbolic Uses of Platforms: The Politics of Platform Governance in the United States," *Journal of Digital Media & Policy* 12, no. 2 (2021): 215–30.
33. Sara Fischer, "Scoop: Google Threatens to Pause Google News Initiative Funding in U.S.," *Axios*, May 21, 2024, https://www.axios.com/2024/05/21/google-news-initiative-journalism-funding-california.
34. Richard Gingras, "Setting the Record Straight on News," *Google* (blog), June 26, 2020, https://blog.google/outreach-initiatives/google-news-initiative/setting-record-straight-news/.
35. "How Google Supports Journalism and the News Industry," *Google* (blog), https://blog.google/supportingnews/#overview.

5. A GLOBAL NETWORK

36. W. Richard Scott, "Lords of the Dance: Professionals as Institutional Agents," *Organization Studies* 29, no. 2 (2008): 219–38.
37. Scott, "Lords of the Dance."
38. Kate Conger, "Google Removes 'Don't Be Evil' Clause from Its Code of Conduct," *Gizmodo*, May 18, 2018, https://gizmodo.com/google-removes-nearly-all-mentions-of-dont-be-evil-from-1826153393.
39. Kari Steen-Johnsen, Vilde Schanke Sundet, and Bernard Enjolras, "Theorizing Policy-Industry Processes: A Media Policy Field Approach," *European Journal of Communication* 34, no. 2 (2019): 197.
40. Philip M. Napoli, *Social Media and the Public Interest: Media Regulation in the Disinformation Age* (Columbia University Press, 2019); José Van Dijck, "Governing Digital Societies: Private Platforms, Public Values," *Computer Law & Security Review* 36 (2020): 105377.
41. Napoli, *Social Media and the Public Interest*, 135, 136.
42. Philip M. Napoli, "Social Media and the Public Interest: Governance of News Platforms in the Realm of Individual and Algorithmic Gatekeepers," *Telecommunications Policy* 39, no. 9 (2015): 751–60.
43. Napoli, *Social Media and the Public Interest*, 134.
44. Krystal Hu, "ChatGPT Sets Record for Fastest-Growing User Base—Analyst Note," *Reuters*, February 2, 2023, https://www.reuters.com/technology/chatgpt-sets-record-fastest-growing-user-base-analyst-note-2023-02-01/.
45. Nico Grant and Cade Metz, "A New Chat Bot Is a 'Code Red' for Google's Search Business," *New York Times*, December 21, 2022, https://www.nytimes.com/2022/12/21/technology/ai-chatgpt-google-search.html.
46. Liz Reid, "Generative AI in Search: Let Google Do the Searching for You," *Google* (blog), May 14, 2024, https://blog.google/products/search/generative-ai-google-search-may-2024/.
47. Nico Grant and Katie Robertson, "Google's A. I. Search Leaves Publishers Scrambling," *New York Times*, June 1, 2024, https://www.nytimes.com/2024/06/01/technology/google-ai-search-publishers.html.
48. Emma Roth, "OpenAI Will use Associated Press News Stories to Train Its Models," *The Verge*, July 13, 2023, https://www.theverge.com/2023/7/13/23793810/openai-associated-press-ai-models.
49. Grant and Robertson, "Google's A. I. Search Leaves Publishers Scrambling."
50. Shayne Longpre, Robert Mahari, Ariel Lee, Campbell Lund, et al., "Consent in Crisis: The Rapid Decline of the AI Data Commons," Data

5. A GLOBAL NETWORK

Provenance Initiative, 2024, https://www.dataprovenance.org/Consent_in_Crisis.pdf; Richard Fletcher, "How Many News Websites Block AI Crawlers?," Reuters Institute, February 22, 2024, https://reutersinstitute.politics.ox.ac.uk/how-many-news-websites-block-ai-crawlers.
51. *The New York Times Company v. Microsoft Corporation, OpenAI, Inc., OpenAI LP, OpenAI GP, LLC, OpenAI, LLC, OpenAI OpCo LLC, OpenAI Global LLC, OAO Corporation, LLC, and OpenAI Holdings, LLC*, 2024, Case 1:23-cv-11195, doc. 1. 3.
52. *The New York Times Company v. Microsoft Corporation* . . . , 27.
53. *The New York Times Company v. Microsoft Corporation* . . . , 4.
54. *The New York Times Company v. Microsoft Corporation* . . . , 27.
55. Longpre et al., "Consent in Crisis."
56. Longpre et al., "Consent in Crisis."
57. *The New York Times Company v. Microsoft Corporation* . . . , doc. 52, 8.
58. *The New York Times Company v. Microsoft Corporation* . . . , 8.
59. *The New York Times Company v. Microsoft Corporation* . . . , 3.
60. Pamela J. Shoemaker and Stephen D. Reese, *Mediating the Message in the Twenty-First Century: A Media Sociology Perspective* (Routledge, 2013); Qun Wang, Philip M. Napoli, and Yi Ma, "Problems and Solutions for American Political Coverage: Journalistic Self-Critique in the Wake of the 2016 Presidential Election," *Journalism Practice* 12, no. 10 (2018): 1241–58.
61. Adam Satariano, "E. U. Agrees on Landmark Artificial Intelligence Rules," *New York Times*, December 8, 2023, https://www.nytimes.com/2023/12/08/technology/eu-ai-act-regulation.html.
62. Adam Satariano and Milan Schreuer, "Facebook's Mark Zuckerberg Gets an Earful from the E. U.," *New York Times*, May 22, 2018, https://www.nytimes.com/2018/05/22/technology/facebook-eu-parliament-mark-zuckerberg.html.
63. "EU AI Act: First Regulation on Artificial Intelligence," European Parliament, https://www.europarl.europa.eu/topics/en/article/20230601STO93804/eu-ai-act-first-regulation-on-artificial-intelligence.
64. "Artificial Intelligence Worldwide." Statista.com, 2024, https://www.statista.com/outlook/tmo/artificial-intelligence/worldwide#users.
65. "7 Key AI Investment Statistics Every Investor Should Know," *Edge Delta*, May 24, 2024, https://edgedelta.com/company/blog/ai-investment-statistics.
66. "China's Ambitions in Artificial Intelligence," European Parliament, https://www.europarl.europa.eu/RegData/etudes/ATAG/2021/696206/EPRS_ATA(2021)696206_EN.pdf.

5. A GLOBAL NETWORK

67. Yang Xiujun [杨秀君], "Logics, Essence, and Practical Strategies of Xi Jin Ping's Important Statement on AI Technology," [习近平关于人工智能重要论述的形成逻辑、核心要义及实践方略], December 27, 2024, https://www.cssn.cn/jjx/shzyjjysj/202412/t20241227_5827810.shtml.
68. "National Security Commission on Artificial Intelligence," NSCAI, 2021, https://assets.foleon.com/eu-central-1/de-uploads-7e3kk3/48187/nscai_full_report_digital.04d6b124173c.pdf
69. "National Security Commission on Artificial Intelligence," 14.
70. Cat Zakrzewski, Nitasha Tiku, and Elizabeth Dwoskin, "OpenAI Prepares to Fight for Its Life as Legal Troubles Mount," *Washington Post*, April 9, 2024, https://www.washingtonpost.com/technology/2024/04/09/openai-lawsuit-regulation-lawyers/.

BIBLIOGRAPHY

Adgate, Brad. "Nielsen: How the Pandemic Changed at Home Media Consumption." *Forbes*, August 21, 2020. https://www.forbes.com/sites/bradadgate/2020/08/21/nielsen-how-the-pandemic-changed-at-home-media-consumption/.
AFP. "Paid Content Takes Hit as News Corp Drops $32m Project Alesia 'Digital Newsstand.'" *News.com.au*, October 23, 2010. https://www.news.com.au/breaking-news/paid-content-takes-hit-as-news-corp-drops-32m-project-alesia-digital-newsstand/news-story/b547dbdef6f14cc9ca12cf798d2b4e7c.
"AGCM Annual Report." AGCM, 2011. http://www.agcm.it/en/component/joomdoc/annual-reports/AnnualReport2010_Catrical.pdf/download.html.
Agichtein, Eugene, Eric Brill, Susan Dumais, and Robert Ragno. "Learning User Interaction Models for Predicting Web Search Result Preferences." *Proceedings of the 29th Annual International ACM SIGIR Conference on Research and Development in Information Retrieval* (2006): 3–10.
Alexander, Jeffrey C., and Paul Burbank Colomy. *Differentiation Theory: Problems and Prospects*. Columbia University Press, 1990.
Ali, Rafat. "Google News Starts Publishing Full Stories; AP, AFP, PA and Canadian Press; Still No Ads." *Gigaom*, August 31, 2007. https://gigaom

BIBLIOGRAPHY

.com/2007/08/31/419-google-starts-publishing-full-stories-on-its-news-section-ap-afp-pa-and/.

Althaus, Scott L. "American News Consumption During Times of National Crisis." *PS: Political Science & Politics* 35, no. 3 (2002): 517–21.

American Medical Association. "Ama, Google Launch Health Care Interoperability & Innovation Challenge." Press release. April 9, 2018. https://www.ama-assn.org/press-center/press-releases/ama-google-launch-health-care-interoperability-innovation-challenge.

Anderson, Christopher W. "What Aggregators Do: Towards a Networked Concept of Journalistic Expertise in the Digital Age." *Journalism* 14, no. 8 (2013): 1008–23.

Apple. "Apple Launches Apple News+ an Immersive Magazine and News Reading Experience." Press release. March 25, 2019. https://www.apple.com/newsroom/2019/03/apple-launches-apple-news-plus-an-immersive-magazine-and-news-reading-experience/.

Athey, Susan, Markus Mobius, and Jeno Pál. *The Impact of Aggregators on Internet News Consumption.* National Bureau of Economic Research, 2021.

Auchard, Eric. "AFP, Google News Settle Lawsuit Over Google News." *Reuters*, April 7, 2007. https://www.reuters.com/article/us-google-afp/afp-google-news-settle-lawsuit-over-google-news-idUSN0728115420070407.

"Axel Springer Concludes Its Data Documentation: Major Losses Resulting from Downgraded Search Notices on Google." *Axel Springer*, November 5, 2014. https://www.axelspringer.com/en/presse/Axel-Springer-concludes-its-data-documentation-Major-losses-resulting-from-downgraded-search-notices-on-Google_22070687.html.

Bakker, Piet. "Aggregation, Content Farms, and Huffinization: The Rise of Low-Pay and No-Pay Journalism." *Journalism Practice* 6, no. 5–6 (2012): 627–37.

Baram, Marcus. "Facebook Finally Admits It's a Giant Media Company—Almost." *Fast Company*, January 11, 2017. https://www.fastcompany.com/3067148/facebook-finally-admits-its-a-giant-media-company-almost.

Barnett, Emma. "Rupert Murdoch Has Warned That His Paywall Plans Could Be Delayed." *Telegraph*, November 13, 2009. https://www.telegraph.co.uk/finance/newsbysector/mediatechnologyandtelecoms/digital-media/6559694/Rupert-Murdoch-to-remove-News-Corps-content-from-Google-in-months.html.

BIBLIOGRAPHY

Beatty, John. "Perceptions of Online Styles of News Video Production." *Journal of Visual Literacy* 35, no. 2 (2016): 126–46.

Becker, Andreas. "German Publishers vs. Google." *DW*, October 30, 2014. https://www.dw.com/en/german-publishers-vs-google/a-18030444.

Beckmann, Chris. "Google News Changes Reflect Your Feedback." *Google*, July 15, 2010. https://news.googleblog.com/2010/07/google-news-changes-reflect-your.html.

Beddoe, Kate. "Google News Initiative Kicks Off Asia-Pacific Innovation Challenge." *Google*, November 20, 2018. https://blog.google/outreach-initiatives/google-news-initiative/asia-pacific-challenge/.

Beech, Mark. "COVID-19 Pushes Up Internet Use 70% and Streaming More Than 12%, First Figures Reveal." *Forbes*, March 25, 2020. https://www.forbes.com/sites/markbeech/2020/03/25/covid-19-pushes-up-internet-use-70-streaming-more-than-12-first-figures-reveal/?sh=22341b193104.

Bell, Emily. "Facebook Is Eating the World." *Columbia Journalism Review*, March 7, 2016. https://www.cjr.org/analysis/facebook_and_media.php.

Bell, Emily, Taylor Owen, Peter Brown, Codi Hauka, and Nushin Rashidian. "The Platform Press: How Silicon Valley Reengineered Journalism." *Columbia Academic Commons*, May 26, 2017. https://academiccommons.columbia.edu/catalog/ac:15dv41ns27.

Bemis, Alec H. "Remains of the Day." *LA Weekly*, September 12, 2001. https://www.laweekly.com/news/remains-of-the-day-2133806.

Bender, Brad. "Google News Showcase, One Year In." *Google*, November 16, 2021. https://blog.google/products/news/news-showcase-one-year-/.

———. "A New Licensing Program to Support the News Industry." *Google*, June 25, 2020. https://www.blog.google/outreach-initiatives/google-news-initiative/licensing-program-support-news-industry-/?_ga=2.236282177.1122694280.1593072794-752983740.1593072794.

Bender, Brad, and Olivia Ma. "Read All About It: A New Look for Google News." *Google*, June 22, 2022. https://blog.google/products/news/google-news-anniversary-local-reporting-funding/.

"Berne Convention for the Protection of Literary and Artistic Works." WIPO, 1979. https://www.wipo.int/wipolex/en/treaties/textdetails/12214.

"The Berne Convention for the Protection of Literary and Artistic Works from 1886 to 1986." WIPO, 1986. https://www.wipo.int/edocs/pubdocs/en/copyright/877/wipo_pub_877.pdf.

BIBLIOGRAPHY

Benson, Rodney. *Shaping Immigration News: A French-American Comparison.* Cambridge University Press, 2013.

Blecher, Ludovic. "Digital News Innovation Fund: More Than €21m of Funding to Reach €115m to Date for Innovation in News." *Google* (blog), July 24, 2018. https://www.blog.google/around-the-globe/google-europe/digital-news-innovation-fund-more-21m-funding-reach-115m-date-innovation-news/.

———. "Digital News Innovation Fund: Three Years In, and 662 Total Projects Supported." *Google* (blog), March 21, 2019. https://www.blog.google/around-the-globe/google-europe/digital-news-innovation-fund-three-years-and-662-total-projects-supported/.

———. "More Than EUR 21 Million in Funding from Round 3 of the Digital News Initiative Fund." *Google* (blog), July 6, 2017. https://www.blog.google/around-the-globe/google-europe/21-million-funding-round-3-digital-news-initiative-fund/.

Bloom, David. "Online Video Increases Worldwide Even as U.S. and Europe Streaming Slows." *Forbes*, May 18, 2022. https://www.forbes.com/sites/dbloom/2022/05/18/online-video-viewing-growth-flattens-in-us-europe-but-big-screens-roku-rule/?sh=1462833551b3.

Blythe, Stephen E. "The US Digital Millennium Copyright Act and the EU Copyright Directive: Comparative Impact on Fair Use Rights." *Tul. J. Tech. & Intell. Prop.* 8 (2006): 111.

Boczkowski, Pablo J. *Digitizing the News: Innovation in Online Newspapers.* MIT Press, 2005.

Boczkowski, Pablo J., and José A. Ferris. "Multiple Media, Convergent Processes, and Divergent Products: Organizational Innovation in Digital Media Production at a European Firm." *Annals of the American Academy of Political and Social Science* 597, no. 1 (2005): 32–47.

Boom, Daniel Van, and Queenie Wong. "Australia Passes Law Forcing Google and Facebook to Pay News Publications." *CNET*, February 24, 2021. https://www.cnet.com/tech/mobile/australia-passes-law-forcing-google-and-facebook-to-pay-news-publications/.

Branigan, Tania. "Google to End Censorship in China Over Cyber Attacks." *Guardian*, January 12, 2010. https://www.theguardian.com/technology/2010/jan/12/google-china-ends-censorship.

Bruell, Alexandra. "Google to Launch Long-Delayed News Showcase Product in U.S. This Summer." *Wall Street Journal*, June 8, 2023. https://www.wsj.com/articles/google-to-launch-long-delayed-news-showcase-product-in-u-s-this-summer-4aec324d.

BIBLIOGRAPHY

Buckley, Chris. "Q⁺A: Is There a WTO Case Against Chinese Internet Censorship?" Reuters, March 10, 2010. https://www.reuters.com/article/us-china-usa-internet/qa-is-there-a-wto-case-against-chinese-internet-censorship-idUSTRE6290T120100310.

Bump, Pamela. "How Video Consumption Is Changing in 2023." *HubSpot*, April 3, 2023. https://blog.hubspot.com/marketing/how-video-consumption-is-changing.

Byford, Sam. "Google Finally Settles with Belgian Publishers Over Content Scraping Lawsuit." *Verge*, December 13, 2012. https://www.theverge.com/2012/12/13/3764692/google-copyright-lawsuit-settlement-belgium.

Calzada, Joan, and Ricard Gil. "What Do News Aggregators Do? Evidence from Google News in Spain and Germany." *Marketing Science* 39, no. 1 (2020): 134–67.

Campbell, Ian C. "News Corp Gives Up on Its 'Knewz' Aggregator After 18 Months." *Verge*, July 9, 2021. https://www.theverge.com/2021/7/9/22570164/knewz-news-corp-aggregation-google-facebook.

Carlson, Matt. "Facebook in the News: Social Media, Journalism, and Public Responsibility Following the 2016 Trending Topics Controversy." *Digital Journalism* 6, no. 1 (2018): 4–20.

——. "Order Versus Access: News Search Engines and the Challenge to Traditional Journalistic Roles." *Media, Culture & Society* 29, no. 6 (2007): 1014–30.

Carlson, Matt, and Nikki Usher. "News Startups as Agents of Innovation: For-Profit Digital News Startup Manifestos as Metajournalistic Discourse." *Digital Journalism* 4, no. 5 (2016): 563–81.

Carlson, Sean. "Rededicating the Newseum's Journalists Memorial." *Google*, May 18, 2011. https://news.googleblog.com/2011/05/rededicating-newseums-journalists.html.

Carpenter, Serena. "A Study of Content Diversity in Online Citizen Journalism and Online Newspaper Articles." *New Media & Society* 12, no. 7 (2010): 1064–84.

Ceci, Lucia. "Online Video Usage in the United States—Statistics and Facts." *Statista*, July 12, 2021. https://www.statista.com/topics/1137/online-video/#dossierKeyfigures.

Chavern, David. "It's Time to Rein In the Tech Platforms' Anticompetitive Behavior." *News Media Alliance*, August 21, 2008. https://www.newsmediaalliance.org/ceo-time-to-rein-in-platforms/.

Chee, Foo Y. "Google Has Finally Agreed to Pay for News Content in Australia, Brazil, and Germany After Mounting Pressure from Publishers

BIBLIOGRAPHY

and Regulators." Reuters, June 25, 2020. https://www.businessinsider.com/google-to-pay-some-publishers-in-australia-brazil-germany-for-content-2020-6.

Chee, Foo Y., and Klaus Lauer, Klaus. "Google Wins Legal Battle with German Publishers Over Fee Demands." Reuters, September 12, 2019. https://www.reuters.com/article/us-google-germany-publishers-idUSKCN1VX0R2.

Chiou, Lesley, and Catherine Tucker. "Copyright, Digitization, and Aggregation." 2011. https://ide.mit.edu/wp-content/uploads/2016/04/2011.12_Chiou_Tucker_Copyright-Digitization-and-Aggregation_309.pdf?x61816.

Cho, Junghoo, Sourashis Roy, and Robert E. Adams. "Page Quality: In Search of an Unbiased Web Ranking." In *Proceedings of the 2005 ACM SIGMOD International Conference on Management of Data* (2005), 551–62.

Cipriani, Jason. "The New Google News App Has Arrived: Here's What You Need to Know." *CNET*, May 16, 2018. https://www.cnet.com/how-to/new-google-news-app-what-you-need-know/.

Claburn, Thomas. "Google News Becomes a Publisher." *Information Week*, August 31, 2007. https://www.informationweek.com/google-news-becomes-a-publisher/d/d-id/1058737.

Clinton, Hillary. "Remarks on Internet Freedom." *US Department of State*, January 21, 2010. https://2009-2017.state.gov/secretary/20092013clinton/rm/2010/01/135519.htm.

Coddington, Mark. *Aggregating the News: Secondhand News and the Erosion of Journalistic Authority*. Columbia University Press, 2019.

——. "Clarifying Journalism's Quantitative Turn: A Typology for Evaluating Data Journalism, Computational Journalism, and Computer-Assisted Reporting." *Digital Journalism* 3, no. 3 (2015): 331–48.

——. "Normalizing the Hyperlink: How Bloggers, Professional Journalists, and Institutions Shape Linking Values." *Digital Journalism* 2, no. 2 (2013): 140–55. https://doi.org/10.1080/21670811.2013.785813.

Coelho, Fabio. "O PL 2630 pode impactar a internet que você conhece." Google, March 11, 2022. https://services.google.com/fh/files/blogs/gcarta2630.pdf.

Cohen, Josh. "Extending the Associated Press as Hosted News Partner." *Google* (blog), August 30, 2010. https://news.googleblog.com/2010/08/extending-associated-press-as-hosted.html.

——. "Original Stories, from the Source." *Google* (blog), August 31, 2007. https://news.googleblog.com/2007/08/original-stories-from-source.html.

BIBLIOGRAPHY

Cohen, Sabrina, Giada Zampano, and Peppi Kiviniemi. "Italy Opens Antitrust Probe of Local Google News Service." *Wall Street Journal*, August 28, 2009. https://www.wsj.com/articles/SB125137301333663261.

Colella, Raffaele. "Go Beyond the Headlines with Google News." *Google* (blog), November 14, 2019. https://www.blog.google/products/news/beyond-headlines/.

Condliffe, Jamie. "China's New Cybersecurity Rules May Block Western Innovation." *Technology Review*, November 7, 2016. https://www.technologyreview.com/s/602812/chinas-new-cybersecurity-rules-may-block-western-innovation/.

Coner, Altan. "Personalization and Customization in Financial Portals." *Journal of American Academy of Business* 2, no. 2 (2003): 498–504.

Conger, Kate. "Google Removes 'Don't Be Evil' Clause from Its Code of Conduct." *Gizmodo*, May 18, 2018. https://gizmodo.com/google-removes-nearly-all-mentions-of-dont-be-evil-from-1826153393.

Cooke, Lynne. "A Visual Convergence of Print, Television, and the Internet: Charting 40 Years of Design Change in News Presentation." *New Media & Society* 7, no. 1 (2005): 22–46.

Cox, Alex. "Dive Deeper Into Local News with News Showcase." *Google* (blog), February 9, 2022. https://blog.google/products/news/local-news-showcase-product-updates/.

Crawford, Walt. "Turn On the Radio." *EContent* 25, no. 2 (2002): 44–45.

De la Peña, Nonny, Peggy Weil, Joan Llobera, Bernhard Spanlang, Doron Friedman, Maria V. Sanchez-Vives, and Mel Slater. "Immersive Journalism: Immersive Virtual Reality for the First-Person Experience of News." *Presence* 19, no. 4 (2010): 291–301.

DiSilvestro, Amanda. "Google Videos vs. YouTube: Which Is the Best Video Search Engine?" *Search Engine Watch*, October 31, 2017. https://www.searchenginewatch.com/2017/10/31/google-videos-vs-youtube-which-is-the-best-video-search-engine/.

Domingo, David, and Chris Paterson. *Making Online News. Vol. 2: Newsroom Ethnographies in the Second Decade of Internet Journalism*. Peter Lang, 2011.

Duke, Jennifer. "Facebook, Google to Be Probed Over Role in Creating 'Filter Bubbles.'" *Sydney Morning Herald*, February 26, 2018. https://www.smh.com.au/business/companies/facebook-google-to-be-probed-over-role-in-creating-filter-bubbles-20180226-p4z1pj.html.

Dwyer, Colin. "German Publishers' Lawsuit Against Google Threatens to Backfire." NPR, May 10, 2017. https://www.npr.org/sections/thetwo

BIBLIOGRAPHY

-way/2017/05/10/527800498/german-publishers-lawsuit-against-google-threatens-to-backfire.

"Economic Report on the Impact of the New Article 32.2 of the LPI." AEEPP, July 9, 2015. https://www.aeepp.com/noticia/2272/actividades/informe-economico-del-impacto-del-nuevo-articulo-32.2-de-la-lpi-nera-para-la-aeepp.html.

Elder, Robert. "Publishers in the UK Are Uniting Against Google and Facebook." *Business Insider*, August 9, 2016. http://www.businessinsider.com/uk-publishers-unite-to-take-on-google-and-facebook-2016-8.

"Emily Bell: Journalism in the Age of Trump and the Real-Time Social Web." *Conversation*, June 14, 2017. https://theconversation.com/emily-bell-journalism-in-the-age-of-trump-and-the-real-time-social-web-74627.

Enge, Eric. "Ranking Videos on Google and YouTube: Study Shows How They Differ." *Perficient*, July 19, 2017. https://blogs.perficient.com/2017/07/19/ranking-videos-on-google-and-youtube-study-shows-how-they-differ/.

"European Online Video Subscription Growth." *Informitv*, February 9, 2021. https://informitv.com/2021/02/09/european-online-video-subscription-growth/.

European Parliament. "China's Ambitions in Artificial Intelligence." 2021. https://www.europarl.europa.eu/RegData/etudes/ATAG/2021/696206/EPRS_ATA(2021)696206_EN.pdf.

———. "Copyright in the Digital Single Market." March 26, 2019. http://www.europarl.europa.eu/doceo/document/TA-8-2019-0231_EN.pdf.

———. "EU AI Act: First Regulation on Artificial Intelligence." June 1, 2023. https://www.europarl.europa.eu/topics/en/article/20230601STO93804/eu-ai-act-first-regulation-on-artificial-intelligence.

European Union. "Directive 2001/29/EC of the European Parliament and of the Council of 22 May 2001 on the Harmonisation of Certain Aspects of Copyright and Related Rights in the Information Society." WIPO, 2001. https://wipolex.wipo.int/en/text/126977.

Fallows, James. "On Rupert Murdoch's Times Paywall." *Atlantic*, July 16, 2010. https://www.theatlantic.com/technology/archive/2010/07/on-rupert-murdochs-times-paywall/59878/.

Fischer, Sara. "Google to Launch News Showcase Product in U.S." *Axios*, June 8, 2023. https://www.axios.com/2023/06/08/google-news-showcase-us.

BIBLIOGRAPHY

——. "News Aggregation Apps Take on Big Tech." *Axios*, August 23, 2019. https://www.axios.com/2019/08/23/news-aggregation-apps-big-tech-knewz-news-corp.

——. "Scoop: Google Threatens to Pause Google News Initiative Funding in U.S." *Axios*, May 21, 2024. https://www.axios.com/2024/05/21/google-news-initiative-journalism-funding-california.

Fletcher, Richard. "How Many News Websites Block AI Crawlers?" Reuters Institute, February 22, 2024. https://reutersinstitute.politics.ox.ac.uk/how-many-news-websites-block-ai-crawlers.

Fligstein, Neil, and Doug McAdam. "Toward a General Theory of Strategic Action Fields." *Sociological Theory* 29, no. 1 (2011): 1–26.

Fortt, Jon. "What's Google News Worth? $100 Million." *Fortune*, July 23, 2008. http://fortune.com/2008/07/22/whats-google-news-worth-100-million/.

Fox, Vanessa. "Taking Advantage of Universal Search." *Google* (blog), May 17, 2007. https://webmasters.googleblog.com/2007/05/taking-advantage-of-universal-search.html.

Fraga, Isabela. "Brazilian Newspapers Leave Google News En Masse." *Knight Center for Journalism*, October 18, 2012. https://web.archive.org/web/20121023213333/https://knightcenter.utexas.edu/blog/00-11803-brazilian-newspapers-leave-google-news-en-masse.

Franzen, Carl. "What Lies Behind Murdoch's Move to block Google?" *Atlantic*, November 9, 2009. https://www.theatlantic.com/entertainment/archive/2009/11/what-lies-behind-murdoch-s-move-to-block-google/347627/.

Friedland, Lewis, Philip Napoli, Katherine Ognyanova, Carola Weil, and Ernest J. Wilson III. "Review of the Literature Regarding Critical Information Needs of the American Public." Unpublished manuscript submitted to the Federal Communications Commission, 2012.

Gagne, Christopher. "Canon AEDE: Publishers' Protections from Digital Reproductions of Works by Search Engines Under European Copyright Law." *Temp. Int'l & Comp. LJ* 29 (2015): 203.

Gallagher, Ryan. "Google Employees Uncover Ongoing Work on Censored China Search." *Intercept*, March 4, 2019. https://theintercept.com/2019/03/04/google-ongoing-project-dragonfly/.

Garber, Megan. "Google News Experiments with Human Control, Promotes a New Serendipity with Editors' Picks." *Nieman Lab*, June 10, 2010. http://www.niemanlab.org/2010/06/google-news-experiments-with-human-control-promotes-a-new-serendipity-with-editors-pick/.

BIBLIOGRAPHY

———. "Google News Founder Krishna Bharat: For News Consumers, 'The Whole Experience Is What Counts.'" *Nieman Lab*, April 8, 2011. http://www.niemanlab.org/2011/04/google-news-founder-krishna-bharat-for-news-consumers-the-whole-experience-is-what-counts/.

García, Mario R. "*USA Today* Turns 30: Part 1." *García Media*, September 9, 2012. https://www.garciamedia.com/blog/usa_today_turns_30-part_1-looking_into_the_attic_for_those_early_sketches/.

Geerts, Thierry. "Partnering with Belgian News Publishers." *Google* (blog), December 12, 2012. https://europe.googleblog.com/2012/12/partnering-with-belgian-news-publishers.html.

Geremia, Sabrina. "Our Concerns with Bill C-18, the Online News Act." *Google* (blog), May 16, 2022. https://blog.google/intl/en-ca/our-concerns-with-bill-c-18-the-online-news-act/.

Gill, Sam. "Should Platforms Be Regulated? A New Survey Says Yes." *Medium*, August 15, 2018. https://medium.com/trust-media-and-democracy/should-platforms-be-regulated-a-newsurvey-says-yes-2f3f4d0d1f00.

Gillespie, Tarleton. "Governance of and by Platforms." In *The SAGE Handbook of Social Media*, ed. Jean Burgess, Thomas Poell, and Alice E. Marwick, 254–78. Sage, 2017.

———. "The Politics of 'Platforms.'" *New Media & Society* 12, no. 3 (2010): 347–64.

Gingras, Richard. "Helping Local News Thrive." *Google* (blog), February 24, 2014. https://news.googleblog.com/2014/02/helping-local-news-thrive.html.

———. "Labeling Fact-Check Articles in Google News." *Google* (blog), October 13, 2016. https://blog.google/outreach-initiatives/google-news-initiative/labeling-fact-check-articles-google-news/.

———. "Setting the Record Straight on News." *Google* (blog), June 26, 2020. https://blog.google/outreach-initiatives/google-news-initiative/setting-record-straight-news/.

Ginsburg, Jane C. "Copyright and Control Over New Technologies of Dissemination." In *Law and Society Approaches to Cyberspace*, 385–419. Routledge, 2017.

Glaser, Mark. "Google News to Publishers: Let's Make Love Not War." *Mediashift*, February 4, 2010. http://mediashift.org/2010/02/google-news-to-publishers-lets-make-love-not-war035/.

Goffey, Andrew. "Algorithm." In *Software Studies: A Lexicon*, ed. M. Fuller, 15–20. MIT Press, 2008.

BIBLIOGRAPHY

Golder, Joe. "Google's News Showcase Teaches Executives What Not to Do." *Forbes*, October 25, 2021. https://www.forbes.com/sites/zengernews/2021/10/25/googles-news-showcase-teaches-executives-what-not-to-do/.

Goldman, Eric. "Search Engine Bias and the Demise of Search Engine Utopianism." *Yale Journal of Law & Technology* 8 (2005): 188.

Goldman, David. "Worst Year for Jobs Since '45." CNN, January 9, 2009. https://money.cnn.com/2009/01/09/news/economy/jobs_december/.

Gorwa, Robert. "What Is Platform Governance?" *Information, Communication & Society* 22, no. 6 (2019): 854–71.

Granger, Jacob. "Google News Showcase: Is It Viable for the Smallest of Newsrooms?" *journalism.co.uk*, July 7, 2022. https://www.journalism.co.uk/news/google-news-showcase-is-it-viable-for-the-smallest-of-newsrooms-/s2/a944419/.

Granka, Laura A. "The Politics of Search: A Decade Retrospective." *Information Society* 26, no. 5 (2010): 364–74.

Grant, Nico, and Cade Metz. "A New Chat Bot Is a 'Code Red' for Google's Search Business." *New York Times*, December 21, 2022. https://www.nytimes.com/2022/12/21/technology/ai-chatgpt-google-search.html.

Grant, Nico, and Katie Robertson, "Google's A.I. Search Leaves Publishers Scrambling." *New York Times*, June 1, 2024. https://www.nytimes.com/2024/06/01/technology/google-ai-search-publishers.html.

Groklaw. "An Update on the Copiepresse/Google Dispute—ACAP Enters the Picture." *Groklaw*, October 16, 2008. http://www.groklaw.net/articlebasic.php?story=20081016024354825.

Grove, Steve. "Our Next Steps in the Google News Initiative." *Medium*, March 20, 2018. https://medium.com/@grove/our-next-steps-in-the-google-news-initiative-ec5b7fe4dcb8.

Gunther, Marc. "Tech Execs Get Grilled Over China Business." CNN, February 16, 2006. https://money.cnn.com/2006/02/15/news/international/pluggedin_fortune/index.htm.

Haggart, Blayne, and Clara Iglesias Keller. "Democratic Legitimacy in Global Platform Governance." *Telecommunications Policy* 45, no. 6 (2021): 102152.

Hågvar, Yngve Benestad. "Labelling Journalism: The Discourse of Sectional Paratexts in Print and Online Newspapers." *Nordicom Review* 33, no. 2 (2012): 27–42.

Haim, Mario, Andreas Graefe, and Hans-Bernd Brosius. "Burst of the Filter Bubble? Effects of Personalization on the Diversity of Google News." *Digital Journalism* 6, no. 3 (2018): 330–43.

BIBLIOGRAPHY

Halavais, Alex. "Part 3. The Rise of Do-It-Yourself Journalism After September 11." Pew Research Center, September 5, 2002. http://www.pewinternet.org/2002/09/05/one-year-later-september-11-and-the-internet/.

Hallin, Daniel C. "Field Theory, Differentiation Theory, and Comparative Media Research." In *Bourdieu and the Journalistic Field*, ed. ed. Rodney Benson and Eric Neveu, 224–43. Polity, 2005.

Hallin, Daniel C., and Paolo Mancini. *Comparing Media Systems: Three Models of Media and Politics*. Cambridge University Press, 2004.

"Hamburg Declaration Regarding Intellectual Property Rights." FIEG, June 26, 2009. https://www.fieg.it/upload/documenti_allegati/Hamburg_Declaration.pdf.

Hammonds, Keith H. "How Google grows . . . and grows . . . and grows." *Fast Company*, March 31, 2003. https://www.fastcompany.com/46495/how-google-growsand-growsand-grows.

Hartley, Sarah. "An Innovation Challenge for Europe." *Google* (blog), April 7, 2022. https://blog.google/outreach-initiatives/google-news-initiative/innovation-challenge-europe/.

Hebbard, D. B. "German Publishers 'Bow to Pressure,' Will Allow Google to Display Search Result Snippets." *Talking New Media*, October 23, 2014. http://www.talkingnewmedia.com/2014/10/23/german-publishers-bow-to-pressure-will-allow-google-to-display-search-result-snippets/.

Helberger, Natali. "On the Democratic Role of News Recommenders." *Digital Journalism* 7, no. 8 (2019): 993–1012.

Helberger, Natali, Kari Karppinen, and Lucia D'acunto. "Exposure Diversity as a Design Principle for Recommender Systems." *Information, Communication & Society* 21, no. 2 (2018): 191–207.

Helmore, Edward. "Google Made $4.7bn from News Sites in 2018, Study Claims." *Guardian*, June 10, 2019. https://www.theguardian.com/technology/2019/jun/10/google-news-revenue-2018-new-study.

Hern, Alex. "News Corp Agrees deal with Google Over Payments for Journalism." *Guardian*, February 17, 2021. https://www.theguardian.com/media/2021/feb/17/news-corp-agrees-deal-with-google-over-payments-for-journalism.

Holt, Kris. "Facebook Can't Find Enough Local News for Its Local News Service." *Endadget*, March 18, 2019. https://www.engadget.com/2019-03-18-facebook-local-news-availability-today-in-journalism-project.html.

BIBLIOGRAPHY

Hu, Krystal. "ChatGPT Sets Record for Fastest-Growing User Base—Analyst Note." Reuters, February 2, 2023. https://www.reuters.com/technology/chatgpt-sets-record-fastest-growing-user-base-analyst-note-2023-02-01/.

Hugenholtz, P. Bernt. "Copyright and Freedom of Expression in Europe." In *Expanding the Boundaries of Intellectual Property: Innovation Policy for the Knowledge Society*, ed. Rochelle Cooper Dreyfuss, Diane Leenheer Zimmerman, and Harry First, 343–63. Oxford University Press, 2001.

Ingram, Mathew. "External Traffic to Spanish News Sites Plummets After Google Move." *Gigaom*, December 16, 2014. https://gigaom.com/2014/12/16/traffic-to-spanish-news-publishers-plummets-after-google-move/.

Isaac, Mike. "Facebook 'Trending' List Skewed by Individual Judgment, Not Institutional Bias." *New York Times*, May 20, 2016. https://www.nytimes.com/2016/05/21/technology/facebook-trending-list-skewed-by-individual-judgment-not-institutional-bias.html.

Isaac, Mike, Daisuke Wakabayashi, Damien Cave, and Edmund Lee. "Facebook Blocks News in Australia, Diverging with Google on Proposed Law." *New York Times*, February 17, 2021. https://www.nytimes.com/2021/02/17/technology/facebook-google-australia-news.html.

Isbell, Kimberley. "The Rise of the News Aggregator: Legal Implications and Best Practices." *Citizen Media Law*.

Jarboe, Greg. "YouTube Algorithm: 7 Key Findings You Must Know." *Search Engine Journal*, March 13, 2019. https://www.searchenginejournal.com/youtube-algorithm-findings/296291/.

Jenkins, Henry, and Mark Deuze. "Convergence Culture." *Convergence* 14, no. 1 (2008): 5–12.

Jeon, Doh-Shin, and Nikrooz Nasr. "News Aggregators and Competition Among Newspapers on the Internet." *American Economic Journal: Microeconomics* 8, no. 4 (2016): 91–114.

Jiang, Min. "The Business and Politics of Search Engines: A Comparative Study of Baidu and Google's Search Results of Internet Events in China." *New Media & Society* 16, no. 2 (2014): 212–33.

Johnson, Bobbie. "Murdoch Could Block Google Searches Entirely." *Guardian*, November 9, 2009. https://www.theguardian.com/media/2009/nov/09/murdoch-google.

Johnson, Cathryn, Timothy J. Dowd, and Cecilia L. Ridgeway. "Legitimacy as a Social Process." *Annual Review of Sociology* 32 (2006): 53–78.

Kahney, Leander. "Who Said the Web Fell Apart?" *Wired*, September 12, 2001. https://www.wired.com/2001/09/who-said-the-web-fell-apart/.

Kalogeropoulos, Antonis, Federica Cherubini, and Nic Newman. "The Future of Online News Video." *Digital News Project* (2016).

Kalogeropoulos, Antonis, and Rasmus Kleis Nielsen. "Investing in Online Video News: A Cross-National Analysis of News Organizations' Enterprising Approach to Digital Media." *Journalism Studies* 19, no. 15 (2018): 2207–24.

Keith, Susan. "Searching for News Headlines: Connections Between Unresolved Hyperlinking Issues and a New Battle Over Copyright Online." In *Die wachsende Macht von Suchmaschinen im Internet/The Power of Search Engines*, ed. Marcel Machill and Markus Beiler, 202–19. Herbert von Halem, 2007.

Kincaid, Jason. "Google Video Prepares to Enter the Deadpool for Good." *TechCrunch*, April 15, 2011. https://techcrunch.com/2011/04/15/google-video-prepares-to-enter-the-deadpool-for-good/.

Kiss, Jemima. "My Taptu App Takes the Visual News Aggregator to Mobile." *Guardian*, November 9, 2010. https://www.theguardian.com/technology/pda/2010/nov/09/taptu-app-aggregator.

Kleis Nielsen, Rasmus, and Sarah Anne Ganter. "Dealing with Digital Intermediaries: A Case Study of the Relations Between Publishers and Platforms." *New Media & Society* 20, no. 4 (2018): 1600–17.

Kosslyn, Justin, and Cong Yu. "Fact Check Now Available in Google Search and News Around the World." *Google* (blog), April 7, 2017. https://www.blog.google/products/search/fact-check-now-available-google-search-and-news-around-world/.

Kramer, Staci. "AP's Curley, Google's Mayer Talk Aggregation—Carefully; AP-Google Deal?" *Gigaom*, April 25, 2006. https://gigaom.com/2006/04/25/nab-aps-curley-googles-mayer-talk-aggregation-carefully-ap-google-deal/.

——. "Google News Creator Watches Portal Quiet Critics with 'Best News' Webby." *OJR*, September 25, 2003. http://www.ojr.org/ojr/kramer/1064449044.php.

——. "Parsing & Breaking Down the AP-Google Agreement." *Gigaom*, August 2, 2006b. https://gigaom.com/2006/08/02/parsing-breaking-down-the-ap-google-agreement/.

Krazit, Tom. "AP, Yahoo Strike Content Deal; AP, Google Still Talking." *CNET*, February, 2010. https://www.cnet.com/news/ap-yahoo-strike-content-deal-ap-google-still-talking/.

BIBLIOGRAPHY

———. "Google, AP Reach Deal for Google News Content." *CNET*, August 30, 2010. https://www.cnet.com/news/google-ap-reach-deal-for-google-news-content/.

Krebs, Isabelle, Philipp Bachmann, Gabriele Siegert, Rafael Schwab, and Raphael Willi. "Non-journalistic Competitors of News Media Brands on Google and YouTube: From Solid Competition to a Liquid Media Market." *Journal of Media Business Studies* 18, no. 1 (2021): 27–44.

"Law on Copyright and Related Rights." *Federal Law Gazette*, 2013. https://www.gesetze-im-internet.de/englisch_urhg/englisch_urhg.html.

Lee, Angela M., and Hsiang Iris Chyi. "The Rise of Online News Aggregators: Consumption and Competition." *International Journal on Media Management* 17, no. 1 (2015): 3–24.

Lenssen, Philipp. "Google News Adds Most Popular, Recommended." *Blogoscoped*, January 21, 2006. http://blogoscoped.com/archive/2006-01-21-n38.html.

Lewinski, John Scott. "Medical Experts Employ Social Media to Battle Coronavirus." *Forbes*, February 6, 2020. https://www.forbes.com/sites/johnscottlewinski/2020/02/06/medical-experts-employ-social-media-to-battle-coronavirus/.

Liu, Yangyue. "The Rise of China and Global Internet Governance." *China Media Research* 8, no. 2 (2012).

Loecherbach, Felicia, Judith Moeller, Damian Trilling, and Wouter van Atteveldt. "The Unified Framework of Media Diversity: A Systematic Literature Review." *Digital Journalism* 8, no. 5 (2020): 605–42.

Longpre, Shayne, Robert Mahari, Ariel Lee, Campbell Lund, et al. "Consent in Crisis: The Rapid Decline of the AI Data Commons." *Data Provenance Initiative*, 2024. https://www.dataprovenance.org/Consent_in_Crisis.pdf.

Lubianco, Júlio. "Big Tech Companies Unite Against Payment for News Content in Brazil; Journalists Are Divided." *LatAm Journalism Review*, March 30, 2022. https://latamjournalismreview.org/articles/big-techs-payment-news-brazil/.

Ma, Olivia. "A Call to News Publishers: How to Share Your Video." *Google* (blog), June 28, 2009. https://news.googleblog.com/2009/06/call-to-news-publishers-how-to-share.html.

MacKinnon, Rebecca, Elonnai Hickok, Allon Bar, and Hae-in Lim. *Fostering Freedom Online: The Role of Internet Intermediaries*. UNESCO, 2015.

BIBLIOGRAPHY

Mahone, Jessica, Qun Wang, Philip Napoli, Matthew Weber, and Katie McCollough. "Who's Producing Local Journalism? Assessing Journalistic Output Across Different Outlet Types." DeWitt Wallace Center for Media & Democracy Report, 2019. https://dewitt.sanford.duke.edu/wp-content/uploads/2019/08/Whos-Producing-Local-Journalism_FINAL.pdf.

Makhortykh, Mykola, Aleksandra Urman, and Roberto Ulloa. "Detecting Race and Gender Bias in Visual Representation of AI on Web Search Engines." In *Advances in Bias and Fairness in Information Retrieval: Second International Workshop on Algorithmic Bias in Search and Recommendation, BIAS 2021, Lucca, Italy, April 1, 2021, Proceedings*, 36–50. Springer, 2021.

Margolis, Michael, and David Resnick. *Politics as Usual*. Vol. 6. Sage, 2000.

Masnick, Mike. "A Look at Rupert Murdoch's History of Internet Failures." *Techdirt*, December 21, 2010. https://www.techdirt.com/articles/20101219/22155912331/look-rupert-murdochs-history-internet-failures.shtml.

———. "Study of Spain's 'Google Tax' on News Shows How Much Damage It Has Done." *Techdirt*, July 29, 2015. https://www.techdirt.com/2015/07/29/study-spains-google-tax-news-shows-how-much-damage-it-has-done/.

May, Carl, and Tracy Finch. "Implementing, Embedding, and Integrating Practices: An Outline of Normalization Process Theory." *Sociology* 43, no. 3 (2009): 535–54.

Mazotte, Natalia. "Newspapers in Brazil Say Their Boycott Turned Google News 'Deficient,' Reiterate Request for Payment." *LatAm Journalism Review*, October 22, 2012. https://latamjournalismreview.org/articles/newspapers-in-brazil-say-their-boycott-turned-google-news-deficient-reiterate-request-for-payment/.

McCarthy, Caroline. "Google Reveals Payment Deal with AP." *CNET*, August 4, 2006. https://www.cnet.com/uk/news/google-reveals-payment-deal-with-ap/.

"Measures for the Administration of Internet Information Services." CECC, September 25, 2000. https://www.cecc.gov/resources/legal-provisions/measures-for-the-administration-of-internet-information-services-cecc.

Mehta, Yogita. "Google News Highlights Unique Content with Editors' Picks." *Google* (blog), August 4, 2011. https://news.googleblog.com/2011/08/google-news-highlights-unique-content.html.

Meikle, Graham, and Sherman Young. *Media Convergence: Networked Digital Media in Everyday Life*. Macmillan International Higher Education, 2011.

BIBLIOGRAPHY

Metz, Cade. "Google Pockets Half of 'Unlicensed' News Dollars, Says Study." *Register*, December 1, 2009. https://www.theregister.com/2009/12/01/fair_trade_consortium_news_study/.

———. "Google Redirects China to Uncensored Hong Kong Servers." *Register*, March 22, 2010. https://www.theregister.co.uk/2010/03/22/google_redirects_china_to_hong_kon.

Meyer, David. "German Parliament Passes 'Google Tax' Law, Forcing Royalty Payments for News Snippets." *Gigaom*, March 1, 2013. https://gigaom.com/2013/03/01/german-parliament-passes-google-tax-law-forcing-royalty-payments-for-news-snippets/.

Mikkelson, David. "Palestinians Dancing in the Street." Snopes.com, September 23, 2001. https://www.snopes.com/fact-check/false-footaging/.

Miller, Robin. "From Niche Site to News Portal: How Slashdot Survived the Attack." *Online Journalism Review* 14 (2001).

Miners, Zack. "Facebook Will Be Mostly Video in 5 Years, Zuckerberg says." *PC World*, November 6, 2014. https://www.pcworld.com/article/2844852/facebook-will-be-mostly-video-in-5-years-zuckerberg-says.html.

Mitchell, Amy, J. Baxter Oliphant and Elisa Shearer. "Americans Are Turning to Media, Government and Others for COVID-19 News." Pew Research Center, April 29, 2020. https://www.journalism.org/2020/04/29/1-americans-are-turning-to-media-government-and-others-for-covid-19-news/.

Mitchell, Amy, Jesse Holcomb, Kenneth Olmstead, and Nancy Vogt. "Developments in Online News Video Content." Pew Research Center, March 26, 2014. https://www.pewresearch.org/journalism/2014/03/26/developments-in-online-news-video-content/.

Molyneux, L., and R. R. Mourão. "Political Journalists' Normalization of Twitter: Interaction and New Affordances." *Journalism Studies* 20, no. 2 (2019): 248–66. https://doi.org/10.1080/1461670X.2017.1370978.

Mortaigne, Véronique. "Zelnik Report Advocates a 'Google Tax.'" *Lemonade*, July 1, 2010. https://www.lemonde.fr/technologies/article/2010/01/07/le-rapport-zelnik-prone-une-taxe-google_1288659_651865.html.

Moses, Lucia. "For News Publishers, Smart Speakers Are the Hot New Platform." *Digiday*, July 23, 2018. https://digiday.com/media/news-publishers-smart-speakers-hot-new-platform/.

Mui, Ylan. "Congress Takes on Big Tech in Hearing on Anti-competitive Behavior Among Digital Giants." CNBC, June 10, 2019. https://www.cnbc.com/2019/06/10/congressional-hearingtakes-on-antitrust-behavior-among-digital-giants.html.

BIBLIOGRAPHY

Muskita, Putra. "Indonesia to Require Google, Meta to Compensate News Publishers." *Tech in Asia*, February 20, 2024. https://www.techinasia.com/indonesia-require-google-meta-compensate-news-publishers.

Napoli, Philip M. "Deconstructing the Diversity Principle." *Journal of Communication* 49, no. 4 (1999): 7–34.

———. "Exposure Diversity Reconsidered." *Journal of Information Policy* 1 (2011): 246–59.

———. "Evolutionary Theories of Media Institutions and Their Responses to New Technologies." In *Communication Theory: A Reader*, ed. Linda Costigan Lederman, 315–29. Kendall/Hunt, 1998.

———. "Requiem for the Long Tail: Towards a Political Economy of Content Aggregation and Fragmentation." *International Journal of Media & Cultural Politics* 12, no. 3 (2016): 341–56.

———. "Social Media and the Public Interest: Governance of News Platforms in the Realm of Individual and Algorithmic Gatekeepers." *Telecommunications Policy* 39, no. 9 (2015): 751–60.

———. *Social Media and the Public Interest: Media Regulation in the Disinformation Age*. Columbia University Press, 2019.

———. "The Symbolic Uses of Platforms: The Politics of Platform Governance in the United States." *Journal of Digital Media & Policy* 12, no. 2 (2021): 215–30.

Napoli, Philip M., and Robyn Caplan. "Why Media Companies Insist They're Not Media Companies, Why They're Wrong, and Why It Matters." *First Monday* 22, no. 5 (2017). https://doi.org/10.5210/fm.v22i5.7051.

"National Security Commission on Artificial Intelligence." NSCAI, 2021. https://assets.foleon.com/eu-central-1/de-uploads-7e3kk3/48187/nscai_full_report_digital.04d6b124173c.pdf.

Nechushtai, Efrat., and Seth C. Lewis. "What Kind of News Gatekeepers Do We Want Machines to Be? Filter Bubbles, Fragmentation, and the Normative Dimensions of Algorithmic Recommendations." *Computers in Human Behavior* 90 (2019): 298–307.

Netanel, Neil. *Copyright: What Everyone Needs to Know*. Oxford University Press, 2018.

Ng, Alfred. "Google, Facebook and Amazon Spending More Than Ever Lobbying Congress." *CNET*, January 23, 2019. https://www.cnet.com/news/google-facebook-amazon-spending-more-than-ever-lobbying-congress/.

Nguyễn, Trân. "California Bill Requiring Big Tech to Pay for News Gains Momentum." AP, June 1, 2023. https://apnews.com/article/google-meta

BIBLIOGRAPHY

-big-tech-journalism-fee-california-lawmakers-ec3a926252f59e589e5d48 b067c7904e.
NPC. "Cybersecurity Law of the People's Republic of China." National People's Congress of the People's Republic of China, 2016. http://www.npc.gov.cn/npc/xinwen/2016-11/07/content_2001605.htm.
Nystedt, Dan. "Update: Google News, YouTube Blocked in China Amid Tibet Riots." *Infoworld*, March 17, 2008. https://www.infoworld.com/article/2334051/update-google-news-youtube-blocked-in-china-amid-tibet-riots.html.
Oberbeck, Kay. "A Law to the Detriment of All." Google, August 21, 2012. https://plus.google.com/+KayOberbeck.
O'Brien, Frederick. "What Newspapers Can Teach Us About Web Design." *Smashing Magazine*, November 8, 2019. https://www.smashingmagazine.com/2019/11/newspapers-teach-web-design/.
Olmedo, Míchel, and José Luis Caballero. "A Battle Without Winners, as Spain Examines Early Results of Its 'Google Tax.'" *Ecija*, 2015. https://ecija.com/sala-de-prensa/a-battle-without-winners-as-spain-examines-early-results-of-its-google-tax-2/.
Outing, Steve. "Where's the Money?" *Editor & Publisher* 12, no. 7 (1996): 81, 341.
Owen, Laura H. "News Apps Are Making a Comeback. More Young Americans Are Paying for News. 2017 Is Weird." *Nieman Lab*, June 21, 2017. http://www.niemanlab.org/2017/06/news-apps-are-making-a-comeback-more-young-americans-are-paying-for-news-2017-is-weird/.
Page, Larry, and Sergey Brin. "2004 founders' IPO letter." Google, 2004. https://abc.xyz/investor/founders-letters/2004-ipo-letter/#_ga=2.16562 6872.610004439.1532311821-929489725.1521479135.
Page, Lawrence, Sergey Brin, Rajeev Motwani, and Terry Winograd. "The PageRank Citation Ranking: Bringing Order to the Web." *Stanford InfoLab*, 1999. http://ilpubs.stanford.edu:8090/422/1/1999-66.pdf.
Paka, Anand. "Redesigning Google News for Everyone." *Google* (blog), June 27, 2017. https://www.blog.google/outreach-initiatives/google-news-initiative/redesigning-google-news-everyone/.
Parasie, Sylvain, and Eric Dagiral. "Data-Driven Journalism and the Public Good: 'Computer-Assisted-Reporters' and 'Programmer-Journalists' in Chicago." *New Media & Society* 15, no. 6 (2013): 853–71.
Parfeni, Lucian. "Google News Gets a Most Shared Section." *Softpedia*, December 1, 2010. https://news.softpedia.com/news/Google-News-Gets-a-Most-Shared-Section-169797.shtml.

BIBLIOGRAPHY

Paterson, Chris A. "Convergence in the News Wholesalers: Trends in International News Agencies." In *Making Online News: Newsroom Ethnography in the Second Decade of Internet Journalism*, ed. David Domingo and Chris A. Paterson, 129–40. Peter Lang, 2011.

Paterson, Chris A., and David Domingo, eds. *Making Online News: The Ethnography of New Media Production*. Vol. 1. Peter Lang, 2008.

Paul, Kari. "Zuckerberg Defends Facebook as Bastion of 'Free Expression' in Speech." *Guardian*, October 17, 2019. https://www.theguardian.com/technology/2019/oct/17/mark-zuckerberg-facebook-free-expression-speech.

Peil, Corinna, and Sergio Sparviero. "Media Convergence Meets Deconvergence." In *Media Convergence and Deconvergence*, 3–30. Palgrave Macmillan, 2017.

Perez, Juan Carlos. "AFP-Google Settlement Leaves Open Questions." *Infoworld*, April 6, 2007. https://www.infoworld.com/article/2662703/techology-business/afp-google-settlement-leaves-open-questions.html.

———. "AP Renews Licensing Deal with Yahoo, Not Yet with Google." *Computer World*, February 1, 2010. https://www.computerworld.com/article/2761104/ap-renews-licensing-deal-with-yahoo--not-yet-with-google.html.

Pfanner, Eric. "French Publishers Forge Deal with Google, Breaking Ranks with Europe." *New York Times*, February 17, 2013. https://www.nytimes.com/2013/02/18/technology/a-first-step-on-continent-for-google-on-use-of-content.html.

———. "A Google Worry Recedes, for Now, as Italy Ends Investigation Into News Service." *New York Times*, January 17, 2011. https://www.nytimes.com/2011/01/18/technology/18iht-google18.html.

Plantin, Jean-Christophe, Carl Lagoze, Paul N. Edwards, and Christian Sandvig. "Infrastructure Studies Meet Platform Studies in the age of Google and Facebook." *New Media & Society* 20, no. 1 (2018): 293–310.

Pichai, Sundar. "How We're Helping Get Vaccines to More People." *Google* (blog), January 25, 2021. https://blog.google/technology/health/vaccines-how-were-helping/.

Potts, Kevin. *Web Design and Marketing Solutions for Business Websites*. Apress, 2007.

Rabenstein, Gerrit. "Google News Remains an Open Platform for All German Publishers." *Google* (blog), June 21, 2013. https://germany.googleblog.com/2013/06/google-news-bleibt-offene-plattform-fuer-verlage.html.

Raj, Sushant. "Krishna Bharat—the Indian guy Who Invented Google News." *Medium*, January 17, 2019. https://medium.com/@sushantraj436/krishna-bharat-the-indian-guy-who-invented-google-news-8b6caf606468.

BIBLIOGRAPHY

Rappoport, Paul N. "The Internet and the Demand for News." *Prometheus* 20, no. 3 (2002): 255–62.

Rashidian, Nushin. "Platforms and Publishers: The Great Pandemic Funding Push." *Columbia Journalism Review*, December 17, 2020. https://www.cjr.org/tow_center_reports/platforms-publishers-pandemic-funding-news.php.

Rashidian, Nushin, George Civeris, Pete Brown, Emily Bell, and Abigail Hartstone. "Platforms and Publishers: The End of an Era." *Columbia Journalism Review*, November 22, 2019. https://www.cjr.org/tow_center_reports/platforms-and-publishers-end-of-an-era.php.

Rashidian, Nushin, Pete Brown, Elizabeth Hansen, Emily Bell, Jonathan Albright, and Abigail Hartstone. "Friend and Foe: The Platform Press at the Heart of Journalism." *Columbia Journalism Review*, June 14, 2018. https://www.cjr.org/tow_center_reports/the-platform-press-at-the-heart-of-journalism.php.

Reid, Liz. "Generative AI in Search: Let Google Do the Searching for You." *Google* (blog), May 14, 2024, https://blog.google/products/search/generative-ai-google-search-may-2024/.

Reilly, Liam. "Google Agrees to First-in-the-Nation Deal to Fund California Newsrooms, but Journalists Are Calling It a Disaster." CNN, August 22, 2024. https://www.cnn.com/2024/08/21/media/google-california-pay-newsrooms-journalists-content-deal/index.html.

Ricknäs, Mikael. "Belgian Newspapers Ask Google for $77.5 Million in Damages." *PC World*, May 28, 2008. https://www.pcworld.com/article/146380/article.html.

Robinson, Sue. "'Journalism as process': The Organizational Implications of Participatory Online News." *Journalism & Communication Monographs* 13, no. 3 (2011): 137–210.

Rogers, Simon. "Turning Official Figures Into Understandable Graphics, at the Press of a Button." *Guardian*, December 18, 2008. https://www.theguardian.com/help/insideguardian/2008/dec/18/unemploymentdata.

Rogers, Tony. "6 Ways Reporters Can Avoid Conflicts of Interest." *ThoughtCo*, February 13, 2019. https://www.thoughtco.com/avoid-conflicts-of-interest-2073885.

Roth, Emma. "OpenAI Will Use Associated Press News Stories to Train Its Models." *Verge*, July 13, 2023. https://www.theverge.com/2023/7/13/23793810/openai-associated-press-ai-models.

Sadlier, Allison. "Americans Are Streaming 8 Hours a Day During Coronavirus Lockdown." *New York Post*, April 14, 2020. https://nypost.com

BIBLIOGRAPHY

/2020/04/14/average-american-streaming-content-8-hours-a-day-during-covid-19-according-to-new-research/.

Salinas, Sara. "Amazon's Ad Business Will Steal Market Share from Google This Year, Says eMarketer." CNBC, February 20, 2019. https://www.cnbc.com/2019/02/20/amazon-advertisingbusiness-stealing-market-share-from-google.html.

Saltmarsh, Matthew. "Murdoch Finalizes Paywall for Two British Papers." *New York Times*, March 26, 2010. https://www.nytimes.com/2010/03/27/business/media/27paper.html.

Saoji, Mayuresh. "Google News & Weather Now on the Play Store with a New Look." *Google* (blog), August 27, 2014. https://news.googleblog.com/2014/08/google-news-weather-now-on-play-store.html.

Sarno, David. "Murdoch Accuses Google of News 'Theft.'" *Los Angeles Times*, December 2, 2009. https://www.latimes.com/archives/la-xpm-2009-dec-02-la-fi-news-google2-2009dec02-story.html.

Sasseen, Jane, Kenny Olmstead, and Amy Mitchell. "Digital: By the numbers." Pew Research Center, March 18, 2013. http://www.stateofthemedia.org/2013/digital-as-mobile-grows-rapidly-the-pressures-on-news-intensify/digital-by-the-numbers/.

Satariano, Adam. "E.U. Agrees on Landmark Artificial Intelligence Rules." *New York Times*, December 8, 2023. https://www.nytimes.com/2023/12/08/technology/eu-ai-act-regulation.html.

Satariano, Adam, and Milan Schreuer. "Facebook's Mark Zuckerberg Gets an Earful from the E. U." *New York Times*, May 22, 2018. https://www.nytimes.com/2018/05/22/technology/facebook-eu-parliament-mark-zuckerberg.html.

Sayer, Peter. "Google Faces Broad Antitrust Investigation in Italy." *PC World*, September, 4, 2009. https://www.pcworld.com/article/171460/article.html.

Schechner, Sam. "Google Pledges to Negotiate Fair Licenses with French News Publishers." *Wall Street Journal*, June 21, 2022. https://www.wsj.com/articles/google-pledges-to-negotiate-fair-licenses-with-french-news-publishers-11655807346.

Schindler, Philipp. "The Google News Initiative: Building a Stronger Future for News." *Google* (blog), March 20, 2018. https://blog.google/outreach-initiatives/google-news-initiative/announcing-google-news-initiative/.

Schmidt, Eric. "Google Creates €60m Digital Publishing Innovation Fund to Support Transformative French Digital Publishing Initiatives." *Google*

BIBLIOGRAPHY

(blog), February 1, 2013. https://blog.google/topics/journalism-news/google-creates-60m-digital-publishing/.

Schonfeld, Erick. "The Times UK Lost 4 Million Readers to Its Paywall Experiment." *TechCrunch*, November 2, 2010. https://techcrunch.com/2010/11/02/times-paywall-4-million-readers/.

Schrage, Elliot. "Testimony of Google Inc." *New York Times*, 2006. http://www.nytimes.com/packages/pdf/business/GoogleStatement.pdf.

Schroeder, Roland, and Moritz Kralemann. "Journalism Ex Machina—Google News Germany and Its News Selection Processes." *Journalism Studies* 6, no. 2 (2005): 245–47.

Schudson, Michael. *Discovering the News: A Social History of American News papers*. Basic Books, 1981.

Schwartz, Jason. "Murdoch Embraces Liberal Approach to Curb Facebook, Google." *Politico*, May 18, 2018. https://www.politico.com/story/2018/05/18/rupert-murdoch-facebook-google-news-social-media-algorithm-596738.

Schweigert, Adam. "Towards a Better Definition of Curation in Journalism." *Adam Schweigert* (blog), June 14, 2012. https://adamschweigert.com/towards-a-better-definition-of-curation-in-journalism/.

Scolari, Carlos A. "Media Evolution." In *Mediated Communication*, 149–68. De Gruyter, 2018.

Scott, W. Richard. "Lords of the Dance: Professionals as Institutional Agents." *Organization Studies* 29, no. 2 (2008): 219–38.

"Senator Klobuchar and Representative Cicilline Introduce Legislation to Protect Journalism in the United States." March 10, 2021. https://www.klobuchar.senate.gov/public/index.cfm/2021/3/senator-klobuchar-and-representative-cicilline-introduce-legislation-to-protect-journalism-in-the-united-states.

Seward, Zachary M. "Google News Shines a Spotlight on 'In-Depth' Journalism." *Nieman Lab*, September 3, 2009. https://www.niemanlab.org/2009/09/google-news-shines-a-spotlight-on-in-depth-journalism/.

——. "What the Associated Press Is Saying to Google, Microsoft, and Yahoo." *Nieman Lab*, October 9, 2009. http://www.niemanlab.org/2009/10/what-the-associated-press-is-saying-to-google-microsoft-and-yahoo/.

Shakil, Ismail. "Canada Introduces Legislation to Compel Facebook, Google to Pay for News." *Reuters*, April 5, 2022. https://www.reuters.com/world/americas/canada-lays-out-details-proposed-law-compel-facebook-google-pay-news-2022-04-05/.

BIBLIOGRAPHY

Sherman, Chris. "Humans Do It Better: Inside the Open Directory Project." *Online* 24, no. 4 (2000): 43–48.

Sheth, Swapneel Kalpesh, Jonathan Schaffer Bell, Nipun Arora, and Gail E. Kaiser. "Towards Diversity in Recommendations Using Social Networks." Computer Science Technical Reports, Columbia University, 2011.

Shiels, Maggie. "Building Google News for Everyone—a Retrospective." *Google*, September 18, 2018. https://www.blog.google/products/news/building-google-news-everyone-retrospective/.

Shoemaker, Pamela J., and Stephen D. Reese. *Mediating the Message in the Twenty-First Century: A Media Sociology Perspective.* Routledge, 2013.

Shoemaker, Pamela J., and Timothy Vos. *Gatekeeping Theory.* Routledge, 2009.

Silverthorne, Sean. "Tracks of My Tears: Reconstructing Digital Music." Harvard Business School, November 30, 2009. https://hbswk.hbs.edu/item/tracks-of-my-tears-reconstructing-digital-music.

Singer, Jane B. "The Political J-Blogger: 'Normalizing' a New Media Form to Fit Old Norms and Practices." *Journalism* 6, no. 2 (2005): 173–98.

Singh, Jitendra V., David J. Tucker, and Robert J. House. "Organizational Legitimacy and the Liability of Newness." *Administrative Science Quarterly* (1986): 171–93.

Sjøvaag, Helle. "Media Diversity and the Global Superplayers: Operationalising Pluralism for a Digital Media Market." *Journal of Media Business Studies* 13, no. 3 (2016): 170–86.

Skyquest. "Global Online Video Platforms Market Drives Over 80% of Total Internet Traffic." Global News Wire, August 2, 2022. https://www.globenewswire.com/en/news-release/2022/08/02/2490661/0/en/Global-Online-Video-Platforms-Market-Drives-over-80-of-Total-Internet-Traffic-Skyquest-Technology.html.

Slawski, Bill. "Extracting Knowledge Base Facts for Entities from Sources Such as Wikipedia Titles and Infoboxes." *SEO by the Sea*, August 31, 2014. https://www.seobythesea.com/2014/08/extracting-facts-for-entities-from-sources/.

Slocum, Mac. "What Qualifies as a Spotlight Story on Google News? Here's a Few Clues." *Nieman Lab*, January 6, 2010. http://www.niemanlab.org/2010/01/what-qualifies-as-a-spotlight-story-on-google-news-heres-a-few-clues/.

Smith, Ben. "Project Strobe: Protecting Your Data, Improving Our Third-Party APIs, and Sunsetting Consumer Google+." *Google* (blog), October 8, 2018. https://www.blog.google/technology/safety-security/project-strobe/.

BIBLIOGRAPHY

Smith, Graham. "Copiepresse v Google—the Belgian Judgment Dissected." *Two Birds*, March 13, 2007. http://www.twobirds.com/en/news/articles/2007/copiepresse-v-google.

Smydra, David. "Recognizing Publishers' Standout Content in Google News." *Google* (blog), September 24, 2011. https://news.googleblog.com/2011/09/recognizing-publishers-standout-content.html.

"SPJ Code of Ethics." Society of Professional Journalists, September 6, 2014. https://www.spj.org/ethicscode.asp.

"South Africa to Probe Meta, Google Competition with News Publishers." Reuters, October 17, 2023. https://www.reuters.com/world/africa/south-africa-probe-meta-google-competition-with-news-publishers-2023-10-17/.

Statcounter. "Search Engine Market Share Worldwide." *Statcounter GlobalStats*, 2023. https://gs.statcounter.com/search-engine-market-share.

Statista. "Most Popular Video Content Type Worldwide in 4th Quarter 2022, by Weekly Usage Reach." *Statista*, 2020. https://www.statista.com/statistics/1254810/top-video-content-type-by-global-reach/.

Statt, Nick. "Facebook Strikes News Corp Deal to License News from Australian Media Outlets." *The Verge*, March 15, 2021. https://www.theverge.com/2021/3/15/22332658/facebook-news-corp-rupert-murdoch-deal-australia-sky-news.

Steen-Johnsen, Kari, Vilde Schanke Sundet, and Bernard Enjolras. "Theorizing Policy-Industry Processes: A Media Policy Field Approach." *European Journal of Communication* 34, no. 2 (2019): 190–204.

Sterling, Greg. "Germany Wants to Force Google to Pay License Fees for Links." *Search Engine Land*, August 22, 2012. https://searchengineland.com/germany-wants-to-force-google-to-pay-license-fees-for-links-131288.

———. "Google Gives Publishers New Content 'Showcase' on News, Search, Discover." *Search Engine Land*, October 1, 2020. https://searchengineland.com/google-gives-publishers-new-content-showcase-on-news-search-discover-341393.

———. "Google News Still Available in Spain Despite Closure Deadline." *Search Engine Land*, December 16, 2014. https://searchengineland.com/google-news-still-available-spain-despite-closure-deadline-210990.

Stier, Lauren. "Making Google News Work on Every Phone, Everywhere." *Google* (blog), September 10, 2018. https://www.blog.google/products/news/making-google-news-work-every-phone-everywhere/.

BIBLIOGRAPHY

Stinchcombe, Arthur L. *Constructing Social Theories*. University of Chicago Press, 1987.

"Stimulate Engage Innovate: Digital News Initiative Innovation Fund." Google, 2016. https://newsinitiative.withgoogle.com/dnifund/insights/2016-2017-dni-innovation-fund-report-available-now-download/.

Stolt, Kevin. "Extra! Extra! Google News Redesigned to Be More Customizable and Shareable." *Google* (blog), June 30, 2010. https://googleblog.blogspot.com/2010/06/extra-extra-google-news-redesigned-to.html.

Suchman, Mark C. "Managing Legitimacy: Strategic and Institutional Approaches." *Academy of Management Review* 20, no. 3 (1995): 571–610.

Sullivan, Danny. "AFP & Google Settle Over Google News Copyright Case." *Search Engine Land*, April 6, 2007. https://searchengineland.com/afp-google-settle-over-google-news-copyright-case-10926.

———. "Where's AP in Google News? Apparently in Limbo, as Contract Running Out." *Search Engine Land*, January 8, 2010. https://searchengineland.com/wheres-ap-in-google-news-33164.

———. "The Yahoo Directory—Once the Internet's Most Important Search Engine—Is to Close." *Search Engine Land*, September 26, 2014. https://searchengineland.com/yahoo-directory-close-204370.

Sundar, S. Shyam, and Sampada S. Marathe. "Personalization Versus Customization: The Importance of Agency, Privacy, and Power Usage." *Human Communication Research* 36, no. 3 (2010): 298–322.

Swisher, Kara. "Project Alesia: News Corp.'s Roman Battle Cry—Does That Cast Googlers as the Gauls?" December 23, 2009. https://allthingsd.com/20091223/project-alesia-news-corp-s-roman-battle-cry-does-that-cast-googlers-as-the-gauls/.

———. "What's Really Behind the Rope-a-Dope with Google and Microsoft? Here Are Five Possibilities!" November 24, 2009. http://kara.allthingsd.com/20091124/whats-really-behind-the-rupe-a-dope-with-google-and-microsoft-here-are-five-possibilities/.

Tandoc, Edson C., Jr., and Tim P. Vos. "The Journalist Is Marketing the News: Social Media in the Gatekeeping Process." *Journalism Practice* 10, no. 8 (2016): 950–66.

Tartakoff, Joseph. "Google News Stops Hosting New AP Content." *Gigaom*, January 8, 2010. https://gigaom.com/2010/01/08/419-google-stops-hosting-new-ap-content/.

Taylor, Catharine P. "Web Hits Rise." *Adage*, September 17, 2001. https://adage.com/article/news/web-hits-rise/53814.

BIBLIOGRAPHY

Thornton, Leslie-Jean, and Susan M. Keith. "From Convergence to Webvergence: Tracking the Evolution of Broadcast-Print Partnerships Through the Lens of Change Theory." *Journalism & Mass Communication Quarterly* 86, no. 2 (2009): 257–76.

Tobitt, Charlotte. "Times and Sunday Times Hit 500,000 Subscribers as Digital Outnumbers Print for First Time." *Press Gazette*, July 6, 2018. https://www.pressgazette.co.uk/times-and-sunday-times-hits-500000-subscribers-as-digital-outnumbers-print-for-first-time/.

Toor, Amar. "Google News Launches Fact Check Feature Ahead of Election Day." *The Verge*, October 14, 2016. http://www.theverge.com/2016/10/14/13283200/google-news-fact-check-election.

Towle, Chrissy. "These 25 Publishers Want to Know Their Communities." *Google*, November 16, 2021. https://blog.google/outreach-initiatives/google-news-initiative/innovation-challenge-publishers/.

Tracy, Marc. "Google Made $4.7 Billion from the News Industry in 2018, Study Says." *New York Times*, June 9, 2019. https://www.nytimes.com/2019/06/09/business/media/google-news-industry-antitrust.html.

Travis, Hannibal. "Opting Out of the Internet in the United States and the European Union: Copyright, Safe Harbors, and International Law." *Notre Dame Law Review* 84 (2008): 331.

Tremayne, Mark, Amy Schmitz Weiss, and Rosental Calmon Alves. "From Product to Service: The Diffusion of Dynamic Content in Online Newspapers." *Journalism & Mass Communication Quarterly* 84, no. 4 (2007): 825–39.

Trielli, Daniel, and Nicholas Diakopoulos. "Search as News Curator: The Role of Google in Shaping Attention to News Information." *Proceedings of the 2019 CHI Conference on Human Factors in Computing Systems* (2019): 1–15.

Turvill, William. "Why US Publishers Aren't Signing Up to Google News Showcase." *Press Gazette*, December 16, 2021. https://pressgazette.co.uk/google-news-showcase-us-launch/.

Unkel, Julian, and Alexander Haas. "The Effects of Credibility Cues on the Selection of Search Engine Results." *Journal of the Association for Information Science and Technology* 68, no. 8 (2017): 1850–62.

Upstill, Tystan. "The New Google News: AI Meets Human Intelligence." *Google* (blog), May 8, 2018. https://www.blog.google/products/news/new-google-news-ai-meets-human-intelligence/.

Urman, Aleksandra, Mykola Makhortykh, and Roberto Ulloa. "Auditing Source Diversity Bias in Video Search Results Using Virtual Agents." In *Companion Proceedings of the Web Conference 2021*, 232–36. 2021.

BIBLIOGRAPHY

US Department of the Interior. "Standards for Maintaining, Collecting, and Presenting Federal Data on Race and Ethnicity." https://www.doi.gov/pmb/eeo/directives/race-data.

Van Couvering, Elizabeth. "Navigational Media: The Political Economy of Online Traffic." In *The Political Economics of Media: The Transformation of the Global Media Industries*, ed. Dal Yong Jin and Dwayne Winseck, 183–200. Bloomsbury Academic, 2011.

Van Dijck, José. "Governing Digital Societies: Private Platforms, Public Values." *Computer Law & Security Review* 36 (2020): 105377.

———. "Seeing the Forest for the Trees: Visualizing Platformization and Its Governance." *New Media & Society* 23, no. 9 (2021): 2801–19.

Van Dijck, José, David Nieborg, and Thomas Poell. "Reframing Platform Power." *Internet Policy Review* 8, no. 2 (2019): 1–18.

Veale, Michael, and Reuben Binns. "Fairer Machine Learning in the Real World: Mitigating Discrimination Without Collecting Sensitive Data." *Big Data & Society* 4, no. 2 (2017): 2053951717743530.

Verney, Al. "Let's Work Together to Support Quality Journalism." *Google* (blog), April 28, 2015. https://europe.googleblog.com/2015/04/lets-work-together-to-support-quality.html.

Viana, Natalia. "Should Google Pay for News in Brazil? It's Complicated." *Nieman Lab*, June 2, 2022. https://www.niemanlab.org/2022/06/should-google-pay-for-news-in-brazil-its-complicated/.

Vieira, Alessandro. "Relatório do Grupo de Trabalho Aperfeiçoamento da Legislação Brasileira—Internet." *Senado Federal*, June 21, 2021. https://desinformante.com.br/wp-content/uploads/2022/03/PL-Fake-News_Parecer-Substitutivo-2022_v6.pdf.

Vincent, James. "Google News Gets More Personal with Desktop Redesign." *The Verge*, June 22, 2022. https://www.theverge.com/2022/6/22/23178163/google-news-desktop-redesign-personal-local-content.

———. "This Is What Google Says Search Will Look Like Under EU Copyright Laws." *The Verge*, January 17, 2019. https://www.theverge.com/2019/1/17/18186879/google-eu-copyright-laws-search-news-link-tax.

Vos, Tim P., and Frank Michael Russell. "Theorizing Journalism's Institutional Relationships: An Elaboration of Gatekeeping Theory." *Journalism Studies* 20, no. 16 (2019): 2331–48.

Vranica, Suzanne, and Jack Marshall. "Plummeting Newspaper Ad Revenue Sparks New Wave of Changes." *Wall Street Journal*, October 20, 2016. https://www.wsj.com/articles/plummeting-newspaper-ad-revenue-sparks-new-wave-of-changes-1476955801.

BIBLIOGRAPHY

Walter, Jan D. "Brazil's Papers Without Google News." *DW*, October 24, 2012. https://www.dw.com/en/brazils-papers-without-google-news/a-16326960.
Wang, Qun. "A Complicated Picture: Media Diversity in the Case of Google's Video Search During the Pandemic." *Internet Policy Review* 12, no. 4 (2023): 1–32.
——. "Differentiation and De-differentiation: The Evolving Power Dynamics Between News Industry and Tech Industry." *Journalism & Mass Communication Quarterly* 97, no. 2 (2020): 509–27.
——. "Dimensional Field Theory: The Adoption of Audience Metrics in the Journalistic Field and Cross-Field Influences." *Digital Journalism* 6, no. 4 (2018): 472–91.
——. "Normalization and Differentiation in Google News: A Multi-Method Analysis of the World's Largest News Aggregator." PhD diss., Rutgers University. Publication no. 27672379, ProQuest Dissertations Publishing.
——. "Participatory Journalism in the Chinese Context: Understanding Journalism as Process in China's Participatory Culture." *Journalism* 18, no. 4 (2017): 501–17.
Wang, Qun, Philip M. Napoli, and Yi Ma. "Problems and Solutions for American Political Coverage: Journalistic Self-Critique in the Wake of the 2016 Presidential Election." *Journalism Practice* 12, no. 10 (2018): 1241–58.
Wang, Qun, and Susan Keith. "News Aggregators and Copyright in the European Union and the United States in the Digital Age: Evolution, Comparisons, and Implications." *First Monday*, 2021.
Wang, Qun, and Vikki Katz. "Ethnic Digital Media as Agenda Setters and Agenda Marketers: The Case of WXC and the *Jimmy Kimmel Live!* Controversy." In *Ethnic Media in the Digital Age*, ed. Sherry S. Yu and Matthew D. Matsaganispp, 23–32. Routledge, 2018.
Wang, Shan. "Google Announces a $300M 'Google News Initiative.'" *Nieman Lab*, March 20, 2018. http://www.niemanlab.org/2018/03/google-announces-a-300m-google-news-initiative-though-this-isnt-about-giving-out-grants-directly-to-newsrooms-like-it-does-in-europe/.
Watanabe, Kohei. "The Western Perspective in Yahoo! News and Google News: Quantitative Analysis of Geographic Coverage of Online News." *International Communication Gazette* 75, no. 2 (2013): 141–56.
Weigle, Eric. "Credit Where Credit Is Due." *Google* (blog), November 16, 2010. https://news.googleblog.com/2010/11/credit-where-credit-is-due.html.
Weissbrot, Alison. "Daytime Is Streaming Time: TV Viewing Habits in the Time of COVID-19." *Ad Exchanger*, April 9, 2020. https://www.adex

changer.com/tv-and-video/daytime-is-streaming-time-tv-viewing-habits-in-the-time-of-covid-19/.
Welch, Chris. "Google Begins Shutting Down Its Failed Google⁺ Social Network." *The Verge*, April 2, 2019. https://www.theverge.com/2019/4/2/18290637/google-plus-shutdown-consumer-personal-account-delete.
———. "Google Ends Standoff with French Publishers, Commits to €60 Million 'Innovation' Fund." *The Verge*, February 1, 2013. https://www.theverge.com/2013/2/1/3941854/google-ends-standoff-french-news-sites-digital-publishing-innovation-fund.
Whetstone, Rachel. "About the Google News Case in Belgium." *Google* (blog), September 2006. https://googleblog.blogspot.com/2006/09/about-google-news-case-in-belgium.html.
Whitney, D. Charles, Marilyn Fritzler, Steven Jones, Sharon Mazzarella, and Lana Rakow. "Geographic and Source Biases in Network Television News 1982–1984." *Journal of Broadcasting & Electronic Media* 33, no. 2 (1989): 159–74.
Wiggins, Richard W. "The Effects of September 11 on the Leading Search Engine." *First Monday* 7, no. 10 (2001).
Wohlsen, Marcus. "Spain's Google News Shutdown Is a Silly Victory for Publishers." *Wired*, December 16, 2014. https://www.wired.com/2014/12/google-news-shutdown-spain-empty-victory-publishers/.
Wojazer, Philippe, and Nicholas Vinocur. "Google to Pay 60 Million Euros Into French Media Fund." Reuters, February 1, 2013. https://www.reuters.com/article/us-france-google/google-to-pay-60-million-euros-into-french-media-fund-idUSBRE91O11Z20130201.
World Intellectual Property Organization. "Summary of the WIPO Copyright Treaty (WCT)." 1996. https://www.wipo.int/treaties/en/ip/wct/summary_wct.html.
Xalabarder, Raquel. "Google News and Copyright." In *Google and the Law*, ed. Aurelio Lopez-Tarruella, 113–67. TMC Asser, 2012.
Yang, Xiujun 杨秀君. "Logics, Essence, and Practical Strategies of Xi Jin Ping's Important Statement on AI Technology" [习近平关于人工智能重要论述的形成逻辑、核心要义及实践方略]. December 27, 2024. https://www.cssn.cn/jjx/shzyjjysj/202412/t20241227_5827810.shtml.
Zakrzewski, Cat, Nitasha Tiku, and Elizabeth Dwoskin. "OpenAI Prepares to Fight for Its Life as Legal Troubles Mount." *Washington Post*, April 9, 2024. https://www.washingtonpost.com/technology/2024/04/09/openai-lawsuit-regulation-lawyers/.

BIBLIOGRAPHY

Zara, Christopher. "Rupert Murdoch vs. Google—Google Wins." *International Business Times*, 2012. http://www.ibtimes.com/rupert-murdoch-vs-google-google-wins-796615.

Zhang, Lucy. "Would You Like Video with That?" *Google* (blog), August 21, 2007. https://news.googleblog.com/2007/08/would-you-like-video-with-that.html.

Zheng, Zhihai. "Google Incident Does Not Break WTO Rules." *China Daily*, March 9, 2010. http://www.chinadaily.com.cn/china/2010-03/09/content_9562138.htm.

Zhou, Tao, Zoltán Kuscsik, Jian-Guo Liu, Matúš Medo, Joseph Rushton Wakeling, and Yi-Cheng Zhang. "Solving the Apparent Diversity-Accuracy Dilemma of Recommender Systems." *Proceedings of the National Academy of Sciences* 107, no. 10 (2010): 4511–15.

INDEX

ABCNews.com, 69, 70
ACAP. *See* Automated Consent Access Protocol
Accelerated Mobile Pages (AMP), 173
active personalization, 86
AdSense, 112–13
advertising. *See* digital advertising
AEDE. *See* Asociación de Editores de Diarios Espanoles
AEEPP. *See* Asociación Espanola de Editoriales de Publicaciones Periódicas
AFP. *See* Agence France Presse
Africa, Google News Initiative in, 172–73, 176–77, 181. *See also* South Africa
Agence France Presse (AFP), 99, 101; algorithms for, 103; copyrightability and, 102–3; journalistic traditions for, 103–5

Agence France Presse v. Google Inc., 101–5, 114
AI. *See* artificial intelligence
AI Act, EU (2024), 202–3
"AI Overviews" feature, 196, 201
algorithms: for Agence France Presse, 103–4; algorithmic gatekeeping, 13; computational, 11, 147; datafication and, 11, 145–64; design of, 150; General Data Protection regulation and, 154–55; for Google News, 11, 74–75, 77, 96, 147, 187; human-designed, 11; input, 145–46, 148; I-T-O, 145–46; journalistic approaches to, 151; media diversity and, 155–64; news aggregator and, 12–13; news data and, 150; oppression by, 11–12; originality for, 151–52; output, 145–46, 148; PageRank, 12, 37;

INDEX

algorithms (*continued*)
  throughput, 145–46, 148;
  transparency for, 145; user data
  in, 153–54; workflow and, 146–48
AltaVista, 35, 37
amateur journalism, amateur
  journalists and, 52–55
Amazon, 1; digital advertising
  on, 27
America Online, 19
AMP. *See* Accelerated Mobile
  Pages
Ancillary Copyright Law for Press
  Publishers, Germany (2013),
  114–16, 121
ANJ. *See* National Association of
  Newspapers
antiracism movements, 177–78
antitrust investigations: global
  reforms in, 190; against Google
  News, 111–12; in Italy, 111–12
AOL, 36
AP. *See* Associated Press
Apple (corporation), 6
Apple News, 6–7; establishment
  and launch of, 11, 33
AR. *See* augmented reality
artificial intelligence (AI), 21; "AI
  Overviews" feature, 196, 201;
  ChatGPT, 195, 198–200, 203–4;
  in China, 202–3; Common
  Crawl and, 199; crawlers, 197;
  E-A-T principle, 149, 159;
  E-E-A-T principle, 201; in EU,
  202–3; generative, 144; Google
  News Initiative and, 179–80;
  "Google way" and, 195–205;
  legitimacy of, 203; news

aggregation with, 86, 90; *New
  York Times* challenges to,
  199–200, 203–4; OpenAI,
  195–96, 198, 200–201, 203–4;
  robot exclusion protocols, 108,
  197; technology development for,
  203; US investment in, 202–3
Asahi Shimbun, 50
Asia Pacific Innovation Challenge,
  180
ask.com, 132
Asociación de Editores de Diarios
  Espanoles (AEDE), 118–21
Asociación Espanola de Editoriales
  de Publicaciones Periódicas
  (AEEPP), 121
Associated Press (AP), 4; business-
  to-business model, 123;
  contractual agreements for, 123;
  Google News and, 13–14,
  122–24, 163–64; *International
  News Service v. Associated Press*,
  129; licensing agreements for,
  123; OpenAI and, 196
*Associated Press v. Meltwater
  Holdings Inc.*, 128
Atlantic, The, 196–97
augmented reality (AR), 21
Australia, news media in:
  commercial agreements among,
  98; Facebook ban on, 1–2;
  Google News in, 95; Google
  News Initiative and, 172–73,
  176–77, 183–84; News Corp and,
  98; News Media and Digital
  Platforms Mandatory
  Bargaining Code in, 97–98;
  traditional news industry, 189

■ 278 ■

INDEX

Australian (newspaper), 98
Automated Consent Access Protocol (ACAP), 109
autonomy: differentiation and, 22, 28; institutionalization and, 28; normalization and, 28–29; specialization and, 22–23
Axel Springer, 117, 196

back-end personalization, 87
BBC America, 55
BBC News, 50
Belgium: caching technique in, 106; Copyright and Related Rights Act, 105; European Copyright Directive and, 107; *Google Inc v. Copiepresse*, 105–11, 114; Google News in, *100*, 105–11
Bernault, Carine, 108–9
Berne Convention, 101; copyright law and, 124–27; US membership in, 128
Bharat, Krishna, 43, 56–59, 77–78. *See also* Google News
big data, 20
Bild, 117
Bing News, 7, 160; establishment and launch of, 10–11, 33, 124
Biondo, Carlo D'Asaro, 178
blogging, 18–19; Google News Initiative and, 176–78
Brazil: division of media system in, 136; Google Brazil, 134; Google News in, *100*, 133–36; journalism traditions in, 135; Law of Freedom, Responsibility, and Transparency, 134–35; National Association of Newspapers in, 133–34; newspaper circulation in, 133–34; search engine market in, 135–36
breaking news, 45, 129, 151
bundling: debundling, unbundling, rebundling news, 9–10, 73–74; as editorial decision, 73–74
business-to-business models, 123
Buzzfeed, 196

caching technique: in Belgium, 106; *Field v. Google, Inc.*, 130
California Journalism Preservation Act, US (2024), 92–93
Canada: convergence between digital media and journalism in, 20; Google News in, 95; Online News Act, 98; Radio-Television and Telecommunications Commission in, 98; traditional news industry in, 189
Canon AEDE, 118–21
Canopy, 7
ChatGPT, 195, 198–200, 203–4
Chicago Tribune, 21
China: artificial intelligence investment in, 202–3; news aggregators in, 7
ClaimReview, 220n25
ClaimReview techniques, 80–81
CNET.com, 50
CNN, 7, 10, 50, 55, 159
CNN.com, 45
Coffey, Danielle, 191
Columbia Journalism School, 16
Communications Decency Act, US (1996), Section 230, 27
computational algorithms, 11, 147

INDEX

computational journalism, 20
convergence: in Canadian journalism, 20; cultural, 19; of tech-media, 16; in traditional news industry, 17–21; in US journalism, 20; waves of, 18–21. *See also* divergence; webvergence
Cooperative Patent Classification system (CPC system), 141
Copyright Act, Germany (1965), 116
Copyright and Related Rights Act, Belgium (1994), 105
copyright law: in Belgium, 105, 107; Berne Convention and, 124–27; Copyright Act, 116; Copyright and Related Rights Act, 105; Digital Millennium Copyright Act, 128–30; in EU, 124–25, 130–31; European Copyright Directive, 107, 125–28; in Germany, 114–16, 121, 125–26; global reforms in, 190; harmonization of, 224n24; Ley de Propiedad Intelectual, 118; in Spain, 118; in US, 130; World Intellectual Property Organization and, 125, 128
copyrights, copyrightability and: Agence France Presse and, 102–3; Ancillary Copyright Law for Press Publishers, 114–16; under Berne Convention, 124–27; Copyright Act, 116; Copyright and Related Rights Act, 105; Digital Millennium Copyright Act, 128–30; European Copyright Directive, 107, 125–28; news aggregation and, 83–84
Council of the European Union, 224n24
COVID-19 pandemic: anti-Asian violence, 162, 177; fact-checking during, 81; Google News Initiative and, 176–77; health disparities influenced by race during, 161–63; "infodemic" and, 159; media diversity and, 155–64; video content demand during, 156–58
CPC system. *See* Cooperative Patent Classification system
crawlers: AI and, 197; search engine, 34
crawl rates, 218n2
crawl technique, for Google News Search, 66–67, 106–7
Curley, Tom, 123
Curtis, Drew, 53–54
customization, of Google News, 87–88, 90

DailyHunt, 7
data, datasets and: algorithms and, 146; analysis of, 20; as capital, 148–49, 165; under General Data Protection Regulation, 154–55; journalism, 20; metadata, 85–86; mining of, 20; privatization of, 75; processing of, 20; visualization of, 20. *See also* datafication; data protections
data breaches, 82
datafication: algorithms and, 11, 145–64; content and, 152;

INDEX

data-driven business model and, 148–49, 165; differentiation and, 188–89; of news, 148–55; news sources and, 149–52; user data, 153; values and, 148
data journalism, 20
data protections: under EU General Data Protection Regulation, 154–55; global reforms in, 190
debundled news, 9–10, 73–74
deep linking technology, 86, 113
deinstitutionalization, 205
deliberative democracy, 166
democracy, media diversity and, 166
differentiation: autonomy and, 22, 28; datafication of news and, 188–89; differentiating shifts, 22; divergence and, 21–24; legitimacy and, 28; N-D-N framework and, 188–90; resistance and, 22, 28; specialization and, 28, 188; tech-media and, 16; theory of, 21–22
digital advertising: AdSense, 112–13; market shares for, 27
digital journalism. *See* online/digital journalism
Digital Millennium Copyright Act (DMCA), US (1998), 128–30
Digital News Innovation (DNI), 171, 178–80, 190–91
digital platforms, 1, 4–5; Google News Initiative and, 175; journalism and, 16, 20; news aggregators and, 8; News Media and Digital Platforms Mandatory Bargaining Code,

97–98; platform governance and, 25, 166; platforms, 27; vertical integration of, 75. *See also specific platforms*
directory models. *See* web directory models
divergence: in tech-media, 16; waves of, 23–24
DMCA. *See* Digital Millennium Copyright Act
DuckDuckGo, 7, 160

E-A-T principle, 149, 159
EC Treaty. *See* Treaty establishing the European Economic Community
"Editors' picks" feature, 147, 182–83
E-E-A-T principle, 201
ethnic media, 162
EU. *See* European Union
EUCD. *See* European Copyright Directive
European Commission, 115
European Copyright Directive (EUCD), 107; in France, 125–26; in Germany, 125–26; new EUCD, 125–27; opt-in model, 127; opt-out trend, 127
European Parliament, 125, 224n24
European Publishers Council, 116
European Union (EU): AI Act, 202–3; artificial intelligence in, 202–3; copyright law in, 124–25, 130–31; Council of the European Union, 224n24; General Data Protection Regulation in, 154–55; Google lawsuits in, 84; Google News Initiative in,

• 281 •

INDEX

European Union (EU) (*continued*) 172–73; intellectual property in, 124–25; news aggregators in, 8; Treaty establishing the European Economic Community, 112. *See also specific countries*
Excite, 36

Facebook: Australian news ban on, 1–2; digital advertising on, 27; Facebook News, 7; Google and, 81–82; Google News and, 143; Instant Article, 25; journalism and, 19–20; "Today in" feature, 163
Facebook News, 33
"Fact Check" feature, 80–81, 147
fact-checking: ClaimReview and, 220n25; during COVID-19 pandemic, 81; Google News Initiative and, 179; International Fact-Checking Network, 81
FactCheck.org, 81
fair use doctrine: *Field v. Google, Inc.*, 130; in US, 128–29
Fake News Bill. *See* Law of Freedom, Responsibility, and Transparency
Fark.com, 53–55
Federal Communications Commission (US), 4
Field v. Google, Inc., 130
Financial Times, 196
Floyd, George, 177
Fox News, 50
France: Agence France Presse, 99, 101–5; *Agence France Presse v.*

Google Inc., 101–5, 114; European Copyright Directive in, 125–26; Google News lawsuits in, 99–105; journalism traditions in, 101
"Full Coverage" feature, 88

"Gadget" section, 79
GameStop, 1
gatekeepers, gatekeeping and, 49; algorithmic gatekeeping, 13; in journalism, 12–13, 104
Gawker, 6–7
General Data Protection Regulation (GDPR), EU, 154–55
Germany: Ancillary Copyright Law for Press Publishers, 114–16, 121; *Bild* in, 117; Copyright Act in, 116; European Copyright Directive in, 125–26; Google News in, *100*, 114–17; traditional news industry in, 189; VG Media in, 115
Gingras, Richard, 119, 155
GNI. *See* Google News Initiative
Goddard, Taegan, 6
Golvers, Luc, 108
Google (corporation): algorithms by, 145–48; crawl rate and, 218n2; digital advertising on, 27; early years of, 36–40; establishment and launch of, 34; Facebook and, 81–82; homepage for, 41–42, 48–50, 64; introduction of the history of investment in news-related business, 2–3; News Corp deal with, 2, 184; 9/11 search statistics for, *48*;

■ 282 ■

INDEX

before 9/11 terrorist attacks, 34–43; Open Directory Project and, 41, 60; PageRank, 12, 37–38, 42; patents held by, 140–41, 149–50; privacy policies, 89; social media attempts by, 81–82; traditional news industry in conflict with, 4; Twitter and, 81–82; vertical integration within, 112; web directory model adopted by, 38–39; Yahoo! and, 37. *See also* Google News; Google News Initiative; Google Search; "Google way"; search engines; *specific topics*

Google Ad Manager, 173

Google Analytics, 89, 173

Google Brazil, 134

Google Buzz, 81–82, 143

Google Data, 173

Google Earth, 173

Google Image, 173

Google Inc v. Copiepresse, 105–7, 110–11; Automated Consent Access Protocol, 109; implied consent in, 108; robot exclusion protocols and, 108

Google Maps, 173

Google News: Agence France Presse and, 99–100, 101–5; *Agence France Presse v. Google Inc.*, 101–5, 114; "AI Overviews" feature, 196, 201; AI-powered news aggregation for, 86, 90; algorithms for, 11, 74–75, 77, 96, 147, 187; anniversary of, 142–43; antitrust investigations against, 111–12; Associated Press and, 13–14, 122–24, 163–64; in Belgium, *100*, 105–11; beta version of, 50, 58–60, 69–70, 142; in Brazil, *100*, 133–36; ClaimReview techniques for, 80–81; clicks per month for, 3; color-coded design for, 73; copyright violations by, 109–10; customization of, 87–88, *90*; datafication processes, 85–86; debundled news and, 9–10, 73–74; deep linking technology and, 86; development of, 3; Directory services, 71; early form of, 57–60; early news sources for, 50; E-A-T principle, 149, 159; editorial influences on, 77; "Editors' picks" feature, 147, 182–83; establishment and launch of, 2–3, 10–11, 56–57; evolution of, 3, 63, 96; Facebook and, 143; "Fact Check" feature, 80–81, 147; *Field v. Google, Inc.*, 130; in France, 99–105; "Full Coverage" feature, 88; "Gadget" section, 79; generative AI and, 144; in Germany, *100*, 114–17; *Google Inc v. Copiepresse*, 105–11, 114; Google News Search, 64; Google Reader and, 81; Groups services, 71; "Headline News" page, 59; homepage design for, 70–84, *76*, *85*, *92*; in India, 95; "In the News" section, 73–74, *74*; institutionalization of, 25–29; international coverage of, 95; international editions of, 95; international lawsuits with, 99,

• 283 •

INDEX

Google News (*continued*)
101–5; in Italy, *100*, 111–14; labels for, 84–86; licensing agreements for, 123; "Local coverage/news" section, 78, 147; media diversity and, 155–64; metadata for, 85–86; "Most Popular" section, 79; natural language processing by, 73; news aggregation by, 6, 13, 58–59, 67, 107–8; News Corp and, 98, *100*; "News for you" feature, 143; "News Showcase" feature, 91–94, 182–84; 9/11 terrorist attacks and, 43–60, *46*; origins of, 33; overview of, 10; PageRank algorithm for, 37, 58; personalization features of, 86–89, 94–95, 143–44; publishing partners for, 93, 172; "Recent" section, 77; redesigns of, 70–71; as search engine, 67; in Spain, 14–15, *100*, 118–22; specialization for, 144; "Special topics" section, 77–78; "Spotlight" section, 79, 147; as standalone service, 59–60; traditional news industry influenced by, 3; traffic rates, 77; Twitter and, 143; 2002 redesign for, 71–75; 2010 redesign for, *76*, 76–83; 2017–2018 redesign for, 83–90; 2022–2023 redesign, 91–95; in UK, 95, *100*, 131–33; in US, *100*, 122–31; video search results, 158–59; web search model for, 44–45; Web services, 71. *See also* "Google way"
Google News Beta, launch of, 69–70

Google News Initiative (GNI): in Africa, 172–73, 176–77, 181; artificial intelligence and, 179–80; Asia Pacific Innovation Challenge and, 180; in Australia, 172–73, 176–77, 183–84; blogs for, 176–78; collaborative relationships and, 172–73; contractual partnerships, 174, 184; COVID-19 pandemic and, 176–77; Digital News Innovation Fund, 171, 178–80, 190–91; in Europe, 172–73; evolution and development of, 169–70; fact-checking and, 179; financial support for, 172; Google News Showcase, 91–94, 182–84; Google Project Team, 179; "Google way" and, 174; Innovation Challenge program, 178, 180–81; institutionalization of, 170, 175; international coverage of, 172–73, 176–77; licensing program, 171; machine learning and, 179–80; N-D-N framework, 32, 170, 184–95, 203; in North America, 176–77, 181; origins of, 169; payment models and, 179–80; in South America, 172–73, 176–77, 181; technological support for, 172; traditional news industry and, 171–72; in Turkey, 181; in US, 172–73, 176–77
Google News Lab, 169
Google News Search, 68, 70; beta version, 64, *66*; crawl technique and, 66–67; homepage, *66*; logo design for, 64–65, 67, *68*, 69;

INDEX

sections of, 65–66; webpage design for, 65–66
Google News Showcase, 91–94, 182–84
Google Project Team, 179
Google Reader, 81; "Revenue Manager," 93
Google Search, 120, 173; clicks per month for, 3
Google Sheets, 173
Google Translate, 173
Google Trends, 173
Google Wave, 143
"Google way": artificial intelligence and, 195–205; Google News and, 72; Google News Initiative and, 174; N-D-N framework and, 185, 194; network building and, 194; patent analysis and, 139–41; resistance against, 111; technological innovations and, 140–45, 164; traditional news industry relationship, 137–38; two-sided market, 93
Guardian, 20

hard news, 15
"Headline News" page, 59
homepages: for Google, 41–42, 48–50, 64; for Google News, 70–84, 76, 85, 92; for Google News Search, 66
"Hot news" doctrine, 128–29
House of Commons Bill. *See* Online News Act
Huffington Post, 6–8
hybridity, hybrids and: Google News and, 15–16, 165; media, 18

immersive journalism, 21
India: Google News in, 95; news aggregators in, 7–8
Indonesia: licensing agreements in, 136; Publisher Rights Decree, 136
InfoSeek, 35–36, 41
"In the News" section, 73–74, *74*
Inktomi, 37
Innovation Challenge program, 178, 180–81
input algorithms, 145–46, 148
InShorts, 8
Instagram, 195
institutionalization: of autonomy, 28; cultural-cognitive pillar for, 27–29, 192; deinstitutionalization and, 205; of digital journalism, 25–29; of Google News, 25–29; of Google News Initiative, 170, 175; normative pillar of, 27–29, 192–93; regulative pillar for, 26–27, 192; of tech sector, 191–92; three pillars of, 26–29, 192–93
integration. *See* vertical integration
intellectual property: in Europe, 124–25; Ley de Propiedad Intelectual, 118; World Intellectual Property Organization and, 125, 128
International Fact-Checking Network, 81
International News Service v. Associated Press, 129
internet: evolution of, 52; 9/11 terrorist attacks as influence on, 51–60. *See also specific topics*
investigative journalism, 20, 79
Ireland, Google News in, 112

■ 285 ■

INDEX

Italian Federation of Newspaper Publishers, 111–14
Italy: antitrust investigations in, 111–12; Google News in, *100*, 111–14
I-T-O process. *See* input algorithms; output algorithms; throughput algorithms

Japan, news aggregators in, 7
journalism, journalistic traditions and: for Agence France Presse, 103–4; amateur, 52–55; in Brazil, 135; under California Journalism Preservation Act, 92–93; Columbia Journalism School, 16; digital journalism types, 20; Facebook and, 19–20; in France, 101; gatekeeping in, 12–13; Google and, 19–20; independence for, 175; investigative, 79; normalizing technologies, 18; as process model, 24; as public service, 53; public trust in, 57; social function of, 57; Society of Professional Journalists, 175; Tow Center for Digital Journalism, 16; Twitter and, 18. *See also* online/digital journalism; *specific topics*
Journalism Competition and Preservation Act, US (2023), 78–79, 131, 177

Kasi, Srinandan, 4
Kelly v. Arriba Soft Corp., 130
Knewz, 7

Law of Freedom, Responsibility, and Transparency (Fake News Bill), Brazil (2020), 134–35
legitimacy, legitimation and: of artificial intelligence development, 203; of Google, 37–39, 61; N-D-N framework and, 186–87; normalization and, 28–29, 186–88; organizational, 17–18; as social capital, 28
Leonardi, Marcel, 134
Ley de Propiedad Intelectual (LPI), Spain (2014), 118
liberal democracy, 166
licensing, licensing programs and: for Associated Press, 123; for Google, 92; for Google News, 123; Google News Initiative and, 171; Google News Showcase, 91–94, 182–84; in Indonesia, 136
"Local coverage/news" section, 78, 147
LPI. *See* Ley de Propiedad Intelectual
Lycos, 34–35
Lynch, Roger, 197

machine learning, 86; Google News Initiative and, 179–80
Malda, Rob, 53
Margolis, Michael, 17
Mayer, Marissa, 110
media diversity: COVID-19 pandemic and, 155–64; democracy and, 166; ethnic media and, 162; format-type, 160; Google News and, 155–64; Google News Initiative and,

INDEX

164; output diversity, 163–64; source, 95, 158–59; structural diversity, 161–63; video content and, 156–58

media evolution theory, 18, 20, 22

metadata, 85–86, 152–53

Microsoft, 124, 132; *New York Times* and, 198–200, 203–4. *See also* Bing News

mixed reality (MR), 21

mobile journalism, 20

"Most Popular" section, 79

MSNBC, 45, 50

multimedia journalism, 20

Murdoch, Rupert, 2, 4, 131–32. *See also* News Corp

Musk, Elon, 1, 83

Named enitities: in algorithm systems, 151–52; feature, 73–74; unambiguous named entities, 75, 218n9

National Association of Newspapers (ANJ), 133–34

National Public Radio (NPR), 50

N-D-N framework (normalization-differentiation-negotiation framework): differentiation stage, 188–90; institutionalization, 191–95; N-D-N, 184–95; negotiation stage of, 190–95; normalization stage, 185–88; public interest model and, 193–94

Netscape, 36

NewHoo, 36

news aggregators, news aggregation and: algorithms and, 12–13;

bundling, unbundling, rebundling by, 9–10, 73–74; in Germany, 114–17; by Google News, 10–15; *Huffington Post*, 6–8; human approach to, 8; international, 7–8; machine-based approach to, 8; News Corp and, 7; during 9/11 terrorist attacks, 55–56; overview of, 5–10; in Spain, 119; in UK, 132; unbundling by, 9–10; in US, 128–29; Yahoo! News and, 6, 41. *See also* Google News

News Corp, 4; in Australia, 98; Google deal with, 2, 184; Google News and, 98, *100*; Knewz and, 7; Myspace and, 24; news aggregation by, 7; News International and, 131–32; OpenAI and, 196

"News for you" feature, 143

news industry, traditional: in Australia, 189; in Canada, 189; decline of, 24; disputes with Google, 97; in Germany, 189; Google in conflict with, 4; Google News as influence on, 3; Google News Initiative and, 171–72; "Google way" and, 137–38; media divergence, 21–25; N-D-N framework, 184–95; news aggregation by, 5; normalization in, 17–21; public interest, 193–94; social function of, 57; in Spain, 189; tech industry and, 15–21; in US, 189–90. *See also specific media*

News International, 131–32

INDEX

news media: genres for, 15; Google investment in, 2–3; Google payments to, 2, 184; "Google way" and, 3, 139, 144–45; new sectors, 15; during 9/11 terrorist attacks, 43–60; old sector in, 15. *See also* news industry; *specific countries*; *specific news companies*; *specific topics*

News Media and Digital Platforms Mandatory Bargaining Code, 97–98

newspapers: in Brazil, 133–34; Italian Federation of Newspaper Publishers, 111–14; National Association of Newspapers, 133–34. *See also specific newspapers*

news paralysis, during 9/11 attacks, 43–45, 61

NewsPoint, 8

"News Showcase" feature, 91–94, 182–84

news snippets, 73, 83–84, 115–17, 133

New York Post, 50

New York Times, 2, 10, 25, 159; AI technology challenged by, 198–200, 203–4; Microsoft and, 198–200, 203–4; OpenAI and, 198–200, 203–4; virtual reality initiative, 21

New Zealand, Google News in, 95

9/11 terrorist attacks, 216n27; amateur journalism during, 52–55; Fark.com and, 53–55; Google before, 34–43; Google News and, 43–60, *46*; internet use influenced by, 51–60; N-D-N framework and, 186; news aggregation during, 55–56; news media during, 43–60; news paralysis during, 43–45, 61; news-related searches during, 45–47; online journalism during, 43–60; Slashdot.org and, 53–54, *54*; WTCA On-Line, 44–45

normalization: of autonomy, 28–29; convergence, 18–21; legitimacy and, 28–29; N-D-N framework and, 185–88; resistance and, 28; sociological, 17–18; specialization and, 28

normalization-differentiation-negotiation framework. *See* N-D-N framework

North America: Google News Initiative, 176–77, 181. *See also* Canada; United States

NPR. *See* National Public Radio

Nytimes.com, 45; ChatGPT and, 199

ODP. *See* Open Directory Project

Olson, Barbara Kay, 216n27

online/digital journalism, online/digital journalists and: employment for, 23–24; institutionalization of, 25–29; print journalists and, 23; professional status of, 23–24; Tow Center for Digital Journalism, 16

Online News Act (House of Commons Bill), Canada (2022), 98

• 288 •

INDEX

OpenAI, 201; Associated Press and, 196; ChatGPT, 195, 198–200, 203–4; *New York Times*, 198–200, 203–4; in US, 196
Open Directory Project (ODP), 35–36; Google adoption of, 41, 60
organizational legitimacy, 17–18
output algorithms, 145–46, 148
output diversity, 163–64

PageRank, 12, 37–38, 42; for Google News, 58
Parler, 1
participatory democracy, 166
passive personalization, 86
patents: analysis of, 140–41; classification categories for, 141–44; Cooperative Patent Classification system, 141; definition of, 140; US Patent and Trademark Office, 140–41
personalization: active, 86; back-end, 87, 89; DNI and, 179; front-end, 86, 88; Google News and, 86–90; passive, 86; system-initiated, 86; technological innovation and, 143–44; user-initiated, 86
platform governance, 25, 166
platforms. *See* digital platforms
Political Wire, 6
Politics as Usual (Margolis and Resnick), 17
PolitiFact, 81
portals, search engines and, 49
Pravda, 50

privacy, data privacy, GDPR and, 154–55; Google policy and terms, 89; personally identifying information, 89–90
Project Alesia, 132
public interest, public service and: journalism as, 53; N-D-N framework and, 194
Publisher Rights Decree, Indonesia (2024), 136
Pulse, 8

Radio-Television and Telecommunications Commission, in Canada, 98
rebundling, of news, 9–10, 73–74
"Recent" section, 77
Reddit, 1, 8
REP. *See* robot exclusion protocols
resistance: differentiation and, 28; against Google Way, 111; normalization of, 28. *See also specific topics*
Resnick, David, 17
Reuters, 55
robot exclusion protocols (REP), 108–9, 116, 197

Salon, 50
"scarcity news," 15
search engines: biases, 11–12; DuckDuckGo, 7, 160; early search landscape, 34–36; evolution of, 40–43; Google market share, 11; Google News Search, 64–70; mergers and acquisitions, 36; news aggregators and, 8; news and,

search engines (*continued*) 40–43; Open Directory Project, 35–36; Yahoo! and, 35, 160; young Google, 36–40. *See also specific topics*
Section 230, of Communications Decency Act, 27
Signal, 1
Slashdot.org, 53–54, *54*
SmartNews, 7
Snopes.com, 81
social capital, legitimacy as, 28
social media networks: Google attempts at, 81–82. *See also* Facebook; Twitter; *specific topics*
Society of Professional Journalists (SPJ), 175
source diversity, 95
South Africa, 136
South America, Google News Initiative in, 172–73, 176–77, 181
Spain: Asociación de Editores de Diarios Espanoles in, 118–21; Asociación Espanola de Editoriales de Publicaciones Periódicas, 121; Google News in, 14–15, *100*, 118–22; Ley de Propiedad Intelectual in, 118; traditional news industry in, 189
specialization: AI and, 203; autonomy and, 22–23; differentiation and, 28–29, 188–89; for Google News, 142, 144; N-D-N framework and, 186–88
"Special topics" section, 77–78
SPJ. *See* Society of Professional Journalists

"Spotlight" section, 79, 147
Springer, Axel, 117
structural diversity, 161–63
Subscribe with Google, 173
Sunday Times, 131
system-initiated personalization, 86

tech-media: AI and, 201–3; divergence and, 16; global landscape, 97; media convergence, 15–21; media divergence, 21–25. *See also* hybridity; N-D-N framework; *specific companies*
Thompson, Nicholas, 197
throughput algorithms, 145–46, 148
TikTok, 195
Time.com, 50
Times, The (London), 98
Toutiao, 7
Tow Center for Digital Journalism, 16
transparency, for algorithms, 145
Treaty establishing the European Economic Community (EC Treaty), 112
Turkey, Google News Initiative in, 181
Twitter (X), 1, 8; exodus of news professionals from, 83; Google and, 81–82; Google News and, 143; journalism and, 18

UK *See* United Kingdom
unbundling, by news aggregators, 9–10, 73–74
United Kingdom (UK): accusations of news media theft in, 4; Google News in, 95, *100*, 131–33;

INDEX

news aggregation in, 131; News International in, 131–32
United States (US): artificial intelligence investment in, 202–3; Associated Press in, 4, 13–14, 122–24; *Associated Press v. Meltwater Holdings Inc.*, 128; Berne Convention and, 128; California Journalism Preservation Act, 92–93; Communications Decency Act, 27; copyright systems in, 130; Digital Millennium Copyright Act, 128–30; fair use doctrine in, 128–29; Federal Communications Commission, 4; Google News Initiative and, 172–73, 176–77; "Hot news" doctrine, 128–29; *International News Service v. Associated Press*, 129; Journalism Competition and Preservation Act, 78–79, 131, 177; OpenAI use in, 196; 2024 presidential election, 204; USPTO, 140–41. *See also* 9/11 terrorist attacks
Upday, 8
US. *See* United States
USA Today, 50
user-initiated personalization, 86
US Patent and Trademark Office (USPTO), 140–41

vertical integration, of medial companies and digital platforms, 75; within Google, 114
video search: of Google, 157; video consumption and COVID-19 pandemic, 156–57; YouTube and Google's video search, 158. *See also* media diversity
virtual reality (VR), 21
Vox, 25
Vox Media, 196
VR. *See* virtual reality

Wall Street Journal, 98
Walt Disney Company, 75
Washington Post, 25, 81, 159–60
web directory models: Google and, 38–39; limitations of, 35; link rot and, 35; Open Directory Project, 35–36; open-source model and, 36
webvergence, 19
WhatsApp, 1
Wikipedia, 75
WIPO. *See* World Intellectual Property Organization
workflow, algorithms and, 145–48
World Intellectual Property Organization (WIPO), 125, 128
WTCA On-Line, 44–45

X. *See* Twitter

Yahoo!: Google and, 37; search service of, 34; video search of, 160; web directory model of, 35–36
Yahoo! News, news aggregation by, 6, 8, 41
YouTube, 157–59, 164

Zuckerberg, Mark, 157

GPSR Authorized Representative: Easy Access System Europe, Mustamäe tee 50, 10621 Tallinn, Estonia, gpsr.requests@easproject.com

www.ingramcontent.com/pod-product-compliance
Lightning Source LLC
Chambersburg PA
CBHW022038290426
44109CB00014B/902